S0-BQZ-064

WITHDRAWN
L. R. COLLEGE LIBRARY

CARL A. RUDISILL LIBRARY
LENOIR-RHYNE COLLEGE

When Empire
Comes Home

Repatriation
and Reintegration
in Postwar Japan

Harvard East Asian Monographs 317

When Empire Comes Home

Repatriation and Reintegration in Postwar Japan

Lori Watt

Published by the Harvard University Asia Center
and distributed by Harvard University Press
Cambridge (Massachusetts) and London, 2009

CARL A. RUDISILL LIBRARY
LENOIR-RHYNE UNIVERSITY

© 2009 by The President and Fellows of Harvard College

Printed in the United States of America

The Harvard University Asia Center publishes a monograph series and, in coordination with the Fairbank Center for Chinese Studies, the Korea Institute, the Reischauer Institute of Japanese Studies, and other faculties and institutes, administers research projects designed to further scholarly understanding of China, Japan, Vietnam, Korea, and other Asian countries. The Center also sponsors projects addressing multidisciplinary and regional issues in Asia.

Library of Congress Cataloging-in-Publication Data

Watt, Lori
    When empire comes home : repatriation and reintegration in postwar Japan / Lori Watt.
      p. cm. -- (Harvard East Asian monographs ; 317)
    Includes bibliographical references and index.
    ISBN 978-0-674-03342-9 (cloth : alk. paper)
    1. World War, 1939–1945--Forced repatriation. 2. Return migration--Japan--History--20th century. 3. Social integration--Japan--History--20th century. 4. Decolonization--Social aspects--Japan. 5. Japan--Social conditions—1945– 6. National characteristics, Japanese. 7. Japan--History--Allied occupation, 1945–1952. I. Title.
    D809.J3W37 2009
    952.04'4--dc22

2009015124

Index by Kevin Butterfield

♾ Printed on acid-free paper

Last figure below indicates year of this printing

19 18 17 16 15 14 13 12 11 10 09

$39.95

D
809
·J3
W37
2009

OCLC #: 261175580

Feb 2011

CARL A. RUDISILL LIBRARY
LENOIR-RHYNE UNIVERSITY

Acknowledgments

I am grateful to many individuals and institutions for their support while researching and writing this book. Carol Gluck provided inspiration and guidance at all stages of the project. Henry D. Smith II, Madeleine Zelin, Charles Armstrong, Gregory Pflugfelder, and Louise Young gave generously of their time and insight. Moustafa Bayoumi of Brooklyn College was an extremely conscientious dissertation reader and his insights have contributed a great deal to my understanding of the fallout of empire. Barbara Brooks of the City University of New York gave wonderful advice on sources and historical questions. I learned a great deal from my cohort at Columbia University, especially Jonathan Zwicker, Darryl Flaherty, Chris Hill, Leila Wice, Yasu Makimura, Peter Flueckiger, Ari Levine, Ellen McGill, Georgia Mickey, Ananda Martin, Ken Oshima, Jan Poole, Harrison Miller, David Ekbladh, David Lurie, Sarah Kovner, Hide Tanaka, Kerry Ross, Takashi Yoshida, and Laura Neitzel. My final year was enhanced by the company of Christine Kim and Mark Swislocki. Robert Eskildsen did double duty as mentor and friend, and many of the insights and phrasings in this book came from hours-long conversations with him.

Kokaze Hidemasa and Ōguchi Yūjirō of Ochanomizu University in Tokyo took time out of their busy schedules to train me in historical research during the years I spent there, supported by a Monbushō fellowship. Anayama Asako, Watanabe Naoko, and Morita Tomoko gave of their time and friendship. At the University of Tokyo, Ōnuma Yasuaki of the Graduate School of Law and Politics was kind to serve as my advisor. Katō Yōko allowed me to attend her seminar and to present work in progress. Yoshida Yutaka and Nakano Satoshi of Hitotsubashi University shared insight and materials. Mr. and Mrs. Mori Akira, Barak Kushner, Roger Brown, and Paul Dunscomb made excellent companions in Nakano-Shinbashi. Research in Japan was made possible by a Fulbright IIE Graduate Research Fellowship. I found important sources thanks to a Twentieth-Century Japan Research Award to the Gordon W. Prange Collection at the University of Maryland, where I continued to be indebted to Eiko Sakaguchi and Amy Wasserstrom. I benefited from my association with the Yamaguchi Prefecture History research group and especially enjoyed the company of Nakatsuka Fumio, Ueyama Atsushi, Kurita Hisao, Kawamura Katsunori, and Furuya Nobuko. I am grateful to Maekawa Masao for teaching me about the history of Sasebo and introducing me to several people who shared their stories. Okamoto Kōichi of Waseda University has been a consistent resource and friend.

In 1999 to 2000, I conducted and taped nine formal oral history interviews and spoke informally with about a dozen other people repatriated from overseas after the war. During the interviews, all of the interviewees consented on tape to having their names and stories used. Although they were all comfortable with this arrangement, various intermediaries—relatives, care facility administrators, and friends who had introduced us—were not. For this reason, with the exception of Tsukada Asae, who published articles about her experiences and was an activist in commemorating agricultural settlers, I refer to the interviews by date and not by name. I am grateful to all who spoke to me about their experiences.

A Peking University Fellowship for Advanced Research in Chinese Studies facilitated by the University of Hawai'i and an SSRC International Dissertation Research Fellowship supported research in the People's Republic of China. I am grateful to Niu Dayong of Beijing University and Guo Lianyou of Beijing Foreign Studies University for their help. The Whiting Foundation provided support for completing the dissertation.

My experience as a Reischauer Institute Postdoctoral Fellow in 2002–2003 was invaluable in terms of providing the time, space, and resources for thinking through the book. I learned a great deal from my colleagues there, including Franziska Seraphim, Kenji Tierney, Charo D'Etcheverry, and Linda Angst. Andrew Gordon has been supportive of my research across the years. At Yale, Valerie Hansen provided great advice and Johanna Ransmeier, excellent company. I am especially grateful to Simon Kim and Lisa Yoshikawa. Other people have given generously of their time and ideas: Bryna Goodman, Sharon Sievers, Akira Miyazaki, Marlene Mayo, Laura Hein, and Rob Fish.

Colleagues at Washington University in St. Louis have created a congenial atmosphere for thinking about history. Tim Parsons, Derek Hirst, Mark Pegg, and members of the junior faculty reading group, Nancy Reynolds, Corinna Treitel, Christine Johnson, Maggie Garb, Steve Miles, and Guy Ortolano all read parts of the manuscript. Rebecca Copeland shared her insights as well. Members of the Midwest Japan Seminar provided valuable feedback on a chapter in 2005. At Washington University, the Earle H. and Suzanne S. Harbison Faculty Fellowship and a Roland Grimm Traveling Fellowship provided the means to spend months in Japan. An NEH Faculty Fellowship, funded by the National Endowment for the Humanities and the Japan–United States Friendship Commission, supported a sabbatical that provided the time to complete the manuscript. Any views, findings, conclusions, or recommendations expressed in this book do not necessarily reflect those of the National Endowment for the Humanities or the Japan–United States Friendship Commission. I want to thank Satō Tomomi of the Shiseidō Corporate Museum and Ogata Hiromu of the Printing Museum of Tokyo for their generosity in helping me to secure the image for the cover.

Sheldon Garon and an anonymous reader for the Harvard University Asia Center read the entire manuscript and provided thoughtful and productive feedback, and to both I am very grateful. I want to thank William M. Hammell for shepherding the manuscript to publication.

A special secret handshake for the Hamada family (Scott, Lynne, Eric, Claire, and Sara); the Watt families (Ann and Bob; Paul and Yasuko; Michael, Yuki, Hana, Andy, and Julie); and the Lampros, Wright-Rojas, and Norgren-Rohner families; and for Abe Ken, Robert Vodicka, Michelle Polzine, Daniel Guidera, Richard Hendy, Edwina Gibbs, Chika Hyōdō, Adam Penenberg, Aida Harumi, Higashimori Tsutomu, Howard Huang, Robert Story Karem, Kurt Opprecht, Keith Rodgers, and Jamie Newhard. Finally, I am grateful to Slava Solomatov for making my life more interesting.

Contents

Maps, Figure, and Tables

Maps

Figure

Tables

When Empire Comes Home

Repatriation
and Reintegration
in Postwar Japan

INTRODUCTION

Repatriation, Decolonization,
and the Transformations of Postwar Japan

In the sixteen months following the end of World War II in Asia, from September 1945 to December 1946, the Allied military forces repatriated over 5 million Japanese nationals to Japan. During the same period, the Allies also facilitated the deportation from Japan of over a million former colonial subjects—Koreans, Taiwanese, Chinese, and Southeast Asians—to their countries of origin. The Allies viewed these transfers as an unwelcome but unavoidable part of their primary goals: the demobilization of Japan's military forces and the demilitarization of Japan. The transfers were also a part of the dismantling of Japan's fifty-year imperial project. The unmaking of empires everywhere is a complex process, and the human remnants of Japan's empire—those who were moved and those who were left behind—served as sites of negotiation for the process of disengagement from empire and for the creation of new national identities.

Japan acquired its overseas colonies piecemeal, mostly as the spoils of victory in war: Taiwan in 1895, after the Sino-Japanese War; Korea in 1910, five years after the Russo-Japanese War; the South Seas mandate under the League of Nations and special rights in China after World War I; the puppet state of Manchukuo in 1932; and parts of China and Southeast Asia between 1937 and 1945, during Japan's war in Asia. Following these territorial gains, millions of Japanese participated in the imperial project, subduing, managing, and settling these colonial acquisitions. They went overseas in dribs and drabs, as conscripted soldiers, colonial administrators, and entrepreneurs. By the end of the war, their numbers were significant: as of August 1945, 3.2 million Japanese civilians and 3.7 million soldiers—6.9 million people, nearly 9 percent of the total population of 72 million—were outside of the Japanese home islands.[1] The requirements of war and empire also meant that people from the colonies move to Japan as well. At war's end, an estimated 2 million Koreans, 200,000 people from the Ryukyu archipelago, 56,000 Chinese, and 35,000 Taiwanese were in Japan;[2] another 1.5 million Koreans had migrated, or were forced to move to Manchuria, and tens of thousands of others were in China, Taiwan, and Karafuto (now Sakhalin).[3] With its porous internal borders, efficient transportation system, proactive migration policies, and forced labor schemes, Japan's empire facilitated a degree of ethnic mixing in East Asia not seen before or since.

Immediately after defeating Japan, the Allies began to move people in ways that reversed, at high speed, the migrations of the colonial period. Their first priority was to accept the surrender of all 3.7 million Japanese troops abroad, disarm them, and send them home as part of the demobilization of the Imperial Army and Navy. Unlike in Europe, where the Allies prepared for inevitable postwar refugees by establishing the United Nations Relief and Rehabilitation Administration in 1943, few plans had been made for Japanese civilians abroad; however, the spontaneous civilian migrations of August 1945 forced the Allied militaries and the Japanese government to respond.[4] Soon, the trappings of an organized population transfer—repatriation camps, quarantine procedures, identification papers, and a bureaucracy—took shape. Of the 6.7 million who eventually returned to Japan, 5 million arrived by the end of 1946. The flow of people went both ways: by February 1946, nearly

---

1. Ara, ed., *Nihon senryō, gaikō kankei shiryō shū*, 304.

2. Kōseishō engokyoku, *Hikiage to engo 30-nen no ayumi*, 151.

3. Estimates are 1.5 million Koreans in Manchuria in 1940, 100,000 in China in 1941, 2,260 in Taiwan in 1939, 16,056 in Karafuto in 1940. "Nihon oyobi sono shokumin chiiki ni okeru jinkō no hattatsu," in Ōkurashō kanrikyoku, *Nihonjin no kaigai katsudō*, vol. 1, 222–26.

4. For the Allied response to refugees in Europe, see Grossmann, *Jews, Germans, and Allies*, 133.

1 million Koreans, 40,000 Chinese, and 18,000 Taiwanese had been sent away.[5] All had to cross an ocean to reach their destinations.

Although defeat and expediency triggered the population transfer, larger historical forces shaped it as well. These include the impulse to match each person with his or her "appropriate" national territory, a trend that dislocated millions of people, by force or by choice, in the decades during and after the war. It was also the beginning of the end of the remaining colonial empires throughout the world. In 1945, while politicians in the United States and Great Britain bickered about the future of the British empire, and the British, the French, and the Dutch made efforts to regain their colonies in Southeast Asia, Japan's empire was terminated with little discussion. These worldwide trends, in combination with the particularities of empire and war in East Asia, went on to influence the region in unpredictable ways. The postwar settlement, more than the war itself, shaped East Asia in the latter half of the twentieth century.

The story of repatriation and deportation provides the means for exploring three overlapping reconfigurations of postwar Japan, the first of which came with defeat: the redrawing of the map of Asia and Japan's place in it. In wartime conferences at Cairo, Yalta, and Potsdam, representatives from the United States, the Republic of China, the United Kingdom, and the Soviet Union planned for the defeat of Japan and sketched out a map for the postwar surrender and Allied occupation of the territory under Japanese control.[6] Some of the arbitrary lines they drew, such as the line dividing the Korean peninsula at the 38th parallel, approximated national boundaries today. The division of Indochina (now Vietnam) at the 16th parallel, with the northern portion falling under Republican Chinese jurisdiction and the southern portion falling under Great Britain's South East Asia Command, prefigured the 1954 division of Vietnam at the 17th parallel. The new map reduced Japanese sovereignty from its vast imperial reach to the four home islands, removing the colonies and also regions that had been recognized diplomatically as parts of the Japanese state. Okinawa, a prefecture of Japan since 1879, was severed from Japan and placed under American

---

5. Kōseishō engokyoku, *Hikiage to engo 30-nen no ayumi*, 151–52.
6. Borton, *American Presurrender Planning for Postwar Japan*.

control, where it remained until 1972. Karafuto (now Sakhalin), a part of Japan since 1905, and the Chishima archipelago (now the Kuril Islands), a part of Japan since 1875, were turned over to the Soviet Union. Japan emerged from the war trimmed of its outlying territories.

The new map of Asia snapped into place on August 15, 1945, and made into foreigners Japanese abroad and colonials within Japan, requiring either their transfer or redefinition. With the colonial spaces of the Korean peninsula, Taiwan, northeast China, and elsewhere transformed into nascent national ones, the project of matching each person to his or her national space began. American military sources explain that a combination of strategic and humanitarian concerns motivated the Allies to repatriate Japanese civilians. The Allies wanted to prevent former colonial rulers from exercising power in post-colonial Asia and to avert the potential slaughter of Japanese nationals at the hands of people against whom they had waged a brutal war.[7] The rationale behind the rush to rid Japan of colonial subjects is less clear, and judging from contemporary American and Japanese sources, was based on expediency and racism.[8] Moreover, groups of people who lacked a powerful sponsor, such as several thousand Korean forced laborers in Karafuto, were abandoned to their fate when the island became the Soviet territory of Sakhalin.[9] The end result of the Allied population transfer was an East Asian region more ethnically homogeneous than it had been during the time of the Japanese empire. The first chapter of this study traces the relatively slow history of the migrations throughout the Japanese empire in contrast to the abrupt arrival of the Allied forces, and the ramifications of the overnight transformation of people from colonial participants into objects of an Allied population transfer.

The clean and swift lines drawn by the Allies on maps and around national groups had a dramatic impact on the Ryukyu archipelago. Okinawa had occupied an ambiguous zone between Japan and its colonies: the state and intellectuals claimed Okinawa as "Japanese," but Okinawans suffered economic and social discrimination—they were even

---

7. Supreme Commander for the Allied Powers, *Reports of General MacArthur*, 149.

8. Reischauer, "Forward," i; Koshiro, *Trans-Pacific Racisms and the U.S. Occupation of Japan*.

9. Ōnuma, *Saharin kimin*.

grouped with other colonial subjects in some situations.[10] During the 1940s, American anthropologists and military planners began to see the Okinawans as an "ethnologically distinct" group, a process that eased the detachment of Okinawa from Japan.[11] At the end of the war, Okinawans outside of the Ryukyu archipelago and Japanese from the home islands in the Ryukyus were cycled through the processes of repatriation and deportation in ways that closely resembled the population transfers to and from the colonies. The concluding chapter of this book analyzes the case of repatriation and deportation in the Ryukyus as an illustration of American ideas on the need to define ethnic groups and then match them to their appropriate territory, and as an example of the unmaking of the Meiji imperial order.

A second reconfiguration of postwar Japan was the uneven and incomplete process of absorbing and re-categorizing the fragments of empire within Japan. The geographic construction of the metropole (*naichi*, 内地; literally, "inner territory"), in tension with the colonies (*gaichi*, 外地; literally, "outer territories"), collapsed overnight. People who had been defined by this construct—the people of the metropole and the people of the colonies, including colonial Japanese—had to be redefined for a new non-imperial society. The reshaping of the colonial Japanese and colonial subjects in Japan into something that made sense or was perhaps useful in post-imperial Japan was a complicated and multifaceted task, carried out in a number of realms across the postwar period.

The Allied redrawing of the map of Asia, in combination with the political and economic dominance of the United States after World War II, led to the third transformation of postwar Asia: the recasting of Japan from its position at the nexus of a multiethnic empire in East Asia into a new position as a monoethnic nation on the far edge of the American sphere of influence. This was both a geographic and social reorientation. The new map of Asia had cut away the colonies as well as the geographical and psychological links to Asia, in the southeast (Okinawa) and the northeast (Karafuto and the Chishima islands). With the American military occupying Okinawa and South Korea, and the Soviet military occupying North Korea, northeast China, and the northeastern

---

10. Christy, "The Making of Imperial Subjects in Okinawa."
11. Ota, "The U.S. Occupation of Okinawa."

islands, the Allied military presence acted as a shield between Japan and the rest of Asia. From October 1945, the Allied Occupation authorities took control of all of Japan's diplomatic relations and restricted contacts with the outside world. The influx of tens of thousands of Allied Occupation personnel created new links to the United States. With its ties to the Asian continent cut, and the wind blowing from a new direction, Japan came about to face eastward, and took up its new mooring as part of the Pacific Rim.

Detached from the Asian continent, Japan's people needed to be re-invented as well. The discourse on the uniqueness of the Japanese people dates back to the eighteenth century, if not before. During the colonial period, propagandists in Japan did their best to make racial sense of Japan in East Asia, using slogans such as "Japan and Korea as One" and "Harmony Between the Five Races" in Manchuria that implied both racial similarity and difference and insisted on Japan's right to "lead" the Asian races. After the war, this rhetoric of harmonious racial pan-Asianism was shed like a snakeskin, leaving only the underlying structures of racial prejudice in place. As Oguma Eiji explains, the image of Japan as a peace-loving, homogeneous state instead of the prewar militaristic multinational empire appeared immediately after the war.[12] "Japanese uniqueness" did not need the Americans to nurture it, but, as Yukiko Koshiro has shown, the Americans were able to use the notion of the racially and culturally unique Japanese people, who were *in* Asia but not *of* it, in their creation of junior Americans ("like a boy of twelve" in the words of General MacArthur) who could be conditioned and mobilized in a supporting role for the cold war.[13] The result was a resurgence of the idea of the Japanese people as culturally and racially unique in a nation with timeless and natural borders, in sharp contrast to its recent history as an expansive imperial power in a multiethnic setting.

The postwar population transfer both accelerated and vexed these new renderings of Japan and its people. By sorting and deporting people based on their ethnicity, Allied-sponsored repatriation and deportation contributed to the homogenization of Japan, making more true Japan's

---

12. Oguma, *A Genealogy of 'Japanese' Self-Images*, 299.

13. MacArthur quoted in Dower, *Embracing Defeat*, 550; Koshiro, *Trans-Pacific Racisms and the U.S. Occupation of Japan*, 112–21.

perceived uniformity. More importantly, this act of sorting contributed to the notion that one could determine, unequivocally, whether a person was Japanese or not. This placed national hybrids—children of mixed parentage or Japanese women married to foreign men (and therefore no longer Japanese citizens)—in a terrible bind. Indeed, the stranding of such hybrids, an inevitable product of colonialism, was one of the main casualties of the transition from empire to nation. The failure to re-patriate and deport everyone who was "supposed" to have been moved, with thousands of Japanese left behind in China and hundreds of thou-sands of Koreans remaining in Japan, complicated efforts to see Japan as homogeneous and isolated from Asia. The trickle of returnees through-out the postwar decades and the large resident Korean population forced ideologues to redouble their efforts to emphasize Japan's cultural isola-tion and homogeneity.

Colonial returnees complicated the issue of Japaneseness, which was supposed to be an all-or-nothing category: people of Japanese blood who spoke the Japanese language and behaved, socially and culturally, in a recognizably Japanese manner.[14] Repatriates, Okinawans, and in a few cases, former colonials, were barely Japanese or partly Japanese, categories that did not fit easily into the new configuration. People who represented these categories challenged the either/or characterization of "Japanese," forcing a different structure, one of concentric circles demarcating degrees of Japaneseness. This is not to imply a postwar affinity between the different peoples relegated to the edges of Japa-neseness. As in the colonies, their position on the outer edges on the Japaneseness scale caused friction, with the now-repatriated colonial Japanese making distinctions between themselves and former colonial subjects. With few economic choices in the immediate postwar period, however, many repatriates ended up at black market stalls, cheek and jowl with other colonial migrants. This placed them in literal proximity to the former colonial subjects, on the edge of Japanese society.

The re-renderings of Japan and its people had a profound impact on returnees, especially those who tried to depict themselves as "inter-nationalists" and wrote optimistically about their hopes to serve as liai-sons between Japan and Asia in an effort to build new relationships and

---

14. Discussions of Japaneseness include Fukuoka, *The Lives of Young Koreans in Japan.*

to help Japan recover from the war.[15] With diplomacy, trade, and travel between Japan and Asia proscribed by the Occupation, those hopes came to naught. In postwar Japan, experience in Asia was obsolete—unless it was deemed valuable by the Allied Occupation forces. In her recollection of her life as a young adult in Manchuria shortly after the war, Japanese colonist Kazuko Kuramoto told of her resolution to learn Chinese as a means of becoming a true citizen of Dalian. When she visited a Japanese professor of the Chinese language, he counseled her to give up on Chinese and learn English, and indeed, Kuramoto's English skills were of more use to her than any China-related knowledge when she sought work with the Americans back in Occupied Japan.[16] The second chapter examines the official and social creation of two new categories, the "repatriate" (*hikiagesha*, 引揚者), and "third country nationals" (*dai-sangokujin*, 第三国人), a euphemism for former colonials.

Gender played a role in the shaping of the *hikiagesha*. Civilian Japanese women in postwar Manchuria were exposed to tremendous violence, and even for those who escaped assault, the suspicion of sexual contamination remained. One oral history informant talked of damage to her marriage prospects because she had been a child in Manchuria.[17] Male civilian repatriates, particularly those who had respectable professions in the colonies, originally escaped much of the stigmatization that women endured at the end of the war. But the 1949 return of the "red repatriates," men who had been detained by the Soviet Union and indoctrinated with socialist ideology, suffused the word *hikiagesha* with a new set of suspicions. The third chapter examines the historical circumstances that contributed to the creation of these two sets of distinctive repatriates.

Returnees drew fire during the cold war within Japan and throughout Asia. The Japanese government, firmly under the U.S. security umbrella, did not at first establish diplomatic ties with the People's Republic of China (PRC), and was unwilling or unable to negotiate for the return of tens of thousands of its citizens remaining on the continent. Three

---

15. *Kokusaijin*, September 10, 1947.

16. Kuramoto, *Manchurian Legacy*, 73–74.

17. Oral history interview, February 14, 2000.

non-governmental organizations—the Japanese Red Cross, the Japan-China Friendship Association, and the Peace Liaison Society—stepped in to fill the void, but the newly established government of the PRC was willing to use any issue in an effort to win diplomatic recognition and used the release of Japanese citizens as a bargaining tool.[18] Between 1953, when repatriation from the PRC began, and 1958, when diplomatic strains put an end to the possibility of repatriation, roughly 30,000 Japanese civilians returned to Japan from China. As in 1949, the encounter between returnees and their homeland was layered with meanings they had no way to anticipate. Many people in Japan, tutored in anti-communism, associated returnees from socialist countries—and sometimes, by extension, all repatriates—with communism.

From the moment of their return, repatriates offered some counter-interpretations of who they were and what their experiences had meant. They tended to use the same expressions in describing their ordeal, creating a language of the repatriation experience. These included sentiments such as "with only the clothes on my back" (*ki no mi ki no mama*, 着の身着のまま), "without a red cent" (*hadaka ikkan*, 裸一貫; literally, "completely naked"), and "but for the grace of God" (*kami hitoe*, 紙一重; literally, "only a sheet of paper" that separated one from another person's fate). While returnees tried to distance themselves from the negative stereotypes of repatriates, they tended to sympathize with each other. Early returnees, such as those from Korea, helped later ones from Manchuria. They published self-help guides and formed civic organizations. The largest organization, led by people repatriated from the Korean peninsula, put its efforts into the issue of compensation for assets former colonists were forced to leave behind at the end of the war.[19] These efforts came to fruition in two waves of government compensation packages, a symbolic award in 1957 and a more substantial award in 1967.[20]

The colonial project and its abrupt end produced two sets of Japanese children profoundly changed by their immediate postwar experi-

---

18. Seraphim, *War Memory and Social Politics in Japan*; Radtke, "Negotiations between the PRC and Japan."

19. Sun, "The Reverse Impact of Colonialism."

20. Campbell, "Compensation for Repatriates"; Orr, *The Victim as Hero*.

ences: those who were repatriated from the colonies as children and those who were not—that is, children who were left behind in China during the repatriation process. People who had returned from the colonies as children or teenagers were particularly affected, by having their childhood experiences in the colonies invalidated and their authenticity as Japanese called into question by their peers. Although many of these experiences were undoubtedly painful, this alienation contributed to the making of some of Japan's most insightful critics. The novelist Abe Kōbō, the nonfiction writer Sawachi Hisae, the jazz musician Akiyoshi Toshiko, and the conductor Ozawa Seiji are but four of Japan's most famous colonial Japanese, with Ozawa sometimes claiming that Chinese, not Japanese, is his mother tongue.[21] Colonial Japanese children were old enough to have internalized passionate feelings of patriotism during the war years, only to experience a profound sense of betrayal of those ideals, compounded by a sense that their government had abandoned them at the end of the war. Some had believed the rhetoric that Japan was working to free Asia from the grip of white colonialism, but when they returned to Japan, its occupation by the United States military exposed the contradictions in the colonial project. They survived the violent end of empire, but, rejected in some cases by their classmates as insufficiently Japanese, chafed within its borders in a kind of reverse exile. Another factor influencing this generation is their time in history. Most were of the "Shōwa single-digit" generation (born between 1926 and 1934), a group known for its role in shaping postwar Japanese memory.[22] Repatriated children later wrote of their spiritual alienation from "ordinary" Japanese people and their sense that they remained on the edge of Japaneseness.[23] This generation produced critiques of postwar Japan, in works of social criticism, film, and literature. Repatriate popular culture and repatriates in popular culture are discussed in the fourth chapter.

People repatriated as children sometimes pondered the lives of their doppelgängers who had faced a more challenging fate: surviving as the

---

21. "Ozawa's Vienna Debut Will Be a Waltz Worth the Wait," *Boston Globe*, January 1, 2002.

22. Gluck, "The Past in the Present," 78.

23. Honda, "Nihon no 'Kamyu' tachi"; Sawachi, *Mō hitotsu no Manshū*, 287.

orphans of belligerents and colonial settlers left behind on enemy soil. These Japanese children left behind in China—of whom an estimated 3,000 survived—had a range of experience: some were raised by Chinese families to be used as servants or future wives, but others were cherished the same as the family's biological offspring. Some remembered that they were Japanese or came to suspect it; many had been teased in childhood as "little Japs" or persecuted during the Cultural Revolution as foreign spies. But others learned of their ethnic origins only as their adoptive parents began to die off in the 1970s and 1980s, either through deathbed revelations or encounters with family paperwork. With the resumption of diplomatic ties between Japan and the PRC in 1972, people of Japanese descent began to return for the first time since 1958. Born of Japanese parents but otherwise Chinese, they faced serious linguistic, cultural, and social challenges returning "home" to Japan as adults. The issue of "orphans left behind in China" (*Chūgoku zanryū koji*, 中国残留孤児) did not gather momentum until a critical mass of people began to return in the early 1980s, but their arrival in Japan served to remind the general public of something the repatriates had known all along: that wartime ties and unfinished business still existed between Japan and China. The Japanese who returned from Manchuria as children dwelled on their sense of intellectual and spiritual alienation, but the "orphans" lived that alienation, in the PRC and eventually back in Japan, in much more profound ways. With the return of the "orphans" in the 1980s, addressed in the fifth chapter, repatriates once again provided fuel for the fire in the discussion of who really counted as Japanese.

Historians Andrew Gordon, John Dower, and others have noted the lack of scholarly attention to postwar repatriation. Andrew Gordon writes that "while [repatriation] was a relatively swift and smooth process, to absorb such a vast number of people was a complex undertaking which left a legacy that has not yet been fully studied or understood. Repatriates, both civilian and military, often felt out of place back "home," regarded with a mixture of pity for their poverty and scorn for their role in pursuing what now appeared to have been a hopeless war."[24] John Dower notes that, "The fate of these [colonial] Japanese is

---

24. Gordon, *A Modern History of Japan*, 230.

a neglected chapter among the countless epic tragedies of World War II."[25] Since the 1990s, scholars have explored different aspects of repatriation including repatriate housing, the patterns of repatriate employment after the war, and memories of returnees, particularly agricultural settlers.[26]

A combination of historical and historiographical factors contributed to the obfuscation of the story of postwar repatriation and deportation. In the postwar period, and in interpretations of that period, decolonization has been drowned out by more pressing forces: Japan's catastrophic defeat, Allied occupations, civil wars in China and Korea, and East Asia's role as a frontline in the cold war. The breakup of Japan's imperial formation and subsequent turn away from empire are also compelling transitions, but have tended to be buried under these more dramatic plotlines. Moreover, unlike other empires, the Japanese empire was taken apart by the Allies, not through negotiations between the metropolitan state and its former colonies. This process of "third party decolonization" profoundly influenced the uneven, incomplete, and vexed dissolution of Japan's empire in Asia.

The competing forces of collective remembrance in Japan worked to occlude the story as well. In the immediate postwar period, stories of victimization, including those of atomic and conventional bombing, and the abuse of ordinary citizens by a militaristic state, were put to a

---

25. Dower, *Embracing Defeat*, 50.

26. Inaba Jurō has written about repatriates who lived in the Tsuchiura repatriate dormitory and the emergence of a repatriate consciousness (Inaba, "Hikiagesha no sengo," 298). On post-repatriation employment, see Sun, "The Reverse Impact of Colonialism"; Sun, "Nihon no koyō seido"; and Odaka, "Hikiagesha to sensō chokugo no rōdōryoku." On the agricultural settlers, see Tamanoi, "A Road to a Redeemed Mankind"; Tamanoi, "Knowledge, Power, and Racial Classification"; and Guelcher, "Dreams of Empire." In 2002, under the direction of Katō Kiyofumi, Yumani shobō published 35 volumes and two CD-ROMs of primary sources related to repatriation, centralizing many of the disparate and often fragile records related to the history of repatriation (see Katō, ed., *Kaigai hikiage kankei shiryō shūsei*). Asano Toyomi, *Datsu shokuminchika purosesu*, provides an impressive overview of repatriation-related materials in the United States and Japan and argues that repatriation and the issue of Japanese assets abroad shaped postwar East Asian diplomatic relations. An early monograph on the history of repatriation was published by legal scholar Wakatsuki Yasuo in 1991 (Wakatsuki, *Sengo hikiage no kiroku*).

variety of uses in negotiating the transition from war to postwar.[27] As Franziska Seraphim has shown, civic groups across the political spectrum in Japan vigorously tended their versions of war memory, a process that led, in part, to the association of war memory with special interest groups.[28] At least until the 1960s, however, there was an unconscious sealing of the national borders around these stories: only narratives of Japanese suffering that took place on the home islands of Japan qualified as legitimate national remembrances of suffering in World War II. The sufferings and losses of colonial Japanese remained trapped outside, stopped at water's edge, and were not adopted as part of the national story of suffering. As argued further in the Conclusion, the process of separating and buffering the homeland from the history of the colonies made useless, in terms of national victimization, the otherwise compelling stories of Japanese suffering.

The figure of the repatriate accrued and shed meanings across the postwar period, and the meaning of the word changed depending on who used it. For that reason, to define *hikiagesha*, once and for all, would be folly. It is nevertheless revealing to look at some attempts to define the word. The broadest definition of a repatriate is any of the 6 million people who passed through and completed paperwork at a regional repatriation center on the way back to Japan after World War II. People who were documented in this way entered into the records of the bureaucracy most deeply involved with repatriation, the Ministry of Health and Welfare. One problem with this definition is that it fails to make a clear distinction between civilians and military personnel. Overseas civilians became repatriates; military men demobilized from overseas became demobilized soldiers (*fukuinhei*) and eventually "veterans" (*beteran*). But in part to distinguish themselves from military men who were demobilized domestically, soldiers returning from overseas often referred to themselves colloquially as repatriates. A majority of the most notorious repatriates, the Siberian detainees, had been military men and therefore technically not repatriates at all. Returnees from the United States and Europe—that is, places other than the former Japanese empire—

---

27. "What Do You Tell the Dead When You Lose?" in Dower, *Embracing Defeat*, 485–521.

28. Seraphim, *War Memory and Social Politics in Japan*.

were processed at regional repatriation centers but occupied different administrative categories and did not qualify for repatriate compensation or recognition. Nevertheless, some of these returnees from the West, and not the colonies, insisted that they, too, were *hikiagesha*.

A 1957 law that served as the basis for small benefits payments to returnees provided a legal definition of a repatriate: a person whose livelihood had been in the colonies for more than six months preceding defeat.[29] Whereas the 1957 definition clarified some aspects of who, for the purposes of compensation, counted as a repatriate, it clouded others by making room for unrepatriated repatriates: people who were bona fide residents of the colonies but who happened to be in Japan at the end of the war, and therefore did not experience the often searing trip back to Japan. By the time of the second compensation package in 1967, the definition, reflecting a shift in political understandings, had changed.[30] The 1957 definition implied that a repatriate was a poor person in need of welfare. The 1967 definition removed the income ceiling for compensation and included language about a commitment to empire, indicating that a repatriate was now a returnee of any income bracket and who deserved some official recognition for his service and his losses. Later laws included other caveats, reflecting the success of lobbying efforts and changing political understandings. These legal definitions, discussed further in the fifth chapter, were generated in the official realm for the purposes of state compensation. Complex and dynamic understandings of the repatriate also developed in the realms of literature, film, memoirs, and commemorative efforts.

Repatriates were defined in the crucible of imperialism, colonialism, and decolonization. Imperialism is the set of ideas of political, economic, and cultural domination of another territory, ideas that are generated primarily in the metropole, in Japan's case, the home islands or *naichi*. Colonialism is the implementation of those ideas in the colonial setting, in Japan's case, *gaichi*. Resistance to the word "de-imperialization" means

---

29. Hikiagesha kyūfukin tō shikyū hō (Repatriate benefits allowance law). Law no. 109, May 17, 1957.

30. Hikiagesha tō ni taisuru tokubetsu kōfukin no shikyū ni kansuru hōritsu (Repatriate special subsidy allowance law). Law no. 104, 55th Diet Session (Special), August 1, 1967.

that "decolonization" refers to the post-colonial and post-imperial processes in both the former colonies and the metropole. Japan's empire was composed of many different forms of colonies: formal, informal, treaty ports, mandates, wartime acquisitions administered by the military, and the anomalous Manchukuo.[31] The difference in these colonial forms mattered a great deal in the administrative and economic realms, but was less significant with defeat when Japanese nationals stopped being participants in their particular colonial formation and became Japanese abroad.

Although this history of the end of empire in East Asia is interested in every person who passed through a regional repatriation center, the people repatriated from Manchuria are of particular importance. The majority of repatriates came from Korea, Taiwan, China south of the Great Wall, and elsewhere, but the widespread social image of the repatriate is based on the women, men, and children who were in Manchuria after the war. The Japanese in Manchuria were a source of fascination—celebratory and disapproving—for people in the homeland even before 1945, and the lurid (and often censored) stories surrounding the year they spent in Manchuria after the war before repatriation served only to add to the image of a group as a possible threat to people at home. Allied military personnel, including American officers who unexpectedly found themselves responsible for large Japanese civilian populations, played an important role in the process, but the goal of this study is to present this story as it was understood by actors in East Asia. The question of how American military and civil authorities made sense of their role in this population transfer remains to be explored further.

Understandings of hygiene in Japan's colonial spaces influenced domestic perceptions of Japanese colonial returnees. In her remarkable book about how Chinese elites negotiated modernity through various

---

31. For different kinds of colonies, see Beasley, *Japanese Imperialism 1894-1945*; Myers and Peattie, eds., *The Japanese Colonial Empire, 1895–1945*; and Duus, Myers, and Peattie, eds., *The Japanese Informal Empire in China, 1895–1937* and *The Japanese Wartime Empire, 1931–1945*. A large body of scholarship now exists on different aspects of Manchuria. When referring to that geographical region, now the three northeastern provinces of the PRC, I use "Manchuria"; when referring to the Japanese-sponsored state that existed in the region from 1932 to 1945, I use "Manchukuo," the English-language name used by the Japanese architects of the state when writing in English about it.

understandings of hygiene, Ruth Rogaski shows how Meiji medical experts tried to import the "full kit" of modern hygienic practices—including public health and medical institutions, sanitary police, and laboratories—to control germs in their efforts to modernize the nation.[32] Lessons learned in making domestic society hygienic were then applied in the colonies. In Taiwan, Japanese authorities under the leadership of Gotō Shinpei sought to make all of Taiwan a hygienic space, which reduced the need to police boundaries between Japanese and Taiwanese communities.[33] In Korea, authorities sought to raise the level of hygiene by training doctors and modernizing public health and medicine, but Japanese civilians still complained about the unhygienic nature of the Korean people. Rogaski also shows that in China, or at least in the city of Tianjin, Japanese authorities concerned themselves with the health of Chinese people mainly when they perceived that their substandard hygiene might represent a threat to the Japanese population. Especially after 1937, Japanese authorities sought to control the sources of contagious diseases such as cholera by inspecting Chinese homes at gunpoint, quarantining victims of the diseases, and burning infected corpses. Japanese authorities viewed prostitutes in China as potential carriers of venereal disease and therefore a threat to Japanese people, and they placed prostitutes of all nationalities including Japanese under their "sanitary sex" system. But as Rogaski concludes, maintaining places sufficiently hygienic for Japanese people in the informal empire in China had more to do with policing the boundaries between Japanese and Chinese communities than attempting to transform all of China into a hygienic space.[34] For these reasons, returnees from Taiwan and to a certain extent Korea were understood to have come from hygienic spaces and therefore were less of a threat to conditions in Japan. Early returnees from the intact Japanese concessions in China had less time to be exposed to unhygienic China as well. As explored further in the third chapter, the 1946 returnees from Manchuria had spent a year in China after the authorities were no longer able to police the boundaries between Japanese communities and others, and had therefore been ex-

---

32. Rogaski, *Hygienic Modernity*, 136–64.
33. Ibid., 258–59.
34. Ibid., 260–84.

posed to unhygienic conditions, further contributing to the ambivalent reception of the Manchurian Japanese.

Population transfers occurred throughout the world in the twentieth century, and repatriation and deportation in Japan resonated with at least two other movements of people. The end of French rule in colonial Algeria triggered the flight of nearly a million European Algerians in 1962.[35] The *pieds noirs*, as they were known, faced difficulties in integrating into a home to which many of them had never been.[36] Placing *pieds noirs* and *hikiagesha* side by side—as repatriate critic Honda Yasuharu did in a 1979 article—suggests that colonial returnees in many places play roles as buffers in the transition from imperial to postimperial formations.[37] Japanese repatriation began just months after the beginning of the expulsions of an estimated 12 million ethnic Germans from Eastern Europe and elsewhere immediately following the end of the war.[38] A comparison to the German case shows similarities in the postwar fate of Axis belligerents, particularly for those who ended up in Soviet hands, but reveals striking differences in how people in postwar West Germany and Japan made use of these episodes in their national histories. The comparative aspects of Japanese repatriation are addressed further in the Conclusion.

Historians have characterized interwar Japan as a nation mobilized for "total war."[39] John Dower answers, in many ways, the question of what happened after defeat to a people mobilized for total war.[40] As Louise Young has shown, Japan was also a nation mobilized for "total empire," with communities throughout Japan feverish in their support of expansionism.[41] The history of Japan's total empire raises an analogous question of what happened to a people mobilized for empire after the failure of the colonial project. In the immediate postwar period, the 3 million *hikiagesha* repatriated from the colonies underwent a process

---

35. Stora, *Algeria, 1830–2000*.

36. Ibid., 8.

37. Honda, "Nihon no 'Kamyu' tachi," 199; Stora, "The 'Southern' World of the Pieds Noirs."

38. Naimark, *Fires of Hatred*; Bramwell, ed., *Refugees in the Age of Total War*.

39. Barnhart, *Japan Prepares for Total War*.

40. Dower, *Embracing Defeat*.

41. Young, *Japan's Total Empire*.

of stigmatization that allowed metropolitan Japanese to distance themselves from the failed colonial project and ultimately contributed to the obscuring of Japan's imperial history by saddling the responsibility of it onto the colonial returnees. Once the image of the *hikiagesha* had been created, it then served as a convenient domestic "other" and as a vessel for a variety of postwar anxieties, including the contamination of the nation's women by foreigners, possible communist indoctrination in Siberian detainees, and potential social disruption by mavericks in general. In addition to coming to grips with their lost colonial homes and trying to survive in devastated postwar Japan, repatriates also had to negotiate with the stereotype of being someone pitiable, but also possibly contaminated, poorly socialized, or troublesome. By the 1980s, with the last wave of colonial returnees, Japanese society no longer had a need to distance itself from colonial failure, and the *Chūgoku zanryū koji*, instead of being cycled through the extant category of *hikiagesha*, were put to other, non-imperial uses. War and defeat have been defining factors in many aspects of "postwar" Japan. In less visible ways, so have the empire and the loss of the colonies. This book explores how that loss was incorporated into postwar Japan, that is, what happened when empire came home.

ONE

New Maps of Asia

"'State employees,' 'pioneers,' 'pillars of the continent': now they have been labeled 'repatriates' and become destitute."[1] So wrote the sympathetic publisher of Tamana Katsuo's 1947 record of his year in postwar Manchuria, from August 1945 until his repatriation in September 1946, during which time he was transformed from a "state employee" into a repatriate.[2] To understand the creation of these "pioneers" and their transformation into repatriates, we must undertake an overview of the geopolitical changes through which Tamana and others lived. The first part of this chapter recounts the history of Japanese colonial expansion and the migrations to and from the metropole that accompanied it. The second part tells of the imposition of a new geopolitical configuration on East and Southeast Asia with the arrival of the Allied forces. The Allies placed the inhabitants of the former Japanese empire into new categories that were often puzzling to the people who were forced to inhabit them. At their final destinations, yet another set of categorizations awaited them.

---

1. Minakawa, "Hikiagesha mondai ni yosete," 128.

2. The title page identified Tamana as a former employee of the South Manchuria Railway Company (SMRC). Tamana identified himself as employed by "a certain large company in Manchuria" (満州の某大会社). Tamana, *Hadaka no 600-mannin*, 1. The publisher Minakawa indicated that Tamana worked for Nichiman Shōji (日満商事) from about 1935, presumably after his employment with the SMRC. Minakawa, "Hikiagesha mondai ni yosete," 127.

A History of Migration in the Japanese Empire

The years from 1895 to 1945 marked an extraordinary period of move-ment for people to and from the Japanese archipelago, and, as the his-torian Katō Yōko has pointed out, more Japanese people were abroad in 1945 than in 1995.[3] From the time of the "closed country" (*sakoku*) edicts of the 1630s, the early modern state forbade its subjects to leave Japan, and it was not until 1884 that ordinary people were given the right to emigrate. With new possibilities for mobility, people left Japan for any number of reasons. The new tax systems of the Meiji period burdened peasants, some of whom left for Hawaii and the Americas to seek eco-nomic relief and new lives. In East Asia, military service and colonial opportunities circulated millions of Japanese through the region.

Military ventures and colonial expansion were closely linked, and all of Japan's imperial acquisitions were preceded by or tied to some kind of military action. The military required civilian support systems in order to establish colonial rule and to provide for family members who later accompanied them to the colonies. Men who became familiar with the colonies as soldiers sometimes went back later as civilians, often with families in tow.[4] Farming families recruited to settle in Manchuria were trained in how to handle weapons. The line between military and civilian in the colonies was often blurred.

The circulation of military men and Japanese civilians contributed to metropolitan views of the colonies. As reflected in their letters home and in conversations with their relatives and friends, the impressions of individuals who had traveled through or lived in these regions added a personal strand to the official and commercial media voices that worked hard to present the colonies in positive and appealing ways.[5] All of those views, in turn, influenced the reception of overseas Japanese and former colonial subjects after the war.

Meiji Japan's first overseas military engagement, the Taiwan Expedi-tion of 1874, illustrates the intersection between military actions, plans for colonization, and domestic interpretations of the actions in the commercial press at home. In 1874, the Japanese government sent a mil-

---

3. Katō Yōko, "Haisha no kikan," 110.
4. Oral history interview, November 19, 2000.
5. Lone, *Japan's First Modern War*, 59–60.

itary contingent to Taiwan ostensibly to punish aborigines who had killed a group of fishermen from the Ryukyu archipelago—an act that provided the opportunity to test the newly established military and to demonstrate sovereignty over the Ryukyus by displaying state concern for its "citizens." As illuminated by the historian Robert Eskildsen, official sources reveal that the government explored the idea of colonization but made its primary goal the containment of the event. Commercial sources, on the other hand, celebrated the overseas mission, and used it to promote the idea of Japan's civilizing mission in Taiwan.[6] Twenty-one years later, when Japan received rights to colonize Taiwan after the Sino-Japanese War of 1894–95 against the Qing, colonization had already been rehearsed.

After Japan's victory in 1895, men in the Japanese Army were in Taiwan again to pacify the resistance to Japanese colonial rule, an effort that lasted until 1897. Soon, Japanese civilians began to move to Taiwan to help build the colony. Although colonial archives, especially population censuses, need to be used with caution, they can still provide a sense of demographic change over time. In 1900, an estimated 38,000 *naichijin*, Japanese from the home islands, had settled in Taiwan. According to the population censuses instituted in the name of scientific imperial administration by Governor General Gotō Shinpei, the Japanese population grew steadily: 135,400 by 1915; 183,800 by 1925; and 272,700 by 1935.[7] The last Taiwan-wide census conducted by the colonial gov-

---

6. Eskildsen, "Of Civilization and Savages."

7. "Nihon oyobi sono shokumin chiiki ni okeru jinkō no hattatsu," in Ōkurashō kanrikyoku, *Nihonjin no kaigai katsudō.* vol. 1, 204–5. Note on this source: immediately after the war, the Ministry of Finance (MOF) oversaw the compilation of a series of surveys and reports called *Nihonjin no kaigai katsudō ni kansuru rekishiteki chōsa* (A historical survey of the overseas activities of Japanese nationals). The various agencies of the Allied Occupation of Japan needed reference materials for the purpose of calculating reparations; the Japanese government needed information on Japanese people and assets overseas. The MOF reports, directed in part by former colonial officials, were intended to meet those needs, and some of the reports were translated into English. Although much of the information in the reports, including an evaluation of Japanese-owned assets abroad, was of public interest, the MOF never intended to publish the reports, and the courts ruled against early attempts to make the reports publicly available. In 1985, Kōrai shorin published a reproduction of the reports in a 12-volume series in Seoul. In 2002, Yumani shobō, under the direction of the historian Kobayashi Hideo, reprinted the reports in a

ernment took place in 1935, and population figures during the war years are more difficult to pin down. One source listed 365,000 Japanese people in Taiwan 1941;[8] another source gives the number of Japanese people in Taiwan in 1942 as 385,000.[9] By the end of the war, Ministry of Health and Welfare sources estimated 582,000 Japanese people—350,000 civilians, 169,000 Army, and 63,000 Navy—in Taiwan.[10] Migration from the home islands accounted for most of the Japanese population growth, but births in Taiwan contributed as well.

Perhaps more striking than the steady increase of the Japanese population in Taiwan is the amount of traffic between Taiwan and Japan. From 1900 to 1938, the colonial government of Taiwan kept statistics on the number of Japanese people who traveled to and from the home islands. From 1900 to 1904, for example, of the 80,500 Japanese people who traveled to Taiwan, 62,100 returned to Japan and 18,400 remained in Taiwan. Of the 293,500 Japanese people who traveled to Taiwan between 1930 and 1934, 273,700 returned to Japan and 14,800 remained.[11] These numbers indicate not only that the number of Japanese people who settled in Taiwan increased incrementally over time, but also that a much larger number of Japanese people, tens of thousands per year, cycled through the colonies, demonstrating available transportation and close links between the home islands and Taiwan.

The Japanese colonization of Taiwan shaped Chinese demography as well. When the Japanese military arrived to establish the colony in 1895, it gave the Han Chinese residents a choice: they could leave for the mainland by May 1897 or remain under Japanese rule. Many of the gentry did leave, but those who could not, or chose not to leave, remained.[12] The

---

24-volume series. The 1985 and 2002 editions of this source are facsimiles of the original 1947 report and therefore the content is identical. The reports are arranged slightly differently in the two editions. Because my page references come from the 1985 edition, I include titles of the reports for those who refer to the 2002 edition.

8. "Nihon oyobi sono shokumin chiiki ni okeru jinkō no hattatsu," in Ōkurashō kanrikyoku, *Nihonjin no kaigai katsudō*, vol. 1, 205.

9. Tōyō keizai shinpōsha, ed., *Kanketsu Shōwa kokusei sōran dai 3 kan*, 302.

10. Kōseishō shakai engokyoku, *Engo 50-nen shi*, 10–11, 17–18, 29–34.

11. "Nihon oyobi sono shokumin chiiki ni okeru jinkō no hattatsu," in Ōkurashō kanrikyoku, *Nihonjin no kaigai katsudō*. vol. 1, 208.

12. Lamley, "Taiwan Under Japanese Rule," 208.

Taiwanese population of Taiwan grew during the colonial period, nearly doubling from 2,546,000 in 1895 to 4,733,300 in 1935.[13]

After the establishment of colonial rule, Taiwanese continued to travel outside of Taiwan and "foreigners," almost exclusively people from mainland China, traveled to Taiwan. For example, from 1931 to 1935, records indicate that 89,738 Chinese entered Taiwan and 82,819 left Taiwan; in the same period, 60,771 Taiwanese went to "foreign countries" (usually to Fujian and Guangdong Provinces in nearby China) and 61,394 returned. During this period, 33,035 Taiwanese went to Japan and 32,000 returned. Few Taiwanese settled in Japan's other colonies, although the colonial government tried to deploy them to expand the empire.[14] But Taiwanese registered as colonial Japanese, or *sekimin* (籍民), did travel to Japan's other formal and informal holdings on the Chinese mainland.[15] Some of the *sekimin* were indeed from Taiwan, but officials in Japanese enclaves in southern China allowed some Chinese people to register as *sekimin*. As Barbara Brooks explains, the *sekimin*, as subimperialists, gained some of the advantages and bore some of the burdens of their status: the former included extraterritoriality in treaty ports and economic rights, and the latter their position as Chinese people doing the will of the imperial power.[16] Towards the end of the war, the Japanese military actively recruited Taiwanese for the war effort, and at defeat, approximately 207,000 Taiwanese were in the Japanese military.[17] When the war ended, some 25,000 to 35,000 Taiwanese were in Japan.[18]

As Ruth Rogaski has shown, Gotō Shinpei and other colonial leaders implemented parts of the Meiji system of public sanitation and health in

---

13. These figures do not include the aboriginal population, listed as *seibanjin* (生蕃人). According to the figures in the Ministry of Finance reports, the numbers of aborigines dropped from a Chinese estimate of 148,000 in 1886 to a low of 46,300 in 1920, before rising to an estimated 155,700 in 1941. "Nihon oyobi sono shokumin chiiki ni okeru jinkō no hattatsu." In Ōkurashō kanrikyoku, *Nihonjin no kaigai katsudō*, vol. 1, 204–5.

14. Phillips, *Between Assimilation and Independence*, 29.

15. Lamley, "Taiwan Under Japanese Rule," 223–31.

16. Brooks, *Japan's Imperial Diplomacy*, 106. For further analysis of colonial citizenship and migration, see also Brooks, "Japanese Colonial Citizenship" and "Peopling the Japanese Empire."

17. Kōseishō shakai engokyoku, *Engo 50-nen shi*, 23; Chen, "Imperial Army Betrayed."

18. Kōseishō engokyoku, *Hikiage to engo 30-nen no ayumi*, 151.

Taiwan and worked hard to bring the colony in line with Japanese standards of hygiene.[19] In 1947 reports on Taiwan's demography, the authors, still promoting the hygienic nature of Taiwan, imply that Taiwan under Japanese rule had been more sanitary and advanced than the home islands.[20] Leo Ching has challenged the idea of Taiwan as the unproblematic colony, one relatively free from violence, and shows how this discourse on Taiwan was generated in the pre- and post-colonial periods.[21] Nevertheless, from the Japanese point of view, Taiwan was perceived as the most hygienic and peaceful of the colonies and that impression colored the perception of the Japanese civilians. For these reasons, and the relative calm in Taiwan during and after the war, people in the metropole did not usually perceive Japanese colonists from Taiwan as carriers of negative colonial qualities.

Even before its formal annexation in 1910, Korea had been the site of a great deal of Japanese military and colonial circulation. Like Taiwan, the Korean peninsula had been caught up from the beginning of the establishment of the modern Meiji state and its military. The 1873 discussion of whether to send a mission to "punish Korea" split the newly established Meiji government, a division that reverberated through Japanese politics for two decades.[22] The faction against invading Korea won out, and no action was taken. Three years later, however, in 1876, Japan forced on Korea the unequal Kanghwa Treaty and began to use the framework of modern diplomacy on Korea, making the old East Asian order obsolete.[23] From 1876 to 1894, Korea remained under the influence of both Qing China and Japan, but the Kanghwa Treaty created many opportunities for Japanese traders, the early "brokers of empire," in the words of the historian Jun Uchida.[24] Mostly small businessmen, they moved to Korea even before the official colonial apparatus

---

19. "Transforming *Eisei* in Meiji Japan," in Rogaski, *Hygienic Modernity*.

20. The authors of the specific reports are not named, but the introduction indicates that they were written by people with knowledge of the colonies. Kitayama Fukujirō, professor at Taihoku Imperial University in Taiwan, and Kaneko Shigeo of the Bank of Taiwan are identified as editors of the project.

21. Ching, *Becoming "Japanese."*

22. Ravina, *The Last Samurai*, 184.

23. Kim, *The Last Phase of the East Asian World Order*.

24. Uchida, "Brokers of Empire," 153.

had been established. It was the Sino-Japanese War of 1894–95 that brought tens of thousands of ordinary Japanese soldiers to the Korean peninsula, parts of China, and Manchuria, where battles against Qing China were fought. These men recorded impressions of the region and shared them with people back home. As Stewart Lone has shown, the depictions of Korea were uniformly negative, although those of Manchuria were somewhat nuanced.[25] The removal of Qing Chinese influence in Korea put Japan into conflict with the other power in the region, Russia, leading to the Russo-Japanese War of 1904–05. This time, hundreds of thousands of Japanese troops circulated through the region.

The Japanese civilian population in colonial Korea grew steadily. At the time of the Kanghwa Treaty in 1876, an estimated 54 Japanese people lived in Korea. When it became a protectorate of Japan in 1905, at the end of the Russo-Japanese War, the Japanese population of Korea was over 40,000 people. By the time of the 1910 annexation of Korea, the Japanese population was over 170,000, and the population grew over time. The 1942 census indicated a population of 752,823. That number dropped to approximately 710,000 in May 1944, in part because the 1942 census overestimated the population and because of the large-scale military mobilization in the final years of the war.[26] As of September 1945, an estimated 720,100 Japanese civilians (285,000 north and 435,000 south of the 38th parallel) and 294,000 Army personnel were on the Korean peninsula. [27]

The colonization of Korea put Koreans on the move as well. The number of Koreans who were in Japan before annexation in 1910 is unclear, and estimates range from 790 to several thousands.[28] The first

---

25. Stewart Lone suggests that the war was "a kind of tourism." Lone, *Japan's First Modern War*, 58.

26. The numbers on the Japanese population in Korea come from Morita, *Chōsen shūsen no kiroku*, 1.

27. For estimates of civilians in September 1945, see USAMGIK, 7–9. The Ministry of Health and Welfare gives estimates of 294,000 Army and 42,000 Navy personnel on the entire Korean peninsula at the end of the war. Kōseishō shakai engokyoku. *Engo 50-nen shi*, 11, 17. Morita Yoshio gives the number of approximately 600,000 Japanese civilians and military personnel in South Korea at the end of the war (Morita, *Chōsen shūsen no kiroku*, 328).

28. The 790 figure appears in Lee and De Vos, *Koreans in Japan*, 32. Fukuoka Yasunori argues that that figure is too low. Fukuoka, *Lives of Young Koreans in Japan*, 3.

phase of Korean migration to Japan, due to changes in the land-tenure system in colonial Korea in which peasants found it increasingly difficult to survive, took place in the 1920s and 1930s, with an increase in the number of Koreans in Japan from 39,000 in 1921 to 400,000 in 1930.[29] With the war in China in 1937, and the need to conscript Korean labor to replace Japanese men recruited as soldiers, even more Koreans came— or were forced to come—to Japan. By 1945, estimates of the number of Koreans in Japan range from 2 million to 2.4 million.[30]

Colonial forces pushed Koreans to other places as well. Koreans had migrated to the Jiandao region in China north of the Tumen River before colonization, and by 1932, 80 percent of the estimated population was Korean. Japanese acquisition and expansion of railroads in Manchuria facilitated the movement of Koreans between Andong, the city just across the Yalu River from North Korea, to Fengtian (now Shenyang) and points north. Some migrated to remote areas in Manchuria and grew rice in inhospitable regions. According to research by the Public Safety Division of Manchukuo, 1,345,212 Koreans lived in Manchuria in 1940, with about half of that number in the Jiandao region; many were not counted, however, and it is likely that more than 1.5 million Koreans lived in Manchuria at this time. Approximately 100,000 Koreans lived in China south of Manchuria by 1941, mostly in North China. Koreans moved to Japan's other colonial spaces. Census takers counted 2,260 Koreans in Taiwan in 1939, and 16,056 in Karafuto in 1940.[31] These numbers come from a 1947 Japanese report on colonial demography in which the authors stressed that these flows demonstrated good transportation and the freedom to choose one's home under Japanese administration, an interpretation that contradicts policies of forced labor and sex work. They say little about the conditions faced by Koreans abroad, other than to mention that Korean women in Taiwan tended to work in the "hospitality industry."[32] Barbara Brooks, on the other hand, explains

---

29. Mitchell, *The Korean Minority in Japan*, 29.

30. For a discussion of the estimates of the numbers of Koreans in Japan at the end of the war, see note 93 in Chapter 2 of the present study.

31. "Nihon oyobi sono shokumin chiiki ni okeru jinkō no hattatsu," in Ōkurashō kanrikyoku, *Nihonjin no kaigai katsudō*, vol. 1, 223–26.

32. The description "hospitality industry" (*fujin no sekkyakugyō*, 婦人の接客業) is, of course, used euphemistically. Ibid., 226.

that "an official discourse of fear and hatred, embodied in the government records about the 'Korean problem' of *futei Senjin* [不逞鮮人, "malcontent Korean"], spread from the Korean colony, where discrimination against Koreans was strongest, to the popular language of people throughout the empire."[33] The Japanese in Taiwan presented an image of a colonial elite ruling over a well-mannered colonial population, but in Korea, the Japanese mixture of military and colonial administrators, independent-minded small businesspeople and freelancers, ruling over a sometimes hostile colonial population, presented a more complicated picture. This, in turn, influenced the reception of postwar repatriates from Korea and Koreans who remained in Japan in the postwar period.

Like the colonization of Taiwan and Korea, the colonization of Manchuria began with the circulation of soldiers through the region during the Sino- and Russo-Japanese Wars. Japanese attempts to gain rights on the Liaodong peninsula, the foothold into Manchuria, were thwarted in 1895 but succeeded after defeating Czarist Russia in 1905. The South Manchuria Railway, established in 1906, led Japan's railway empire in Manchuria. Japanese soldiers continued to cycle through the region: between 1918 and 1922, more than 72,000 Japanese troops participated in the Siberian Intervention, an expedition initiated by the United States to extricate stranded Czechoslovakian troops from Siberia and to test the stability of the Bolsheviks. Some Japanese military personnel from that expedition remained in Siberia and northern Manchuria as late as 1922, and in the Russian and then Soviet part of Sakhalin (above the 50th parallel) until 1925.[34] These military actions had links with colonialism later, both in terms of establishing a Japanese presence and acquainting individual Japanese people with the region. In 1918, 16-year-old Horiguchi Tatsusaburō went to Siberia for the first time as a member of the Japanese forces fighting against the Bolsheviks. Later in 1937, as a 41-year-old community leader, drawing on his Manchurian and Siberian experience, he cajoled farmers in his village to emigrate to Manchuria.[35]

While civilians relished the opportunity to travel in Manchuria—the novelist Natsume Sōseki went in 1909 and the poet Yosano Akiko in

---

33. Brooks, "Peopling the Empire," 31.
34. Coox, *Nomonhan*, 8–9.
35. Yamakawa, *Manshū ni kieta bunson*, 40–42.

1931—the government and the Kwantung (Guandong) Army (関東軍), the Japanese military in Manchuria, found it difficult to persuade people to settle permanently, especially outside the major urban areas of Dairen (now Dalian), Fengtian (now Shenyang), Xinjing (now Changchun), and Harbin.[36] Even after the Manchurian Incident of 1931 and the establishment of Manchukuo in 1932, the government faced resistance on the part of ordinary Japanese to settle in Manchuria. After 1937, the government increased the incentives and the pressures to motivate people to participate in settlement programs, and only then did large numbers of farmers began to move to Manchuria, intending to stay permanently.

In an attempt both to alleviate the perceived problem of an over-population of poor farmers in Japan and to shore up the borders between Manchukuo and the Soviet Union, the government developed two programs, one for teenage boys and another for farm families, to settle Manchuria and Mongolia.[37] Agrarian enthusiasts never reached their goal of 5 million people, but still managed to recruit a total of about 300,000 people: 240,000 people in farming families for Manchurian agricultural settlements and 60,000 boys in the Manchurian Youth Corps Brigade.[38] For the agricultural settlers, a lack of prospects at home and the possibility of owning their own pieces of land motivated them to move to Manchuria. The promise of exemption from military service was also appealing for young men. Although the agricultural settlers were only a small portion (about 10 percent) of the total number of Japanese civilians abroad at the end of the war, because of their traumatic postwar history, the image of settlers who returned from Manchuria came to serve as the quintessential repatriate in postwar Japan.

---

36. Guelcher, "Dreams of Empire" discusses the early government failures to settle people in Manchuria, 2–17. For Sōseki's journey, see Natsume Sōseki, "Travels in Manchuria and Korea"; for Yosano Akiko, see Yosano, *Travels in Manchuria and Mongolia*; for tourism in Manchuria, see Young, *Japan's Total Empire*, 259–68, and Kushner, *The Thought War*, 45.

37. Young, *Japan's Total Empire*, especially Part IV, "The New Social Imperialism and the Farm Colonization Program, 1932–1945" and Kami, *Man-Mō kaitaku seishōnen giyūgun*, 39.

38. As of the end of May 1945, when all available men had been drafted out of the settlements, the Manchurian "National" Census (Manshūkoku seifu no kokusei chōsa) provides the number of 196,739 settlers in 743 settlements. Man-Mō dōhō engokai, ed., *Man-Mō shūsen shi*, 443–44.

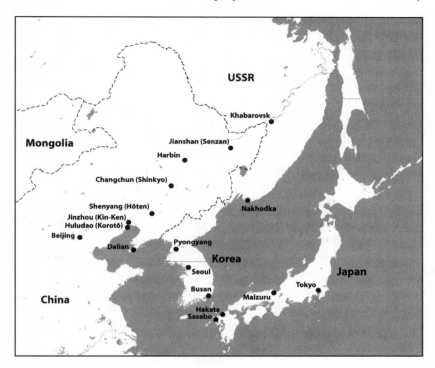

Map 1   Northeast Asia, 1946

Although each Manchurian settler group had its own story, the history of one group, the Senzan Sarashinagō (尖山更科郷) agricultural settlement from Nagano Prefecture, provides an illustration of the motivations and problems settlers faced in Manchuria before and after defeat. In 1940, the local government of the village of Sarashina in Nagano sent 120 households of about 500 people to Manchuria to establish a "branch village."[39] Some went to escape poverty at home; others went out of a sense of civic duty. The Sarashina villagers settled in a reportedly unpopulated area near the mountain Jianshan (Senzan in Japanese), 28 kilometers from the town of Baoqing (寶清; Hōsei in Japanese) in a triangle of Manchuria that jutted into the Soviet Union (see Map 1).

39. Nagano-ken kaitaku jikōkai Manshū kaitakushi kankōkai, *Nagano-ken Manshū kaitaku shi*, vol. 2, 326–36.

Their closest neighbors, 20 to 30 kilometers away, included two other Japanese settler communities and a Manchurian Youth Corps Brigade from Nagano. Photographs show the villagers living in tents in the snow during their first, frigid winter, plowing the vast fields, harvesting their first crop, and celebrating at their new Shinto shrine. In 1941, 30-year-old Tsukada Asae joined the village as an elementary school teacher in the Manchurian "national" school system (*zai Man kokumin gakkō*, 在満 国民学校), where the curriculum was identical to schools back in Japan.[40] For Tsukada, dissatisfied with the opportunities available to her in the 1930s Japanese countryside, and harboring dreams of traveling the world, going to Manchuria as an elementary school teacher for an agricultural community on a government-sponsored program seemed like the only way to escape her limited options in Japan.

Compared to Taiwan and Korea, Manchuria provoked a deep ambivalence in metropolitan Japanese. Depicted as a land of opportunity, a frontier open for the taming, it was also seen as a threatening place, alien to domestic values. It also struck some as deceptive: if it was so wonderful, why did corporations need to be bribed, why did settlers need to be persuaded to go? One early literary example from the 1940s, Tanizaki Jun'ichirō's novel *The Makioka Sisters*, captures this ambivalence toward Manchuria. In one of the plotlines, Taeko, the youngest and least constrained of the four Makioka sisters, seeks a way to end her relationship with her boyfriend, "Kei-boy." His family, weary of the problems caused by the dissolute young man, discusses sending him to Manchuria as a manservant in the Manchurian Imperial Household.[41] Taeko, who is eager to be rid of him, is delighted by the idea. But when her sisters ask her whether she plans to accompany him, she is less than enthusiastic.

---

40. Tsukada, "Kaitaku gakkō no omoide," 332.

41. Tanizaki, *The Makioka Sisters*, 467–71. In the original Japanese, the phrase used is *Manshū ochi* (満州落ち; literally, "falling into Manchuria"), with the meaning of going to Manchuria when no other opportunities are available (Tanizaki, *Sasameyuki*, 252). Tanizaki wrote the novel in the mid-1940s. The timeframe in the novel runs from November 1936 through 1941. Within the story, the discussion of sending Kei-boy to Manchuria occurs in October 1940. The third sister, Yukiko, scolds the fourth sister, Taeko, by saying, "You use [Kei-boy] as long as you can, and then you say you know a good place for worthless young men, and try to send him off to Manchuria" (Tanizaki, *The Makioka Sisters*, 470).

Later, her sister Yukiko challenges her for trying to dispose of Kei-boy in Manchuria, which Taeko has characterized as "a good place for worthless young men."[42] Kei-boy's brothers depict Manchuria as a land of opportunity for men "of good bourgeois origins, in a word, who might even be a little stupid."[43] But Yukiko, indignant about Taeko's shabby treatment of Kei-boy, identifies the real use of Manchuria in this case: a means by which to dispose of inconvenient people.

The demography of Manchuria changed dramatically in the years under Japanese rule. Population statistics from the region were never as reliable as those from Taiwan, for example, but are still informative. The first "national" census in Manchuria, undertaken in 1940, counted a total of 43,203,000 people: 40,858,000 "Manchurians"; 820,000 Japanese; 1,450,000 Koreans; 69,000 stateless persons; and 4,000 third country nationals.[44] The "stateless persons" were "White Russians" who had opposed the Bolshevik revolution and moved to Manchuria, with over half of them residing in or near Harbin. But "White Russian" was a catch-all category that included approximately 45,000 ethnic Russians and also Ukrainians, Jews, Georgians, Armenians, and Tartars.[45] By the end of the war, approximately 45 million people lived in Manchukuo.[46] Census takers struggled to categorize the different kinds of people in Manchuria, and, as Mariko Tamanoi has shown, even official policymakers could not reach a consensus on what to call "Manchurians."[47] Early censuses used a category called "Manchurian" for all Chinese people in addition to the small Manchu minority, although that category was later modified to "people of Han and Manchurian ethnicity" (*Kan-Man kei* 漢満系).[48] The 1947 Ministry of Finance reports, written by colonial bureaucrats and intended to serve as a historical record of Japanese activities and assets in the colonies, presented Manchuria's colonial actors in terms of their ethnicity: people of Manchu-

---

42. Tanizaki, *The Makioka Sisters*, 470.

43. Ibid., 467

44. Tōyō keizai shinpōsha, ed., *Kanketsu Shōwa kokusei sōran*, 551.

45. Man-Mō dōhō engokai, ed., *Man-Mō shūsen shi*, 178.

46. 45,323,000 in 1943, according to Tōyō keizai shinpōsha, ed., *Kanketsu Shōwa kokusei sōran*, 302.

47. Tamanoi, "Knowledge, Power, and Racial Classification."

48. Tōyō keizai shinpōsha, ed., *Kanketsu Shōwa kokusei sōran*, 551.

rian ethnicity (*Mankei* 満系; including Han Chinese); people of Japanese ethnicity (*Nikkei* 日系); and people of Korean ethnicity (*Senkei* 鮮系). These categorizations reflect the colonial effort to highlight the "Manchurian" nature of Manchuria, when in fact the Han Chinese population overwhelmed the tiny Manchu population.

Japan continued to add bits of territory to its empire. During World War I, Japan declared war on Germany in 1914 and took control of German colonial possessions in Shandong in China and in the western Pacific. After the war Japan retained some economic rights in Shandong and received the South Seas mandate under the League of Nations for the islands in the Pacific. The 1941 military thrust into Southeast Asia that accompanied the attack on Pearl Harbor added more territory to the wartime empire (see Map 2).

The pattern of Japanese empire-building—military conflicts that circulated troops through regions adjacent to Japan and presented opportunities for colonization—created a geography particular to the Japanese empire: a core of the home islands, *naichi*, surrounded by an elastic border of the outer reaches of the empire, *gaichi*. As in other imperial formations, people within Japan made a distinction between what they considered to be the homeland, or Japan proper, and the colonies, territory that was part of the empire but not necessarily truly Japan. The conceptualization of "homeland" and "colony" had political, legal, social, and spiritual connotations, all of which were contested and in flux.[49] The outer reaches of Japan, Okinawa in the south and Karafuto and Chishima in the north, were part of the homeland administratively, but few people in Japan, or even in those regions, recognized them as such, and their existence complicated the colonial geography. The outer boundaries of the territory under Japanese control, "the colonies," expanded and contracted depending on diplomatic and military victories

---

49. One example of the plastic nature of *naichi* is the story of the father of the film critic Ishiko Jun who found *naichi* inescapable, even in Manchuria. Ishiko, who grew up in Manchuria, found an unpublished novel written by his father in the 1930s in which the protagonist experienced a sense of liberation on the passage to Manchuria. But when his father, a newspaper reporter, arrived in Manchuria, he found Japanese society there as oppressive and insular as it was back in Japan. Chūgoku hikiage mangaka no kai, eds., *Boku no Manshū*, 237–39.

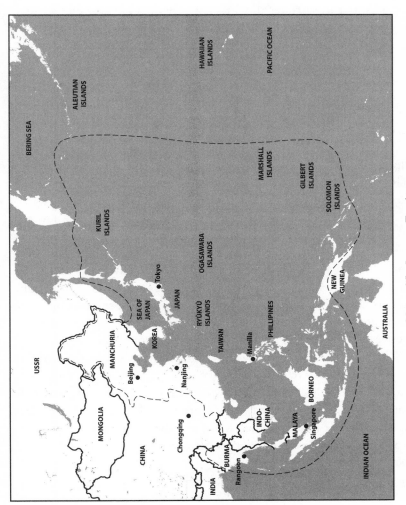

Map 2   The Japanese Empire

and losses. When that elastic boundary went out, Japanese people spread out behind it, and colonial subjects incorporated within it moved as well. In the decades after the war, the government retroactively defined the geographic territories of "the homeland" and "the colonies" for legal purposes, but throughout the imperial period, the boundaries of them were plastic. Regardless of their specific delineations, the homeland and the colonies worked in tension to define each other. These conceptualizations defined people as well. Those within the borders of Japan proper were "people of the homeland" (*naichijin*) in contrast to the "people of the colonies" (*gaichi no hito*). Like the places that defined them, the categories of these two groups of people worked to define and sustain each other.

Factors in addition to the tensions between the homeland and the colonies shaped the colonial Japanese, especially a person's status. For military men during the war, their time overseas was viewed in a state-mandated positive light, of doing their patriotic duty and liberating colonized peoples from white oppressors. Civilians abroad fell into several occupational categories: colonial administrators and their families; employees of semi-governmental companies such as the South Manchuria Railway Company and their families; employees of major corporations, such as the Manchurian Industrial Development Company; teachers at colonial schools and universities; small business people who ran businesses; Manchurian settlers; freelancers or "continental *ronin*." These categorizations shaped to a large extent perceptions at home.

When defeat came, it revealed in urgent terms the immediate differences between the circumstances of colonial and metropolitan Japanese. Some of these tensions hinged on whether one was inside or outside the country in 1945. But fifty years of empire had also built up longer-term understandings of metropolitan Japan and the colonies, and the people who were shaped by them. Those understandings were reworked in postwar Japan.

Defeat in the Colonies

Defeat, communicated by means of Emperor Hirohito's radio address at noon on August 15, 1945, was a shock for most Japanese people at home and in the colonies. For colonists, however, the Japanese government's acceptance of the Potsdam declaration meant that the ground on which they stood ceased to be under Japanese jurisdiction. The movement through the colonies had been relatively gradual, but when the elastic boundary of *gaichi* snapped back to the home island of Japan, the people who had spread out through the colonies were exposed, like fish stranded on a beach after high tide. As colonial governments ceased to function, overseas Japanese experienced a status change and found themselves under the jurisdiction of the Allied forces, whose understanding of geopolitics and priorities differed from the Japanese colonial governments. Koreans, Taiwanese, and other colonial subjects in Japan had a dramatic change of status as well, but their new position was less felicitous than colonial liberation usually entailed: it had the effect of removing the imperial rhetoric, which had, in a way, justified the presence of colonial subjects within the metropole, and reduced them to unwanted migrants from formerly colonial spaces.

Akira Iriye, Bruce Cumings, Michael Schaller, and Marc Gallicchio have written with interpretive clarity about American, Republican Chinese, British, and Soviet maneuverings for positions of power in postwar East Asia.[50] Rather than review extensively the history of the Allied actions in postwar Asia, we will focus on how Allied decisions and actions at the end of the war shaped the fate of Japanese actors in the colonies and colonial subjects in the metropole. It mattered a great deal to the people in Japan's colonies in whose jurisdiction they found themselves at the moment of surrender. A brief review of the process behind the dividing up of the former Japanese empire may be helpful.

Unlike the Japanese government, the Allies had planned for Japanese defeat and the postwar settlement. At conferences in Cairo (December 1943), Yalta (February 1945), and Potsdam (July–August 1945), Allied leaders sought ways to end the war as quickly as possible. In December 1943, Chiang Kai-shek (Jiang Jieshi) joined Roosevelt and Churchill at the Cairo Conference to issue the declaration that stated that Japan would be stripped of all of its territorial possessions in China, Taiwan, and the Pacific; that territories taken from China would be restored to

---

50. Iriye, *The Cold War in Asia*; Cumings, *The Origins of the Korean War*; Schaller, *The American Occupation of Japan*; Gallicchio, *The Cold War Begins in Asia*.

the Republic of China; and that "Japan will also be expelled from all other territories which she has taken by violence and greed."[51]

From February 4 to February 11, 1945, Stalin, Churchill, and Roosevelt met at Yalta to plan military arrangements for the end of the war in Europe and to cooperate in the continuing war against Japan. In secret agreements, Roosevelt and Stalin agreed that the Soviets would enter the war against Japan within three months after German surrender. In return, after Japanese defeat the Soviet Union would acquire all of Sakhalin (the southern half of which had been Japanese territory since 1905) and the Kurils (part of Japan since 1875). The USSR would also receive rights in Manchuria, in particular, Lüshun (Port Arthur), the port near the city of Dalian.[52] The language of these agreements, unknown to almost everyone except Stalin and Roosevelt, emphasized the "safeguarding" of the "preeminent interests of the Soviet Union," and laid the groundwork for Soviet claims of a special position in postwar Manchuria.[53]

From July 17 to August 2, 1945, Stalin, Churchill, and the new U.S. president, Truman, met at Potsdam to discuss Japan's surrender and the postwar occupations. One outcome of the meeting was the Potsdam Declaration, released on July 26, as a warning to the Japanese people—a warning that Japanese leaders discussed, but ultimately ignored.[54] The Potsdam formulation incorporated the wording of the Cairo Declaration stipulating that parts of the Japanese empire would be taken away, but it also finalized the reduction of Japan's borders by defining what was to remain as Japan: "Japanese sovereignty shall be limited to the islands of Honshu, Hokkaido, Kyushu, Shikoku, and such minor islands as we determine."[55] The Potsdam Declaration also made a significant pronouncement on the fate of Japanese soldiers abroad. Article 9 stated "the Japanese military forces, after being completely disarmed, will be permitted to return to their homes with the opportunity to lead peaceful and productive lives." This single sentence later became the legal basis for the

---

51. The Cairo Declaration in United States Senate, Committee on Foreign Relations, *The United States and the Korean Problem*, 1.

52. FRUS, *The Conferences at Malta and Yalta 1945*, xii.

53. Gallicchio, *The Cold War Begins in Asia*, 13.

54. Ibid., 46.

55. Ibid., 46–49; FRUS, *Conference of Berlin (Potsdam), 1945*, 1474–76.

repatriation of Japanese military men abroad. The lack of an equally clear corresponding statement for civilians abroad left them in a diplomatic and legal no-man's land.

With the atomic bombs exploded over Hiroshima on August 6 and Nagasaki on August 9, and the Soviet entry into the war on August 8, Allied civilian and military policymakers scrambled to prepare for Japan's surrender, sooner than many had expected. Allied diplomatic agreements on the future of Europe and Asia had shown signs of breaking down at Yalta, but military leaders needed clear agreements with other Allied forces on what regions each would occupy in order to accept the surrender and disarm the Japanese troops. Those agreements took the form of General Order Number One, which instructed the Imperial General Headquarters, as directed by the Emperor, to cause all of the Japanese and Japanese-controlled armed forces to cease fighting and surrender to military representatives of the United States, the Republic of China, the United Kingdom and the British Empire, and the Soviet Union, depending on where they were located geographically.[56] As Gallicchio has noted, "in short, this order would determine how the Allies divided Japan's empire during the initial period of occupation, a matter of supreme importance for the future of East Asia."[57] Drafted on August 10–11 in the Pentagon by Colonel Charles Bonesteel and other U.S. military men, General Order Number One reflected military reality more than Truman's more ambitious ideas for U.S. military control of all of the Korean peninsula and parts of Manchuria, in part because U.S. policymakers believed that they needed immediate agreement from the other Allies.[58] It sketched out the divisions of the former Japanese em-

---

56. A copy of General Order Number One is available in Takemae, *GHQ shirei sōshūsei*, vol. 2, 1–7, here p. 3: "The Imperial General Headquarters by direction of the Emperor, and pursuant to the surrender to the Supreme Commander for the Allied Powers of all Japanese Armed Forces by the Emperor, hereby orders all of its Commanders in Japan and abroad to cause the Japanese Armed Forces and Japanese-controlled Forces under their command to cease hostilities at once, to lay down their arms, to remain in their present locations and to surrender unconditionally to Commanders acting on behalf of the United States, the Republic of China, the United Kingdom and the British Empire, and the Union of Soviet Socialist Republics, as indicated hereafter as may be further directed by the Supreme Commander for the Allied Powers."

57. Gallicchio, *The Cold War Begins in Asia*, 72.

58. Ibid., 75–92.

pire for the purposes of surrender into American, Chinese, British, and Soviet zones of occupation. When hurriedly circulated among the Allies around August 15, no one was satisfied. The British objected to the fact that Hong Kong ended up in the Chinese Nationalist zone; the French, planning to reoccupy their colonies in Indochina, objected to the assignment of the northern half of Indochina to the Chinese Nationalists; the Soviets insisted on their own broad interpretations of "Manchuria" and asked for Hokkaido; and the U.S. State Department was surprised that the U.S. military was willing to turn the Kurils over to the Soviets. Nevertheless, in part because of the need to respond immediately to the Japanese surrender, leaders of the four parties accepted most of the lines drawn across the former Japanese empire, and the General Order Number One, with instructions specifying to whom Japanese soldiers should surrender, was issued to the Japanese government on September 2, 1945.[59] Based on General Order Number One, each of the Allied militaries prepared to begin processing surrendered Japanese troops in the regions under their administration and to repatriate them to Japan. The execution of that operation reflected the problems and priorities of each military as well as the larger forces of decolonization and postwar population transfers.

Allied Repatriation of the Overseas Japanese

As sketched out in General Order Number One, the U.S. military occupied and administered all the Japanese home islands, the Ogasawara Islands, the Philippines, the South Seas mandate, and Korea south of the 38th parallel. Excluding Japan, these regions contained approximately 990,000 Japanese, 15 percent of the overseas population.[60] The United States set about demobilizing soldiers throughout the region as quickly as possible.

Throughout the Philippines and the rest of the Pacific islands, Japanese troops had suffered severe losses during the American onslaught. Even on islands around Guam and Saipan where the United States did

---

59. Gallicchio, *The Cold War Begins in Asia,* 90.

60. Wakatsuki, *Sengo hikiage no kiroku,* 50–51. Kōseishō engokyoku. *Hikiage to engo 30-nen no ayumi,* 48.

Table 1
Estimates of Japanese Nationals Abroad at the End of World War II

Location	Civilian	Military
Manchuria	1,550,000	664,000 Army
China, including Hong Kong	504,000	1,056,000 Army 71,000 Navy
Korean Peninsula	720,100	294,000 Army 42,000 Navy
Taiwan	350,000	169,000 Army 63,000 Navy
Chishima and Karafuto	390,000	88,000 Army 3,000 Navy
SE & SW Asia and elsewhere	(unavailable)	814,000 Army 270,000 Navy

SOURCE: Kōseishō shakai engokyoku, *Engo 50-nenshi*, 10–11, 17–18, 29–34. Civilian estimates for the Korean peninsula (as of September 1945) are taken from USAMGIK, 7–9.

not attack, troops were near death due to starvation and disease.[61] Eager to demobilize its own forces stationed throughout the Pacific, the U.S. military concentrated the initial demobilization efforts on Japanese in these zones.[62] After the ceasefire, U.S. military personnel disarmed the troops, processed them in camps, and then boarded them on ships bound for Japan. The first official repatriation ship under American auspices, the hospital ship Takasago Maru, arrived at Beppu from Micronesia on September 25, 1945, with 1,600 starving former Imperial Navy personnel.[63] U.S. repatriation from these regions, with a few exceptions, was completed by May 1946.[64]

In light of the Soviet entry into northern Korea on August 8, the United States made it a high priority to establish an American presence on the Korean peninsula. The U.S. military sent an advanced team to Seoul, then called Keijō, on September 6, and landed in force in Inchon on September 8. They entered Seoul and set up camp on the grounds of the Government-General, the colonial government in Korea, on

---

61. Kōseishō engokyoku, *Hikiage to engo 30-nen no ayumi*, 57.
62. Katō Yōko, "Haisha no kikan," 113.
63. Kōseishō shakai engokyoku, *Engo 50-nen shi*, 18–19.
64. Ibid., 14.

September 9.[65] Under the dictates of General Order Number One, the United States began immediately to disarm and repatriate all Japanese military personnel and their families. They instructed a group of Japanese military officers to create the "Liaison Detachment, Japanese Army" that transmitted the orders of the Americans to units of the Japanese military and served as an intermediary between the victorious American and the defeated Japanese troops. One observer noted that with the exception of searches that the Americans conducted on the Japanese before departure, American and Japanese soldiers had little contact with one another, reducing the usual humiliations faced by defeated troops. It was a very efficient transfer during which nearly all of the estimated military personnel in South Korea were sent back to Japan by November 3, 1945.[66]

For the U.S. military, there was no question about what to do with Japanese soldiers abroad, but how to handle Japanese civilians was never outlined as clearly. The U.S. military had a vague notion that territories acquired through Japanese expansionism should be rid of Japanese civilians. One contemporary observer in Korea noted that "the immediate concern of the Military Government was the evacuation of Japanese residents, for their presence in the land which their nation had oppressed for nearly a half century was a constant provocation to violence."[67] At first, though, they received no specific guidelines about their repatriation. For a mixture of pragmatic and humanitarian reasons, the U.S. military soon concluded that civilian repatriation was necessary. Other evidence suggests that General Douglas MacArthur made the decision to repatriate civilians, partly because of humanitarian concerns.[68] One of MacArthur's biographers gives him full credit for repatriation, saying that he

masterminded the vast repatriation program, which, though marred by some cases of delay, confusion, mistreatment, lost belongings, undue overcrowding, and outbreaks of disease, was, all in all, planned well and carried out rapidly

---

65. Morita, *Chōsen shūsen no kiroku*, 274–75.

66. Ibid., 338–49. Morita Yoshio, devoted to chronicling the history of repatriation from the peninsula, was himself repatriated from Korea in March 1946.

67. Gane, "Foreign Affairs of South Korea," 57.

68. McWilliams, *Homeward Bound*, 9.

and efficiently. It was a logistical accomplishment of gigantic proportions, and as a humanitarian achievement it earned for MacArthur and his forces continuing grateful remembrance in millions of Japanese and other Asian homes.[69]

Because the repatriation of civilians was not planned ahead of time, "masterminding" is perhaps an exaggeration. But there was a strong, if not always articulated, impulse on the part of the Americans to move Japanese civilians back to Japan.

Another task facing the U.S. military in Korea was governing the country. At first they intended to rule Korea through the existing Japanese colonial government, but found that politically untenable. On September 14, all members of the colonial government were removed from their posts, and on September 19, the Americans flew Abe Nobuyuki, the last Governor-General of Korea, back to Tokyo. The Americans then established a military government through which to govern, but most of the former colonial officials were kept on as advisors and the extant organization was preserved, meaning that the military government resembled almost exactly the Japanese colonial government.[70] The military government was not well equipped to handle the problems of post-liberation Korea. Elated Koreans besieged the Americans with proposals and candidates for a new Korean government.[71] The Soviet attack in the north triggered a stream of refugees towards the southern half of the peninsula. Japanese civilians in South Korea began returning to Japan on their own at the end of the war, so the ports were clogged with people seeking passage to Japan. Koreans returning from Japan, Manchuria, and China streamed into the country. These movements of people created chaos for the newly arrived Americans in Korea.

The U.S. military was responsible for Japanese soldiers in Korea, but the military government had jurisdiction over Japanese civilians. The Governor-General had made some attempts to govern through the end of the war, and in late August established a Central Liaison Office, an organization that mirrored the Central Liaison Office established by the Japanese government in the home islands to facilitate communication between the occupation apparatus (SCAP) and the organs of the Japa-

---

69. James, *The Years of MacArthur*, vol. 3, 90.
70. Cumings, *The Origins of the Korean War*, 128; Morita, *Chōsen shūsen no kiroku*, 289–91.
71. Cumings, *The Origins of the Korean War*, 140–43.

nese government.[72] The Welfare Section of the Central Liaison Office, led by colonial bureaucrats, was supposed to oversee repatriation transportation and refugee camps to facilitate the movement of people between Japan and Korea. A key American participant in the repatriation process, First Lieutenant William J. Gane, was critical of this organization, which he called the Public Health and Welfare Bureau, saying "incompetence and meddlesomeness characterized some of the members of the PHW."[73] Repatriation was accomplished instead by cooperation between American military personnel and the civilian advocacy organization, the Keijō Nihonjin sewakai.

With defeat it became clear that the colonial government would no longer be able to look after the needs of Japanese civilians. In response, business and civic leaders in Seoul established the Keijō naichijin sewakai, later known as the Keijō Nihonjin sewakai (Seoul Homeland Japanese Support Organization, hereafter Sewakai).[74] The future leaders of the organization met in the days after the war and appointed Hozumi Shinrokurō, president of the Keijō Electricity Company and a former colonial bureaucrat, as president. They outlined the mission of the organization, which was to facilitate communication between Japanese civilians and the new authorities and to protect the lives and property of Japanese civilians in Korea. Unaware that repatriation would be mandatory, some members of the Sewakai argued that their mission should be to facilitate continued Japanese residence in Korea, and in an August 25 speech, President Hozumi indicated that the organization would work to support both those who intended to return to Japan and those who planned to stay in Korea. When local chapters of the Sewakai formed throughout the Korean peninsula, they attracted Japanese members who had the deepest ties in Korea, believing as they did that

---

72. On the Central Liaison Office in Korea, see Morita, *Chōsen shūsen no kiroku*, 148–50; on the Central Liaison Office in Japan, see Takemae, *Inside GHQ*, 113–14.

73. Gane, "Foreign Affairs of South Korea," 101.

74. The organization put out a bulletin every day except Sunday in the immediate aftermath of the war, distributing up to 1,500 copies per day. Reprints of the bulletin, the *Keijō Nihonjin sewakai kaihō* are available: Heiwa kinen jigyō tokubetsu kikin, *Keijō Nihonjin sewakai kaihō*.

the Sewakai would be the central organization for Japanese residents in postcolonial Korea.[75]

Japanese civilians in Korea responded to the end of the war in a variety of ways. Some prepared to leave Korea immediately, withdrawing money from banks, bringing their children in from evacuation in the countryside, and selling off their possessions. Then they headed for Busan or other ports and negotiated passage on any available ship back to Japan. One local leader, Governor Nobuhara Akira of Gyeongsangnam Province in southeastern Korea, anticipated that Japanese residents would not be able to remain in Korea. As soon as the war ended, he instructed people to leave their homes and head for port cities, and for the Japanese police to facilitate this. The long-term Japanese residents of Busan opposed these instructions saying they had no intention to return to Japan, and that Nobuhara was displaying weakness. Instead, they insisted, he should be putting his efforts into establishing a consulate, reorganizing Japanese residents, and establishing schools for the children of the future Japanese community. Nobuhara responded that they had an unrealistic understanding of the new geopolitical situation and that they should pack their bags and leave as quickly as possible.[76] Those who took Nobuhara's advice and left before the process was regulated fared much better than later returnees as there were not yet limits on the amount of cash and belongings early returnees could bring with them.

After the repatriation of Japanese military personnel was underway, the military government then turned its attention to repatriating Japanese civilians. They established a repatriation system on September 23, 1945, following the procedures established by the Sewakai and began to work through them, instructing Japanese people to register with the local association, and then instructing the Sewakai to organize those people for the trip home. On March 8, 1946, the Military Government in Korea indicated that all Japanese except those stipulated by them must leave Korea as soon as possible, and on April 1, added that people who remained would be punished.[77]

---

75. Morita, *Chōsen shūsen no kiroku*, 132–46.
76. Ibid., 124–25.
77. Kōseishō shakai engokyoku, *Engo 50-nen shi*, 35.

The system for receiving repatriates in Japan (discussed in Chapter 2) took shape in late September and early October, and with it came restrictions on what Japanese people could bring home with them. On September 27, 1945, after learning that the Imperial Japanese Navy intended to pay a discharge allowance to its personnel overseas, SCAP issued a statement limiting the amount of money people could bring home with them to 500 yen for commissioned officers, 200 yen for non-commissioned officers and enlisted personnel, and 1,000 yen for civilians.[78] In an October 13 statement, the Japanese Ministry of Finance informed people in Korea of these limits and that they could exchange their colonial currency only at the regional repatriation centers upon arrival.[79] In some cases, the loss of Japanese civilians became the gain of the U.S. military. Long-time residents of Korea found it difficult to believe that access to their homes and belongings in Korea would be severed forever, so they packed, labeled, and stored their belongings in warehouses for later retrieval. The Americans apparently disposed of this property at will, designating the carefully labeled belongings as "abandoned," and then using them in exchange for goods and services provided by Koreans or selling them as souvenirs.[80]

Despite these problems, the existence of a well-organized civilian group in Korea, the Sewakai, contributed a great deal to the rapid and efficient repatriation of Japanese civilians. The U.S. Military Government may have found it difficult to move hundreds of thousands of people in an coordinated manner had they not had help from a group on the ground. Compared to other population transfers, this combination of the powerful U.S. Military Government, and the cooperation of a knowledgeable citizens' group, made for a relatively peaceful transfer.

After repatriation from American-administered regions was under way, the U.S. military worked to hasten the repatriation of Japanese from other parts of Asia, and turned its attention to the Japanese in regions under Republican Chinese jurisdiction. Based on Allied agreements made during the war, Chiang Kai-shek's Nationalists (the Guo-

---

78. "Funds that may be Brought into Japan by Repatriated Japanese." SCAPIN 67, September 27, 1945 in Takemae, *GHQ shirei sōshūsei*, vol. 2, 107.

79. Morita, *Chōsen shūsen no kiroku*, 337–38.

80. McWilliams, *Homeward Bound*, 58–59.

mindang or GMD) bore responsibility for accepting the surrender of Japanese troops and deporting Japanese nationals from all of China south of Manchuria, including Hong Kong, Taiwan, and French Indochina north of the 16th parallel. [81] These regions contained 2 million Japanese, or about 30 percent of the overseas population at the end of the war. [82]

The Japanese military had waged a brutal war on parts of the continent and after the war, Japanese soldiers and civilians in regions under Nationalist jurisdiction suffered the usual humiliations associated with defeat. Compared to the violence inflicted on Japanese by Soviet troops in Manchuria, however, violence was muted. [83] Chiang Kai-shek's widely publicized statement, that "the military of Japan is our enemy, the people of Japan are not," may have contributed to a reduction in anti-Japanese violence in China. [84]

Because of the challenges presented by Mao Zedong's communist revolution in the north, and the general chaos in postwar China, the Nationalists had more pressing concerns than dwelling on the treatment of the vanquished Japanese. Where possible, the Nationalists used defeated Japanese troops for security and for their own geopolitical aims. In the immediate postwar period the Nationalists relied upon armed Japanese troops in Shanghai and Beijing for security. [85] Chiang's government may have struck a deal with the Japanese military to protect the Japanese after defeat in exchange for support against Mao's Eighth Route Army. [86] In some cases, Nationalist, Japanese, and "puppet" forces (Chinese and others who had served the Japanese military) all fought together against the Communists, with occasional help from the U.S. military, who had sent more than 50,000 U.S. Marines to China to secure transportation

---

81. American officials viewed the transfer of Japanese nationals as "repatriation," that is, moving people back to their place of national origin. Japanese sources use the word "to repatriate" (*hikiageru* 引揚げる). Chinese officials, whether Nationalist or Communist, saw the Japanese population transfer as "deportation," that is removing Japanese people from their territory and used the word "to deport" (*kensō* 遣送).

82. Wakatsuki, *Sengo hikiage no kiroku*, 50–51.

83. Kōseishō shakai engokyoku, *Engo 50-nen shi*, 31.

84. Ibid., *Engo 50-nen shi*, 58.

85. Pepper, *Civil War in China*, 10–11; Okamoto, "Imaginary Settings."

86. Gillin and Etter, "Staying On," 499.

facilities and assist with Japanese demilitarization.[87] In this way, the impending Nationalist-Communist conflict paradoxically created less hostile conditions for Japanese troops remaining in Nationalist areas. Deportation of Japanese nationals from the Chinese mainland began in November 1945, from Shanghai, Hong Kong, and Tanggu in Tianjin. Most Japanese nationals were deported from the Chinese mainland and Indochina north of the 16th parallel by July 1946.[88]

At the beginning of the repatriation process, U.S. military forces had stipulated that Japanese demobilization and repatriation would be conducted using only Japanese ships: the remnants of the Imperial Navy and the merchant marine. As they gained a better understanding of the scope of the problem, the United States devoted more of its shipping resources to moving people in East Asia. The U.S. military had already been using its own Liberty cargo ships and LSTs (Landing Ship, Tank) to transport Japanese from regions under their control.[89] By March 1946, the United States made its commitment official and turned over 100 Liberty ships, 85 LSTs, and 6 hospital ships for the Japanese repatriation effort.[90] U.S. military personnel trained Japanese workers on these ships and soon the sailing of repatriation ships was an entirely Japanese operation.

Taiwan, too, fell under Republican Chinese administration. The Nationalists arrived to accept the surrender of approximately 232,000 military personnel and then send them home. They also faced the issue of the Japanese civilian population of approximately 350,000 people.[91] Because of the relative calm in postwar Taiwan, Japanese and Allied Occupation officials believed that repatriation from Taiwan was less urgent than from other areas.[92] But when it began, with the influx of American ships in March 1946, repatriation happened abruptly. On March 19, 1946, the organization responsible for the deportation of Japanese from Taiwan, the Nikkyō kanri iinkai, placed a notice in the *Nichi Shin seihō* newspaper, informing the Japanese residents of Taiwan that with the exception of approximately 7,000 Japanese skilled workers and their families,

87. Boyle, *China and Japan at War*, 328.
88. Kōseishō shakai engokyoku, *Engo 50-nen shi*, 14.
89. Katō Yōko, "Haisha no kikan," 116.
90. Kōseishō engokyoku, *Hikiage to engo 30-nen no ayumi*, 55.
91. Kōseishō shakai engokyoku, *Engo 50-nen shi*, 31.
92. Kōseishō engokyoku, *Hikiage to engo 30-nen no ayumi*, 89.

all Japanese would be repatriated in a process scheduled to be completed by the end of April.[93] The same organization reported that between March 2 and May 24, 1946, 453,913 people, including 447,005 Japanese military personnel and civilians, 4,968 Okinawans, and 1,940 Koreans, had been deported.[94] Taiwanese military men and civilians outside of Taiwan at the end of the war found obstacles to returning home and underwent sudden reclassifications. An Allied Occupation source reports on 770 "Formosans" shipped from the Philippines to Japan, and instructs the Japanese government to care for them because "at present [November 1945] no Formosans can be returned to their homelands."[95]

Publications issued by the Ministry of Health and Welfare depict repatriation from Taiwan as the most peaceful transfer, and film footage and anecdotal accounts suggest that repatriates from Taiwan were better off than repatriates from other parts of Asia.[96] But the process was not without problems. Japanese technicians and their families kept behind in Taiwan, sometimes involuntarily, faced challenging living situations. Another category of people, "Japanese left behind" (*zan'yo Nikkyō* 残余日僑), included people who avoided the mandatory evacuation order to remain behind secretly; people who had married into Taiwanese households; people in welfare facilities such as orphans, the elderly, and mental patients; and prisoners and suspects in jail.[97] Although their numbers were not great, their existence illuminates the kinds of difficulties administrators faced when ordered to remove *every* person of a given nationality from a former colony, especially those without advocates.

The Nationalists had an understanding of the colonial actors in Taiwan that differed from the Japanese understanding and re-categorized

---

93. "Nikkyō kanri shunin iin genmei," reproduced in "Furoku: shūsen zengo no Taiwan ni kansuru shiryō," in Ōkurashō kanrikyoku, *Nihonjin no kaigai katsudō*, vol. 6, 52.

94. "Kensō jin'in," reproduced in Ōkurashō kanrikyoku, *Nihonjin no kaigai katsudō*, vol. 6, 54. The word *kensō* 遣送 is the Japanese reading for the Chinese word "send away" that was used by Chinese officials to describe the deportation of Japanese nationals in their jurisdiction. (The term used more commonly in Japanese would be *sōkan* 送還.) For a discussion of the word *kensō*, see Man-Mō dōhō engokai, ed., *Man-Mō shūsen shi*, 561.

95. "Formosans Shipped to Japan from the Philippine Islands." SCAPIN 274, November 13, 1945. In Takemae, *GHQ shirei sōshūsei*, vol. 2, 430.

96. Kōseishō shakai engokyoku, *Engo 50-nen shi*, 37. RG 342 USAF (11026–11028) film footage. "Japanese Repatriates, Ōtake."

97. Kawahara, *Taiwan hikiage ryūyō kiroku*, vol. 1, 4–7.

everyone accordingly. Japanese people of the home islands, *naichijin*, became "overseas Japanese" (*Nikkyō* 日僑), a formulation parallel to the Chinese rendering of "overseas Chinese" (*Kakyō* 華僑). Koreans (*Chōsenjin*) became "overseas Korean" (*Chōkyō* 朝僑). People from the Ryukyu archipelago were also renamed in postwar Taiwan, appearing in repatriation documents as "overseas Ryukyuans" (*Ryūkyō* 琉僑), in a category distinct from "overseas Japanese."[98] Their treatment differed as well. Okinawans who had been serving as regular Japanese soldiers were reorganized separately from the other soldiers and reassigned as sanitation workers in Taiwanese cities. During the first wave of the repatriation of the "Japanese" from Taiwan, Okinawans were used as laborers to build deportation camps and carry baggage. According to one source, they supported homeland Japanese repatriation in unseen ways while their own return was delayed.[99]

At the end of the war, the British military re-occupied territory throughout Southeast Asia that the Japanese military had occupied during the war. Defined as a military zone in 1943, the Southeast Asian Command (SEAC) originally included Ceylon, Burma, Siam, the Malay Peninsula, Singapore, and parts of what is now Indonesia.[100] On August 15, 1945, MacArthur entrusted the other Supreme Commander of the Allied Powers, Admiral Lord Louis Mountbatten, with additional parts of Southeast Asia including French Indochina south of the 16th parallel, Borneo, Brunei, Sarawak, Java, the Celebes, and Dutch New Guinea.[101] MacArthur had military reasons for turning over parts of Southeast Asia to Mountbatten, but he also managed to extract himself from having to deal directly with French and Dutch desires to re-establish rule in their colonies in Indochina and the Netherlands East Indies.[102] Mountbatten was charged with two tasks: the demobilization and repatriation of Japanese troops and the repatriation of Allied POWs and

---

98. "Furoku: shūsen zengo no Taiwan ni kansuru shiryō," in Ōkurashō kanrikyoku, *Nihonjin no kaigai katsudō*, vol. 6, 54.

99. Kawahara, *Taiwan hikiage ryūyō kiroku*, 7.

100. The military zone of SEAC was the first expression of "Southeast Asia" as a distinct political identity. Bayly and Harper, *Forgotten Wars*, 12.

101. Dennis, *Troubled Days of Peace*, 5.

102. Ibid., 78.

internees. The expanded SEAC included approximately 750,000 Japanese, or 11 percent of the overseas population.[103]

Japanese civilians in large and small businesses had lived in Southeast Asia since before the war, but these regions were incorporated as part of Japan's empire only after 1942. Aggregate figures of civilians in Southeast Asia are hard to grasp. Approximately 5,500 civilians from Burma, Thailand, and Vietnam were interned in Saigon from October 1945 to await repatriation.[104] In a 30-page company report completed within two weeks of his arrival back in Japan, Banba Tsuneo described the lives of the approximately 3,500 Japanese civilians in a camp called Jurong (Joron) outside of Singapore.[105] Informed by the British that they might have to remain there for three years due to the dire conditions in Japan, camp inmates responded by building a school and a baseball field and organizing English-language classes and a driving club.[106] But on November 18, the British told them they were to be deported, and on November 21, most boarded a crammed cargo ship for the repatriation center at Ōtake, a journey that took 14 days. Civilians such as Banba and the others in his camp were sent home whenever shipping resources became available.

Due to British policies and a lack of shipping capacity, the repatriation of Japanese soldiers from Southeast Asia took longer than from U.S.- or Chinese-occupied zones. In the immediate aftermath of the war, the British used Japanese soldiers to maintain order throughout the region. Then, they re-categorized the former Japanese military men, not as POWs, which would require the application of the Geneva Conventions, but rather as Japanese Surrendered Personnel.[107] The British then used these "JSPs" as a pool of labor throughout the region.[108] Japanese troops administered prison camps, maintained security, and sometimes

---

103. Bayly and Harper use the figures of 630,00 armed Japanese and 100,000 civilians, but figures from the Japanese Ministry of Health and Welfare indicate only pockets of several thousand Japanese civilians in the major cities of Singapore, Saigon, and Rangoon. Bayly and Harper, *Forgotten Wars*, 5; Kōseishō shakai engokyoku, *Engo 50-nen shi*, 30.

104. Kōseishō shakai engokyoku, *Engo 50-nen shi*, 30.

105. Banba, "Marai hantō hikiage hōkokusho."

106. Ibid., 14.

107. Bayly and Harper, *Forgotten Wars*, 7.

108. Ibid., 146.

engaged in battles, fighting alongside British troops.[109] The British faced
an array of pressing problems, including anti-colonial nationalist movements throughout the former British colonies as well as demands from
their French and Dutch allies to find the means for them to re-establish
colonial rule over their Southeast Asian possessions. The United States
did not initially share its shipping resources with the British. For these
reasons, former Japanese military men remained in a kind of limbo in
Southeast Asia, some for several years after the war. By April 1946, for
example, when the United States and Nationalist China had repatriated
nearly all of the Japanese military personnel and civilians in their respective regions, the British had sent home only 48,000 of a total of
738,000 men.[110]

In April 1946, MacArthur provided more shipping resources to SEAC,
including 75 Liberty ships, 4 LSTs, and 22 Japanese ships. Repatriation
began in earnest and nearly 600,000 men were shipped home during
May and June 1946.[111] The British detained approximately 100,000 men
(132,000, according to Japanese sources)[112] as a labor force for as long as
two years and four months. The men in the work detail were repatriated
from SEAC from March 1948 to January 1949.[113]

On August 8, 1945, three months after the German defeat, the Soviets joined the war against Japan as Stalin had promised to Roosevelt
at Yalta. Just after midnight, the Soviet military launched simultaneous
attacks against the Kwantung Army, Japan's military in Manchuria, at
several locations in northeast Asia. The Soviets attacked the southern
half of Sakhalin on August 11, and hostilities continued until August 19.
They attacked the Kurils on August 18 and advanced towards Hokkaido.
Soviet troops captured "the Northern Territories" (Hoppō ryōdo), four
small islands off the coast of Hokkaido that remain disputed in the
twenty-first century.[114] As a result of the seven-day war between the
Soviet Union and Japan, and agreements made at Yalta, the Soviets
occupied and administered the regions they invaded: Manchuria, Korea

---

109. Dennis, *Troubled Days of Peace*, 21, 57.

110. Ibid., 223.

111. Ibid., 223–24.

112. Kōseishō shakai engokyoku, *Engo 50-nen shi*, 13.

113. Ibid., 14.

114. Nimmo, *Behind a Curtain of Silence*, 12–13.

north of the 38th parallel, Sakhalin, and the Kurils. Regions that fell under Soviet administration after the war contained the largest number of Japanese: 2,720,000 or 41 percent of the overseas population.[115] Japanese people suffered a great deal in the zones occupied by the Soviet military, in ways that affected their reception back in Japan (Chapter 3).

In the spring of 1946, the Soviet military retreated from Manchuria, although it maintained a presence in North Korea, Dalian, Lüshun (Port Arthur), and Harbin. Chiang Kai-shek's Nationalists then occupied the major cities in Manchuria, but Lin Biao's Communist Eighth Route Army remained in control of much of the countryside. The U.S. military then encouraged the Nationalists to deport all of the remaining Japanese civilians, providing many of the resources for the project. U.S. military personnel orchestrated the building of a deportation staging area near the port of Huludao (Korotō in Japanese), in between Dalian and Tianjian, now a major navy base for the PRC. The U.S. military, the Nationalists, Japanese civilian groups, and at times, local Communist organizations throughout Manchuria cooperated to organize and transport the Japanese for repatriation.[116] Because the men had been drafted by the Japanese military or detained as POWs by the Soviet Union, the remaining Japanese, including those from the agricultural settlements, included a high proportion of women, children, and the elderly.[117] They were loaded onto freight trains and transported to Huludao, where they boarded American ships bound for one of the regional repatriation centers in Japan.

In an event that Japanese sources refer to as "the million person repatriation," approximately 1,010,000 people were deported from Manchuria between May and the end of October 1946. Another 4,300 others who were stranded in Communist-controlled areas or had been working for the Nationalists in Changchun and Shenyang left Manchuria at the end of November 1946. During the summer of 1947, an additional 30,000 stragglers were deported from Manchuria. Because of the Chinese Civil War, which disrupted transportation throughout Manchuria,

---

115. Wakatsuki, *Sengo hikiage no kiroku*, 50–51.

116. Kōseishō shakai engokyoku, *Engo 50-nen shi*, 38; Man-Mō dōhō engokai, ed., *Man-Mō shūsen shi*, 559–690; Hirashima, *Rakudo kara naraku e*, 198–218.

117. Man-Mō dōhō engokai, ed., *Man-Mō shūsen shi*, 446.

repatriation became increasingly difficult. During the summer of 1948, the Nationalists airlifted supplies to their besieged men in Shenyang. They filled the returning planes with Japanese deportees and dropped them off in Jinzhou (Kinshū in Japanese), near Huludao. Between 3,000 and 4,000 people left Manchuria during this period.[118] (The next opportunity to leave did not arrive until 1953.) The deportation of Japanese civilians from Manchuria combined with the repatriation of military men from Southeast Asia to create a flow of an average of 5,500 refugees a day to Japan during the summer of 1946. In September 1946, the peak of repatriation, 56 ships containing 67,000 returnees arrived in Japan.[119] The arrival of a million Japanese people, who had spent a year in postwar Manchuria, helped shape the image of repatriates in postwar Japan.

The Allies sent the overseas Japanese home in waves, with military men and civilians in the American-occupied parts of the Pacific and the Korean peninsula arriving from 1945 through 1946. Republican China also sent home most of the Japanese in areas under its jurisdiction by the end of 1946. Repatriation from Taiwan took place during the spring of 1946. A million people, mainly civilians, arrived in Japan from Manchuria, between May and October 1946, with a trickle continuing through 1948. The British released most of the military men under their control in Southeast Asia by 1947. The Soviet Union released the men they detained between the summers of 1946 and 1950, with approximately 1,000 convicted or suspected war criminals returning from the USSR and the PRC in 1956. Remaining civilians, mostly from northeast China, returned from the PRC between 1953 and 1958 and again after diplomatic relations were re-established between Japan and the PRC in 1972. This reflects a great deal of variation in the degree, timing, and circumstances of the repatriation of all overseas Japanese, due, in part, to varying degrees of commitment to repatriation on the part of the Allied Occupation forces.

Conclusion

With defeat, circumstances seized the colonial Japanese and thrust them into a new jurisdiction as wards of the Allied military forces. They ex-

---

118. Kōseishō engokyoku, *Hikiage to engo 30-nen no ayumi*, 92–93.
119. "Hokuman hikiage fujin no shūdan ninpu chūzetsu shimatsuki," 5.

perienced an abrupt status transformation from the dominant nationality in colonial settings into a national minority shorn of Japanese state protection. They were then forced to negotiate their survival under these new circumstances.

Modern colonial projects categorized people, and Japanese bureaucrats and intellectuals did this with zeal. During the colonial period, a Japanese person abroad might have been counted as "a person of the home islands" (*naichijin* 内地人) in Taiwan and Korea, or as "a person of Japanese ethnicity" (*Nikkeijin* 日系人) in Manchuria. When the Allied forces arrived in East and Southeast Asia, they terminated Japan's colonial project and superimposed a new geopolitical configuration on the former Japanese empire. Then they re-categorized the colonial actors in their assigned zones. In Taiwan, China, and Manchuria, Japanese were reclassified as "overseas Japanese" (*Nikkyō* 日僑); in South Korea, the Americans saw them as "Japanese" (*Nihonjin* 日本人); the government in Japan, meanwhile, discussed them as "brethren overseas" (*kaigai dōhō* 海外同胞). Koreans, who had been categorized as imperial subjects or simply "Koreans" (*Chōsenjin* 朝鮮人) in Korea, Taiwan, and Japan, and "people of Korean ethnicity" (*Senkei* 鮮系) in Manchuria, were re-categorized by the Nationalists in Taiwan as "overseas Koreans" (*Chōkyō* 朝僑), and by the Americans in Japan as "third country nationals" (*daisangokujin* 第三国人). These new names show a set of categorization through which people passed on their way from colonial actor to national citizen.

Japanese at home and abroad experienced the war's end differently. Within wartime Japan, as defeat neared, ordinary civilians were worn down by the increasing harassment from the government, the lack of food, and the conventional and atomic bombings. Many suffered terribly, and even after the war ended, starvation and homelessness continued. Nevertheless, defeat symbolized a new beginning. As John Dower has shown, people experienced crippling despair but also a tremendous sense of renewal.[120] They had dreaded the prospect of foreign occupation, but it was less violent than they had expected. Defeat, for some ordinary Japanese in metropolitan Japan, was a kind of release from misery. For many in the colonies, however, defeat came as a surprise. Some were

---

120. Dower, *Embracing Defeat*, especially Chapter 1.

slow to recognize that it meant having to leave their homes.[121] Occupation, especially in Manchuria, was worse than they expected, and Tamana, the former "state employee," marveled at the well-behaved American soldiers in Japan compared to Soviet soldiers in Changchun.[122] Defeat, for many colonial Japanese, marked the beginning of misery. In this way, August 1945 marked a divergence of experience between metropolitan and colonial Japanese.

At home, people expressed concern about "overseas brethren," but they maintained a kind of unwillingness to recognize overseas experiences of war's end as part of the national experience of defeat or equivalent to the suffering of people in the metropole during and at the end of the war. Although the prospect of American occupation instilled terror, when it came, for most people it was manageable. But it was less possible to keep track of Japanese civilians in American, Chinese, British, or Soviet custody. Foreign military service was somewhat understandable, but the different kinds of foreign exposure in the former colonies were difficult to comprehend and accept. People at home tended to turn away from stories of defeat in the colonies.[123]

Japanese at home and abroad lived through different kinds of space and time in the transition from wartime empire to postwar nation. Metropolitan Japanese remained in the same space after defeat. As for time, it moved forward, from wartime to Occupation, to postwar temporalities. Colonial Japanese lived through spaces that changed from Japanese-dominated colonial spaces to foreign ones. As for time, there was an airlock of an uncertain period in Allied custody—from a few days to as long as several years—bracketed on the other end by repatriation. Their suspension in that period sealed them outside the stories of defeat within Japan.

This combination of factors—different understandings of the colonies, different experiences of the space and time of defeat—was in place when the colonial Japanese began to arrive on the shores of postwar

---

121. Fogel, "Integrating into Chinese Society"; Kuramoto, *Manchurian Legacy*.

122. Tamana, *Hadaka no 600-mannin*, 115.

123. An example of a repatriate feeling that her metropolitan Japanese neighbors dismissed her stories of postwar suffering as not equal to suffering in Japan is discussed in Guelcher, "Dreams of Empire," 220.

and post-imperial Japan. For some, time spent in the jurisdiction of the Allies was relatively benign, but for others, it was violent and sometimes deadly. This exposure changed their understandings of themselves, and shaped how they understood Japanese defeat in World War II. People abroad at the end of the war were changed by their experiences, but they did not anticipate their ambivalent reception at home. Repatriates believed that they were "overseas compatriots," about to become "compatriots." Most were unprepared to be processed first as repatriates, *hikiagesha*, and placed, at least temporarily, in a category slightly outside of "ordinary Japanese."

TWO

The Co-Production of the Repatriate,

1945–49

Writing in the 1990s, Kazuko Kuramoto recalled her 1947 arrival in Japan from Manchuria and her first encounter with *hikiagesha*, the Japanese word for repatriate:

> [My cousin] Taro always referred to us as "repatriates," as if we were of another race, not "real" Japanese. I had first heard this term, *hiki-age-sha* (the repatriates), at the Sasebo Port when we had arrived in Japan. The man who welcomed us had said, "Welcome home my fellow repatriates." He had not said "welcome home, my fellow Japanese."[1]

This passage encapsulates the experience of many returnees upon their arrival back in Japan. People within Japan tagged them with the postwar neologism *hikiagesha* ("repatriate"), viewed them as a group of people distinct from "fellow Japanese," and in some cases questioned the authenticity of their status as Japanese nationals.

Hikiageru, the verb for "to repatriate," means literally to lift and land, as in bringing cargo onto a dock, and was in common usage. But the noun for repatriate, *hikiagesha*, formed by adding the suffix *sha* or *mono* ("person") to the verb, was a word applied exclusively to Japanese people repatriated from former colonies after defeat. *Hikiagesha* differs from

---

1. Kuramoto, *Manchurian Legacy*, 118.

expressions for "colonial returnee" and "repatriate" in other languages. *Pied noir*, the often pejorative word for French Algerians, existed throughout the colonial period, although according to the historian Benjamin Stora, "the French of Algeria did not encounter that characterization until they arrived in the metropolis—in 1962."[2] The English word "repatriate" contains the root *patria*, or fatherland, connoting a relationship between the returnee and the homeland. The Japanese word for repatriate, in contrast, emphasized the act of returning more than the colonial identity of the person or his or her tie to the nation. Many colonial Japanese preferred to remember, sometimes quite nostalgically, their lives in the colonies, but their postwar moniker categorized them based on the moment of their immediate postwar return. This pinned them, like flies in amber, in a timeless postwar moment. It marked them as part of the end of imperial and wartime Japan, allowing others to see new beginnings in defeat. Like most Japanese euphemisms for imperial remnants, *hikiagesha* does not contain any reference to empire.

Kuramoto indicated that she first heard the word *hikiagesha* upon return to Japan, but one source reveals an almost accidental encounter between Japanese in the former colonies and the word. In the August 30, 1946 edition of the *Tōhoku dōhō*, a Japanese-language newspaper in postwar Manchuria, a contributor wrote: "It appears that within Japan, there has been a tendency to categorize the 'repatriates' as somehow a distinctive kind of people."[3] This glimpse of colonial Japanese coming face to face with their future categorization shows just how puzzling the label was for them. As long as Japanese nationals remained abroad, people at home referred to them as "overseas brethren" (*kaigai dōhō* 海外同胞). Linguistically they were still "of the same belly," the literal reading of *dōhō*. It was upon their return to Japan that they came to be viewed as part of a group of a "distinctive kind of people" somehow different from other Japanese.

In the passage above, with the phrase "as if we were another race," Kuramoto raised the issue of people at home calling into question the racial makeup of the returnees. In most cases, people did not doubt that Japanese blood ran in the veins of repatriates. (Indeed, *hikiagesha*

---

2. Benjamin Stora, *Algeria, 1830–2000*, 8.
3. *Tōhoku dōhō*, Shenyang edition, no. 131, August 30, 1946.

ultimately became a category only for people of Japanese blood.) At times, though, people made distinctions between Japanese blood and repatriate Japanese blood. In a scene from a 1946 short story discussed further in Chapter 4, a woman who had recently arrived from Manchuria is in need of a blood transfusion. The metropolitan Japanese could not be galvanized to help, but other returnees volunteer to give their blood, suggesting that the appropriate blood for a repatriate was that of another repatriate.[4] More often than an outright questioning of racial makeup, discussions about the identity of returnees usually took place within the framework of Japaneseness. Their colonial upbringing tended to mark the generation born in the colonies: they spoke standard Japanese and colonial girls in particular had a reputation for more independent thought and behavior than girls back in Japan. The lack of a regional accent, a weak or nonexistent tie to a hometown within Japan, and perceived behavioral differences sometimes added up to a failure to reach the bar of authentic Japaneseness.[5]

Returnees noticed the labeling process immediately and responded in a variety of ways. This exchange of the people at home attempting to label the returnees, and the returnees' responses, worked together to generate the official and social category of the *hikiagesha*. This chapter narrates the co-production of the *hikiagesha* and shows how the process of labeling repatriates was useful in Japan's move away from the imperial project. It also points to some ways in which repatriates responded to and made use of the label themselves.

Japan's disengagement from empire involved the transformations of other groups of people as well. Just as the overseas Japanese were transformed into *hikiagesha*, former imperial subjects in Japan, including Koreans, Taiwanese, Chinese, and Southeast Asians, needed new categorization as well. Although the imperial subjects in the former colonies received barely a second thought—unlike the French in Algeria, the Japanese made no arrangements for their native collaborators—the former

---

4. Imai, "Rira saku gogatsu to nareba," 20–30.

5. In her memoir, Kuramoto writes that the girls raised in Dalian in Manchuria, partly because of their urban upbringing, were more outspoken and less easily intimidated than the metropolitan girls she encountered in nursing school. The girls from Japan proper accused her of being a "snob" and "disrespectful." Kuramoto, *Manchurian Legacy*, 9–10.

colonial people living in Japan could not be ignored. Their transformation from imperial subjects into resident foreigners happened in a process that was simultaneous with and related to the production of the *hikiagesha*.

It is easy to identify some of the obvious reasons metropolitan society stigmatized the colonial returnees. First is the universal problem of returning home. In many societies it is difficult for those who have left home to return, and this is especially true in Japan, where the friction of the return can be channeled into the process of transforming the returnee into an "other."[6] Returning under less than triumphal circumstances, as was the case of defeated soldiers and former colonial residents after 1945, made things worse.

Some circumstances eased the return of particular colonial Japanese. Of the 3.2 million civilians abroad at the end of the war, perhaps half had gone in official or semi-official categories. People who left and returned to Japan under officially or socially condoned circumstances, such as colonial administrators, employees of semi-governmental companies, and their families, usually had an easier time reintegrating. Returnees who had family members willing to take them in also had an easier time in postwar Japan. The novelist Fujiwara Tei, who wrote in a fictionalized memoir about the difficulties she faced in 1945 and 1946 in Manchuria and North Korea, is an example of someone whose return was eased to Japan because of these conditions. The wife of a Japanese man in a semi-official position in Manchuria, Fujiwara and her children were welcomed back into her own parents' home after their arrival in Japan in 1946.[7] People who had resources at their disposal negotiated postwar society quite well. One colorful example was the future prime minister Tanaka Kakuei. Towards the end of the war, because of the firebombings of Japanese cities, leaders in Japan had decided to move weapons manufacturing to the colonies. Tanaka, in the construction business, received a contract and a substantial loan, and was in the process of setting up manufacturing plants in colonial Korea. In August 1945, hearing rumors of the end of the war, Tanaka returned to

---

6. Some *kikoku shijo* (帰国子女), the children of Japanese businessmen posted abroad who have returned to Japan, have experienced this process of othering.

7. Fujiwara, *Nagareru hoshi wa ikiteiru*.

Japan with his money in hand. The loan disappeared, and Tanaka prospered.[8] Tanaka returned before official repatriation procedures limited the amount of money returnees could bring with them back to Japan.

People who went to the colonies under less than official circumstances found their return to Japan more difficult, both in terms of getting home and resettling. In some situations, leaving Japan for the colonies had solved a problem at home. This was true of poor villagers throughout Japan whose move to Manchuria solved a perceived problem of too many farmers and not enough land within the Japanese homeland. Some families attempted to rid themselves of troublesome family members by sending them to the colonies and their return brought the original problem home with them. The reputation of colonial Japanese before defeat conditioned their reception at home. Metropolitan Japanese easily transferred prewar and wartime prejudices against unattached women and adventurers in the colonies to their postwar incarnations as *hikiagesha*. Returnees suspected of having been transformed or contaminated in ways that might threaten the home society faced special problems upon their return. More discussion of these problems will appear in Chapter 3.

The destitution of the returnees shaped views as well. Forced to leave homes, businesses, and personal possessions behind, the overseas Japanese arrived with only what they could carry on their backs and cash limited by the Allies to 1,000 yen, an amount that was slightly less than what an average family spent on food in a month in 1946.[9] People at home, most on the edge of starvation in a country devastated by conventional and atomic bombing, viewed these refugee-like beings with a mixture of pity and contempt. At best, the colonial returnee looked like yet another mouth to feed and at worst a potential menace. In one case, local leaders complained to the national government about its plan to resettle repatriates on the outskirts of their village.[10] Their opposition to the repatriates had nothing to do with empire, but only that they were strangers. If the villagers were forced to share their re-

---

8. Schlesinger, *Shadow Shoguns*, 19–20, 27–30.

9. Iwasaki, *Bukka no sesō 100-nen*, 144.

10. "Hikiage kaitakumin no nyūshoku ni tsuite no shitsumon chūisho ni taisuru tōben no ken."

sources, they argued, they would not be able to meet the needs of their own constituents. The words for casting the repatriates as outsiders were new, but the practices of resisting perceived outsiders and creating new categories of exclusion were not.

It is important to note that although a significant number of repatriates were stigmatized, many—if not most—overseas Japanese were able to reintegrate smoothly into postwar Japanese society. Several repatriates were willing to discuss their experiences in oral history interviews, but others refused, sometimes because they had no desire to recall that part of their past, but in other cases, because they insisted that the experience had not marked them in any particular way at all. Still others depicted being a *hikiagesha* as a temporary condition, like an illness. In one short story, a father affectionately teases his son for having overcome his "repatriate sickness." The son concurs, calling it a "form of psycho-neurosis."[11]

Nevertheless, these easily identifiable reasons behind the stigmatization of the returnees—the universal problems associated with returning home, the pre-existing reputation of those who went abroad in the first place, and the poverty of returnees—do not fully explain the emergence of the *hikiagesha* figure, its various iterations, its longevity, and the purposes it served. In order to grasp the particularities of the *hikiagesha*, we must look first at how the repatriates were marked in official discourse.

Japanese and American Responses to the Postwar Migration

When the Japanese government surrendered to the Allies, it had no plans in place for the 6.9 million Japanese nationals overseas or for the 2 million colonial subjects within Japan. On the contrary, the government had continued to send military personnel and civilians abroad up until the end of the war and continued to bring laborers and others from the colonies to Japan.[12] Not until the first few weeks after sur-

---

11. Kawachi, "Sazanka," 199. The conversation reads: "You have recovered from your repatriate sickness, haven't you?" Kosuke teased him one time. "Repatriate sickness? Well, I wouldn't brush it off as easily as that—but—" He grinned sheepishly. "It was a form of psychoneurosis, I guess."

12. Settlers were sent to Manchuria as late as May 1945. Young, *Japan's Total Empire*, 407–8.

render did the remnants of the Japanese government turn its attention to the fate of overseas Japanese. During this period, the Japanese government reconstituted itself as much as possible and began to address the urgent issues at hand, including how to preserve the monarchy in the face of unconditional surrender; how to respond to the impending foreign occupation of Japan, the first in its history; how to cope with the devastation of Hiroshima, Nagasaki, and the 67 other cities that had been firebombed; as well as how to handle the possible starvation of a portion of the population.

American forces arrived in Japan in late August and began to implement the structures and policies for the Allied Occupation, formally inaugurated on October 2, 1945.[13] During the six weeks between surrender and the official beginning of the Occupation, some Japanese government officials continued to try to act independently in governing Japan. The historian Katō Yōko has provided some insight into this history with an overview of the transitional government and its response to the issue of the overseas Japanese. She outlines the reorganization of the immediate postwar government (August 16–October 2, 1945) and shows how three levels of government—the Management Council (Shori kaigi), the Communications Commission (Renrakukai), and the Directors Commission (Kanjikai)—began to devise plans for repatriating Japanese people from overseas.[14]

On August 22, 1945, the Supreme Council for War Leadership (Saikō senso shidō kaigi),[15] composed of the highest military and civilian leaders

---

13. Takemae, *Inside GHQ*, 66; for discussion of the American arrival, see 3–8, 53.

14. Katō Yōko, "Haisha no kikan," 112. The full names of the three organizations are the Council for Managing the Termination of the War (Shūsen shori kaigi 終戦処理会議), known as the Management Council (処理会議); the Commission for the Management and Communications of the Termination of the War (Shūsen jimu renraku iinkai 終戦事務連絡委員会), known as the Communications Commission (連絡会) *renraku-kai*, but which differed from the other organization with *renraku* in its Japanese name, the Central Liaison Office (Shūsen renraku chūō jimukyoku 終戦連絡中央事務局) and which served as the interface with Occupation officials); and the Directors Commission for the Committee for the Management and Communications of the Termination of the War (Shūsen jimu renraku iinkai kanjikai 終戦事務連絡委員会幹事会), known as the Directors Commission.

15. For more on the Supreme Council for War Leadership, see Coox, "The Pacific War," 369*n*45.

in the Japanese government, was disbanded. Established by the cabinet of Prime Minister Koiso Kuniaki (in office from July 22, 1944 to April 6, 1945), the Council was the body that accepted the Potsdam Declaration—that is, surrendered to the Allies—under Prime Minister Suzuki Kantarō (in office from April 7, 1945 to August 16, 1945). On the same day in August, the Management Council, composed of most of the men from the Supreme Council for War Leadership, was formed in its place to discuss the most pressing issues concerning the end of the war.

Another new organization, the Communications Commission, was established just under the Management Council. The Communications Commission, composed of officials including the bureau heads of all of the Ministries, was charged with managing the details of ending the war. The top leaders of the bureau were too busy to meet often and the day-to-day decisions were assigned to the Directors Commission. These three bodies were in operation for six weeks between surrender and the formal start of the Occupation. Prince Higashikuni had the unenviable job of prime minister during the 54-day period from August 17 to October 8, 1945.

On August 31, 1945, two weeks after surrender, the Management Council issued the first decision on the government's policy on repatriation: due to dire conditions in Japan and a lack of shipping capabilities, Japanese nationals abroad, wherever possible, "should be made to stay put" (*teichaku saseyo*).[16] Five days later, on September 5, the Management Council issued another directive, with three main points: all available Japanese ships should be put toward the effort of demobilization and repatriation; civilians in Manchuria, Korea, and China—areas where the Soviet invasion and local reprisals put Japanese nationals in physical danger—should be repatriated before civilians elsewhere; and Japan should borrow ships from the Allies for the transportation effort. This directive was accepted by the cabinet on September 7 and appeared to indicate a move away from the plan to have people remain where they were. But on September 11, the Directors Commission put out a third directive about Japanese nationals abroad, saying that wherever possible, troops and civilians abroad should remain where they were, protection should be provided for their lives and assets, and that

---

16. Katō, "Haisha no kikan," 110.

for those who needed to come home, the means for their return including transportation should be provided as rapidly as possible. The Ministries approved the plan on September 24. Katō Yōko argues that although this may look like a retreat from the September 5 decision to try to initiate repatriation, it was in fact building on a plan to forego repatriation in the immediate short term but to continue planning for repatriation as soon as possible. Nevertheless, the "stay put" directive issued on August 31, and expressed again on September 24, formed the basis of the charge by overseas Japanese that their government abandoned them.[17] This has remained a source of resentment, and the kernel of numerous lawsuits, across the postwar period.

On September 29, the Japanese government sent a memorandum to Allied Occupation officials about repatriation.[18] This memo informed them that the Japanese government planned to repatriate first the elderly, children, and the sick, and then to send ships to retrieve people from particularly dire situations, beginning with the Philippines, where Japanese troops were dying of starvation. The Supreme Commander for the Allied Powers (SCAP) sent a single-page response to the memorandum that read, in part, that the "repatriation of Jap Nationals is being conducted in accordance with policies formulated by this office and which will be announced in a few days," and that it would be conducted "based on military necessity."[19] This terminated the possibility of Japanese central government leadership on repatriation. On October 16, SCAP issued its first set of orders on the repatriation of Japanese overseas, reflecting their primary goal of demilitarization, and also making it clear that SCAP would negotiate the return of overseas Japanese because

---

17. Another explanation of the "stay put" or *genchi teichaku* (現地定着) policy is Etō, ed., *Senryō shiroku*, 168. References to the "stay put" policy surface in other sources on repatriation, e.g., Gunma-ken kenmin seikatsubu sewaka, ed., *Gunma-ken fukuin engoshi*, 109; Wakatsuki, *Sengo hikiage no kiroku*, 50–52; Kōseishō engokyoku, *Hikiage to engo 30-nen no ayumi*, 48.

18. Katō, "Haisha no kikan," 114–15.

19. "Repatriation of Japanese Nationals," SCAPIN 89, October 2, 1945, in Takemae, ed., *GHQ shirei sōshūsei*, vol. 2, 138. I use "SCAP" to refer to the Occupation apparatus, although in other sources "SCAP" can refer to General Douglas MacArthur as well as to the Occupation.

Japan would be stripped of its ability to conduct foreign relations.[20] Then, on October 25, 1945, SCAP ordered Japan to cease all diplomatic activity.[21] SCAP continued to issue ad hoc instructions concerning repatriation during the first several months of the Occupation, and on March 16, 1946, gathered up all of the individual instructions it had sent to the Japanese government on repatriation into a single memorandum.[22] On May 7, SCAP revised the March 16 memorandum and reissued the comprehensive instructions on repatriation that served as the basic guidelines for the duration of the Occupation.[23]

Immediately after the war, the central government did consider the plight of the overseas Japanese, but this did little to mitigate the sense in the postwar period that overseas Japanese had been abandoned by their government as "disposable people" (*kimin* 棄民). Although the Japanese government may have handled repatriation differently from SCAP, perhaps even giving priority to civilians in Manchuria, who were left to survive for a year on their own, SCAP's takeover of the process removed the burden of decision-making from the Japanese government. SCAP spoke with resources in hand, providing ships, training, and other support for the population transfer they oversaw. In the meantime, people were on the move.

The Repatriate Relief Bureau

While the Japanese government and SCAP were formulating policy at the top, a massive migration had begun. During the summer and fall of 1945, Koreans in Japan and Japanese in Korea began a spontaneous migration between southwest Japan around Hakata and the port of Busan in Korea. It was an unregulated movement, with Korean fishing boats charging whatever they could to move people back and forth. One oral history informant, age fourteen at the time of repatriation, recalled her

---

20. "Policies Governing Repatriation of Japanese Nationals in Conquered Territories," SCAPIN 148, October 16, 1945, in Takemae, ed., *GHQ shirei sōshūsei*, vol. 2, 223–24.

21. "Transfer of Custody of Diplomatic and Consular Property and Archives," SCAPIN 189, October 25, 1945, in Takemae, ed., *GHQ shirei sōshūsei*, vol. 2, 296–97.

22. "Repatriation," SCAPIN 822, March 16, 1946, in Takemae, ed., *GHQ shirei sōshūsei*, vol. 4, 1293–1330.

23. "Repatriation," SCAPIN 927, May 7, 1946, in Takemae, ed., *GHQ shirei sōshūsei*, vol. 4, 1537–1683.

parents lashing her to the sides of a small boat on the three-day trip from Busan to Hakata.[24] In the last days of the war, a similar but smaller exodus took place in the north from Karafuto and Chishima, occupied by Soviet troops, to Hokkaido. Well before any Allied or Japanese government policies were in place, hundreds of thousands of people sought to return home.

In response to the chaos at these port cities, the central government initially turned to local governments to process the people seeking to enter and leave Japan. Then on October 18, 1945, the government determined that the Ministry of Health and Welfare (hereafter MHW) would be the central agency for administering the repatriation process.[25] Established in 1938, the MHW had worked to mobilize human and other resources for the war effort. After defeat, its mission changed and it became responsible for caring for people who had suffered because of the war.[26]

The agencies within the MHW devoted to overseeing repatriation and deportation were frequently reorganized and renamed in an effort to respond to the changing aspects of the process. Briefly tracing the history of the repatriation bureaucracy provides the means to explore how overseas Japanese, both soldiers and civilians, became the administrative objects of the welfare bureaucracy. On October 27, 1945, an internal reorganization of the MHW led to the establishment of the Social Affairs Bureau (Shakaikyoku). [27] On the same day, the MHW also transformed the Emergency Quarantine Section of the Bureau of Hygiene (Eiseikyoku rinji ken'ekika) into the Bureau for Epidemic Prevention (Rinji bōekikyoku), with Sections devoted to Quarantine (Ken'ekika) and Epidemic Prevention (Bōekika). On November 22, 1945, the Repatriate Relief Section (Hikiage engoka) was established within the Social Affairs Bureau. It was this agency that would expand and contract to oversee repatriation.

In January of 1946, the American military provided approximately 200 ships, mainly LSTs and Liberty ships, to the Japanese government

---

24. Oral history interview, May 29, 2000.
25. Kōseishō shakai engokyoku, *Engo 50-nen shi*, 144.
26. Kōseishō engokyoku, Hikiage to engo 30-nen no ayumi, 19.
27. Kōseishō shakai engokyoku, *Engo 50-nen shi*, 144–46.

in order to speed the repatriation process. On March 13, 1946, in part to manage the new shipping resources, the government expanded the Repatriate Relief Section into the extra-ministerial body, the Repatriate Relief Authority (Hikiage engoin). The Authority oversaw the previously established Repatriate Relief and Quarantine Sections and all of the regional repatriation centers, the camps at ports throughout Japan that received the returnees.

While the MHW was building the bureaucracies for overseeing repatriation, the Occupation authorities were dismantling the bureaucracy of the Imperial Japanese Army and Navy. On November 30, 1945, the Ministries of the Army and Navy were abolished and on the following day they emerged as the First Demobilization Ministry (Daiichi fukuinshō) and the Second Demobilization Ministry (Daini fukuinshō). On June 15, 1946, these two ministries were combined into a single Demobilization Agency (Fukuinchō), but the Army-related and Navy-related bureaus remained distinct. The Demobilization Agency continued the work of the previous ministries: demobilizing soldiers, conducting surveys on missing military personnel, and responding to SCAP demands for information on the Japanese military. The Navy-related bureau also assisted SCAP in minesweeping and other shipping related issues.

The Repatriate Relief Authority and the Demobilization Agency intersected in terms of the staff who worked in the Demobilization Departments (Fukuinbu) of the regional repatriation centers.[28] They had the status and responsibilities of employees of the Repatriate Relief Section and Authority, but they also answered to the military bureaucracy that was in the midst of being transformed, giving their position a dual nature. On October 15, 1947, the Demobilization Agency was abolished, and the tasks related to the First Demobilization Bureau, that is, the formerly Army-related tasks, were absorbed into the MHW. The tasks related to the Second Demobilization Bureau, that is, the formerly Navy-related tasks, were absorbed into the Prime Minister's Office. A few months later, on January 1, 1948, the demobilization-related bureaucracy was reorganized again into the Demobilization Bureau (Fukuinkyoku) and all parts of it were placed within the MHW. The repatriate and demobilization bureaucracies had coexisted, but on May 31, 1948 the Re-

---

28. Kōseishō shakai engokyoku, *Engo 50-nen shi*, 145.

patriate Relief Authority was reorganized to include the MHW's portion of demobilization duties and was renamed the Repatriate Relief Agency (Hikiage engochō). It was through these reorganizations that the MHW absorbed the remnants of the bureaucracies of the Imperial Japanese Army and Navy.

In anticipation of the end of the Occupation, MHW authorities turned their attention to the issues of restoring the military pensions that had been forbidden by SCAP and of aiding other war victims, and they developed agencies to address those concerns.[29] On April 1, 1954, the Repatriate Relief Agency was changed back into the Repatriate Relief Bureau and re-incorporated into the MHW, ending its eight-year history as an extra-ministerial entity. In 1961, the term "Repatriate"—which had appeared in the name since 1946—was removed and the agency became the Relief Bureau (Engokyoku).[30] In 1985, a new research department, the Office for Measures Concerning Chinese Orphans (Chūgoku kojitō taisakushitsu), was added to address the problems of resettling the "orphans left behind in China" and their families. In 1993, the Social Affairs and Relief Bureaus were combined into one, the Social Welfare and War Victims' Relief Bureau (Shakai engokyoku), which holds memorial services for the war dead, supports the settlement and independence of the latest arrivals from China, and operates the National Showa Memorial Museum (Shōwakan). In 2001, the MHW and the Ministry of Labour were combined to form the Ministry of Health, Labour, and Welfare, but the Repatriate Relief Bureau—in its current guise as the Social Welfare and War Victims' Relief Bureau—survived, testifying to the longevity of the problem and the vitality of the bureaucracy.

The details of the various reorganizations of the bureau are less important than the results. In their efforts to demilitarize Japan, the Occupation authorities dismantled the military administration and distributed many of the responsibilities for looking after veterans to the repatriate bureaucracies of the MHW. Military men may have chafed at

---

29. On the history of military pensions, see Kimura Takuji, "Sensōbyōsha senbotsusha izokutō engojō no seitei to gunjin onkyū no fukkatsu." For a discussion of the "war-bereaved families" and the revival of pensions, see Seraphim, *War Memory and Social Politics in Japan*, 60–85.

30. Kōseishō shakai engokyoku, *Engo 50-nen shi*, 698–700.

being the administrative objects of a welfare agency. Some former military men staffed the repatriate bureaucracies, to the resentment of civilian returnees, and the members of the two groups did not necessarily see themselves as constituents. Some repatriates blamed the military for what they perceived to be the irresponsible policies of moving civilians into potential zones of conflict, including the Soviet Manchurian border, and then abandoning them while they and their families escaped.[31] Nevertheless, it was the MHW that came to oversee issues related to repatriates, veterans, war victims, and war bereaved families, linking them in bureaucratic processes.

A second issue raised by placing repatriates and veterans under the same administrative roof is that it contributed to a conflation of colonial and wartime ramifications into the single process of "postwar cleanup" (*sengo shori*). From 1937, when the Japanese military began to wage war on its Asian neighbors, the colonial and military projects grew closer together. But before then, the overseas Japanese had been created under the auspices of colonial bureaucracies and were part of a colonial time and space. As *hikiagesha*, they were tagged as colonial participants but their categorization as a postwar and not post-imperial phenomena quarantined them from their colonial past and obscured the links between imperial and post-imperial Japan.

Other ministries, including Education, Foreign Affairs, and Transportation, and organizations, such as the Housing Corporation (Jūtaku eidan), participated in the process of receiving and resettling the returnees, but most of the efforts were coordinated through agencies within the MHW. Although many of its bureaucrats made good faith efforts to receive and resettle the repatriates, and did the best they could with limited resources, the MHW was most responsible in the process of labeling returnees *hikiagesha* as they passed through the various procedures necessary to return home.

---

31. Iiyama Tatsuō, a photographer active in caring for Japanese orphans repatriated from Manchuria in 1946, illustrated civilian resentment of the military in a 1986 magazine article, which states in that title that "Among the orphans left behind in China, there are no family members of the Kwantung Army." Iiyama, "Kimin 41-nen no kokka sekinin," 88–92.

One other way that the MHW shaped the image of repatriates was through the telling of their history. The MHW kept records of the repatriation process and was diligent in publishing detailed institutional histories in five volumes across the postwar period. Individual regional repatriation centers published histories covering their local operations.[32] These publications are important resources and it is difficult to write about the return of the overseas Japanese without referencing them. They are also yet another way in which returnees are deeply, if ambivalently, tied to the bureaucracy that processed and labeled them on their entry into postwar Japan.

The Regional Repatriation Centers

With SCAP issuing orders and the Repatriate Relief Bureau fielding them, the home islands of Japan began to receive the colonial Japanese. American ships manned by former Japanese merchant marines went to ports throughout the empire to pick up the overseas Japanese, gathered and processed by the Allies and local Japanese organizations. Then the ships headed for one of the fifteen regional repatriation centers (see Table 2 and Map 3).

The Occupation forces and the Japanese government had legitimate concerns about the potential health threats posed to people in Japan by the return of the overseas Japanese. Under the heading of "Medical and Sanitary Procedures," SCAP clarified its policies intended to reduce the introduction of disease from abroad. First on the list of requirements to Japanese officials was "physical inspection for detection of louse infestation, and cases of and suspects of quarantinable disease (cholera,

---

32. The MHW published five histories of repatriation, cited throughout: Hikiage engochō, *Hikiage engo no kiroku* (1950); Kōseishō hikiage engokyoku, *Zoku hikiage engo no kiroku* (1955); Kōseishō hikiage engokyoku, *Zoku zoku hikiage engo no kiroku* (1963); Kōseishō engokyoku, *Hikiage to engo 30-nen no ayumi* (1977); Kōseishō shakai engokyoku, *Engo 50-nen shi* (1997). The major regional histories include: Hakata hikiage engo kyoku (Kōseishō hikiage engoin), *Kyoku shi* (August 1947); Sasebo hikiage engokyoku jōhōka, *Sasebo hikiage engokyoku shi*, vols. 1–2 (1949); Maizuru chihō engokyoku, *Maizuru chihō hikiage engokyoku shi* (1961); Kōseishō Senzaki hikiage engokyoku, *Senzaki hikiage engokyoku shi* (1946). The regional histories are now available in Katō Kiyofumi, ed., *Kaigai hikiage kankei shiryō shūsei*, a series of repatriation-related documents.

Table 2
Regional Repatriation Centers in Japan, 1945–1958

Location	Dates of operation	Number of returnees	Number of deportees
Uraga 浦賀	1945.11.24–1947.05.01	approx. 520,000	approx. 12,000
Maizuru 舞鶴	1945.11.24–1958.11.15	664,531	32,997
Kure 呉	1945.11.24–1945.12.14	(not available)	(not available)
Shimonoseki 下関	1945.11.24–1946.10.01	0	0
Hakata 博多	1945.11.24–1947.05.01	1,392,429	505,496
Sasebo 佐世保	1945.11.24–1950.05.05	1,391,646	193,981
Kagoshima 鹿児島	1945.11.24–1946.02.01	360,924	54,773
Hakodate 函館	1945.12.14–1950.01.01	311,452	0
Ōtake 大竹	1945.12.14–1947.02.21	410,783	1,127 Okinawans
Ujina 宇品	1945.12.14–1947.12.31	169,026	41,075
Tanabe 田辺	1946.02.21–1946.10.01	220,332	0
Karatsu 唐津	1946.02.21–1946.10.01	0	0
Beppu 別府	1946.02.21–1946.03.26	(not available)	(not available)
Nagoya 名古屋	1946.03.26–1947.02.01	259,589	28,241
Senzaki 仙崎	1946.10.01–1946.12.16	413,961	339,548

NOTE: Centers are listed in order established.
SOURCES: Kōseishō shakai engokyoku, *Engo 50-nen shi*, 147–58; Kōseishō engokyoku, *Hikiage to engo 30-nen no ayumi*, 32.

plague, smallpox, louse-borne typhus, yellow fever, leprosy, and anthrax) or of communicable disease which might prejudice the health of subsequent contacts."[33] Then they require the "disinfestation" with DDT of people arriving from areas in which louse-borne typhus occurred, nearly everywhere Japanese people ended up after the war. The Americans promoted immunizations for smallpox, typhus, and cholera to all outgoing repatriates and to many of the incoming ones, as well as to staff

33. "Medical and Sanitary Procedures," SCAPIN 822, Annex V, March 16, 1946, in Takemae, ed., *GHQ shirei sōshūsei*, vol. 4, 1309–12; cited passage on 1309. An earlier memorandum on sanitation procedures issued on October 20, 1945, gives similar instructions, although it does not mention DDT. "Medical and Sanitary Procedures for Debarkation and Port Sanitation in Repatriation," SCAPIN 67, October 20, 1945, in Takemae, ed., *GHQ shirei sōshūsei*, vol. 2, 253–56.

on the ships. They ordered autopsies of rats on the ships and at the re-patriation centers in a search for any rodents carrying the plague.[34]

Although it is understandable that authorities within Japan wanted to prevent the introduction of diseases from abroad, enforcing the quarantine and hygiene-related measures had ramifications for return-ees. Ships suspected of or known to be carrying passengers infected with cholera were prevented from landing in Japan and had to remain anchored just off the coast. In one case, quarantine officers detected cholera on repatriate ships from Southeast Asia. Twenty ships carrying 80,000 repatriates were held up for days in Uraga harbor, and supply-ing food, water, and medicine to them was a monumental task.[35] As we will see below, the novelist Abe Kōbō and the Nagano schoolteacher Tsukada Asae were held up on ships quarantined for cholera, in ways that affected their lives.

The practice of "disinfestation" with DDT remained an important symbolic indignity for repatriates and non-repatriates alike in postwar Japan. Takemae Eiji, who was a child during the Occupation, argued:

The American obsession with sanitized environments conveyed to the Japa-nese the message that they were dirty and disease-ridden. To a people tra-ditionally priding themselves on physical cleanliness and propriety, this was one more insult compounding the injury of defeat. Children particularly re-sented the affront to their dignity as nozzles were thrust into collars and sleeves and DDT was pumped into their clothes and hair, turning them as white as the proverbial miller's apprentice.[36]

For repatriates, though, it was part of their chilly reception back home. American military film footage shows Japanese repatriation center offi-cials receiving repatriates from Taiwan, who, from their high-quality clothing and manners appear to be upper-middle class.[37] The officials order them into lines and then marshal them through DDT stations

---

34. "Medical and Sanitary Procedures," SCAPIN 822, Annex V, March 16, 1946, in Takemae, ed., *GHQ shirei sōshūsei*, vol. 4, 1311.

35. Hikiage engochō, *Hikiage engo no kiroku*, 14.

36. Takemae, *Inside GHQ*, 410. For more on the impact of DDT in postwar Japan, see Igarashi, *Bodies of Memory*.

37. United States Air Force. *Japanese Repatriates, Ōtake* (film footage).

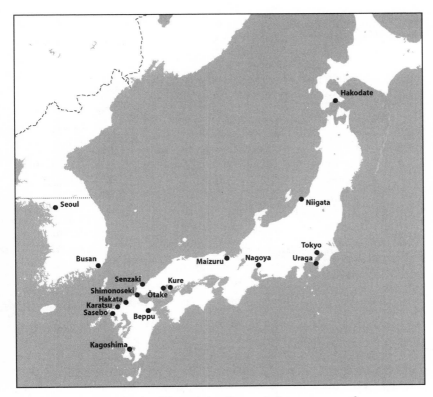

Map 3   Regional Repatriation Centers in Japan, 1945–1958

where uniformed nurses standing a few feet above roughly spray them with DDT. In one encounter, a delicate woman in a kimono leans forward obediently as a sanitation worker grabs the sleeve and fills it with the powder, and then squirts it into her coiffed hair for good measure. The quarantine procedures and the DDT contributed to the sense that the contaminants of the colonies were to be stopped at water's edge.

Inside the regional repatriation centers, officials processed the returnees, immunizing them, sending them to the baths, inspecting their belongings, and disinfecting their clothing.[38] After the initial procedures, officials turned to paperwork, issuing each returnee "repatriate identifi-

---

38. This description of how repatriates were processed is based on accounts of the Maizuru and Ujina centers in Hikiage engochō, *Hikiage engo no kiroku*, 35–42.

cation papers" (*hikiage shōmeisho* 引揚証明書). The moment that repatriates received these forms they received the "qualification" (*shikaku*) of repatriate.[39] One source, a handbook designed to orient returnees to life in postwar Japan, exhorted returnees to be careful with the papers because they would need to show them to receive food rations, facilitate school transfers, and register to vote.[40] MHW sources report problems with counterfeit repatriation papers, suggesting that the documents were valuable enough, in terms of securing extra rations, to reproduce.[41]

In the beginning, these procedures at the staging areas, on the ships, and at the repatriation camps within Japan were disorganized, but within six months or so, they became regulated. Initially, the repatriation camps attempted to comply with SCAP orders to get repatriates in and out of the centers within 24 hours, but the processing time increased. By 1948, returnees remained at repatriation centers for three days and three nights; by 1949, it was four days and nights.[42] When time and resources permitted, the repatriation centers provided other services, and at this point a typical camp ceased to serve just as a transitional area for quarantine, customs, and immigration, and took on the appearance of a small Japanese town with a bank, a post office, a community center, a barber, and a black market set up nearby. The foremost concern of many repatriates was to acquire news of their families and towns in Japan. At some camps, center staff set up information centers that posted maps showing which areas of Japan had suffered war damage.[43] They also fielded and organized letters from relatives to people at the camps. Consultation centers provided advice for people who might face particular hardships or pose problems for authorities: "people with no relatives" (*muenkosha* 無縁故者), widowed women with children likely to face financial problems, people suspected of not holding Japanese citizenship (*hi-Nihonjin* 非日本人), former Manchukuo officials, agricultural settlers, and others.

---

39. Hikiage engochō, *Hikiage engo no kiroku*, 38.
40. Tōkyō-to, *Okaerinasai kikan no minasama*.
41. Hikiage engochō, *Hikiage engo no kiroku*, 41.
42. Ibid., 35.
43. Ibid., 40.

Other agencies provided services in the centers. Ministry of Education officials lectured about the domestic state of affairs, distributed newspapers and magazines, showed movies, and broadcast radio programs.[44] Over time, both Allied officials and the Japanese government became concerned about the ideological state of mind of the returnees. Under the direction of SCAP, the Ministry of Education set up branch offices at the regional repatriation centers to educate and entertain returnees and vet them for possible communist leanings. Concerns about communism inspired Occupation officials to establish a repatriate re-education program administered through the Ministry of Education. Sometimes in conflict with the MHW and the Ministry of Finance, officials from Education sought to shape repatriate education from 1947 through 1951.[45] During the initial rush, however, the goal was to move people through the system as quickly as possible. In the final step, the Transportation Ministry, in cooperation with Japanese Government Railways, issued tickets and made arrangements for meals on the trip home, either in the form of supplies such as tins of bread or meal tickets. In photographs, trains labeled "for repatriates" (*hikiagesha yō* 引揚者用) were clearly marked—one more way that repatriates were, inadvertently perhaps, distinguished from the "ordinary" population of Japan.[46]

When repatriates boarded ships for home, many recall having felt a sense of relief, and looked forward to leaving the sometimes hostile foreign lands behind. The writer Sawachi Hisae, age 14 at the time of deportation from Manchuria, recalled that she thought of nothing else but boarding the repatriation ship. Only then were her ill and weak parents able to reassert their authority, allowing Sawachi to become a child again.[47] In recalling her arrival at a regional repatriation center, Kazuko Kuramoto remembers being taking offense at being treated with DDT, and in the passage below she highlights the additional complication of returning from a Soviet/Chinese communist-occupied zone to Japan under Allied, primarily American, Occupation:

---

44. Ibid., 52.
45. Endō, "J. M. Neruson hikiagesha kyōiku jigyō no tenkai to tokushitsu."
46. Maizuru chihō engokyoku, *Maizuru chihō hikiage engokyoku shi*, xxx.
47. Sawachi, *Mō hitotsu no Manshū*, 24–27.

At the entrance to the temporary barracks set up for the repatriates, we were met by a group of white-jacketed sanitation people. They pulled open each of our collars and stuck in a hose to douse us with a pungent white powder called DDT.

"This is by the order of the occupation forces," they told us, silencing our feeble protest. *The occupation forces! Of course, Japan was occupied by the United States, remember? So why not dunk us, the unwanted cargo kicked out of communist-occupied Manchuria, in DDT? Welcome home, you miserable maggots! Welcome home to the Land of the Rising Sun!* The pungent white powder hissed, crawling down my spine. [italics in original].[48]

Kuramoto's recollection from the 1990s is enriched with insight gained over the postwar period, and contemporary accounts of arrival at the regional repatriation centers tend to emphasize relief and hope.[49] The colonial Japanese began their journeys as "overseas compatriots" and emerged from the centers as repatriates, certified by their repatriate identification papers. It was as designated repatriates, then, that they entered postwar Japan. After moving the returnees through the centers, the MHW provided transportation back to their previously registered domicile in metropolitan Japan, where, the government hoped, returnees would be absorbed back into their communities. Some welcomed the returnees home, but others had been happy to see them go and were less than thrilled about their return. The government tried to address these problems through welfare policies and provided some assistance in the areas of housing, employment services, small business loans, and farm resettlement. All of the efforts were tagged with the ubiquitous modifier "repatriate," contributing to the sense of repatriate distinctiveness.[50] In attempting to aid the repatriates, the government set them just outside of the category of ordinary citizen.

---

48. Kuramoto, *Manchurian Legacy*, 114.

49. Banba, "Marai hantō hikiage hōkokusho," 14.

50. Another illustration of the government distinguishing between "repatriates" and "ordinary citizens" is an April 1946 plan issued to aid returnees upon their final destinations within Japan. Article 9 states that "in addition to educating, comforting, and encouraging repatriates, we will also advocate the policy of promoting understanding of repatriates among ordinary citizens [*ippan kokumin* 一般国民]" ("Teichakuchi ni okeru kaigai hikiagesha engo yōkō," in Kōseishō shakai engokyoku, *Engo 50-nen shi*, 492).

Table 3
Number of Repatriates by Year

Year	Number of repatriates	Cumulative total	Cumulative percentage
Through 1946	5,096,323	5,096,323	77
1947	743,757	5,840,080	88
1948	303,624	6,143,704	93
1949	97,844	6,241,548	95
1950	8,360	6,249,908	95
1951–1995	45,588	6,295,496	95

NOTES: Table includes people who completed repatriation paperwork at their port of arrival. Estimated number of Japanese nationals abroad at war's end: 3,210,000 civilians and 3,670,000 military personnel, a total of 6,880,000 people. Estimated population of Japan in 1945: 72 million. Percentage of the population abroad: 9 percent.

SOURCES: Kōseishō shakai engokyoku, *Engo 50-nen shi.* 729–30; Ara Takashi, ed. *Nihon senryō, gaikō kankei shiryō shū,* 304; Kōseishō 50-nen shi henshū iinkai, ed., *Kōseishō 50-nen shi, shiryō hen,* 618.

Table 3 indicates the numbers of returnees and the year of their return, testifying to the ragged end of empire.

Responses of the Repatriate Community

Repatriates left the repatriation camps on repatriate trains, headed for home, or in some cases, for repatriate housing, repatriate orphanages, repatriate old people's homes, or even unofficial repatriate brothels.[51] Those who had no family or resources in Japan faced poverty. According to a survey of the Ministry of Labour, in July 1946 the average household in Japan spent 1,720 yen on monthly expenses, with 77 percent of that amount going to food and drink.[52] Repatriates returning in the summer of 1946, if they carried the maximum amount of 1,000 yen, had the equivalent of less than half an average family's monthly budget. In 1947, a room in a Tokyo lodging house with three meals a day (assuming that a person could find housing in a city full of homeless bomb victims) cost 1,500 yen per month, 50 percent more than the total amount repatriates could bring home with them.[53] In addition to

---

51. "Hikiagete wa mita keredo," *Shinsō,* 56.
52. Iwasaki, *Bukka no sesō 100-nen,* 144.
53. Shūkan Asahi, ed., *Nedanshi nenpyō,* 62.

finding the means to survive, returnees engaged in the conversation about who they were and what they represented.

The press and other sources began to discuss the plight of repatriates from the moment they arrived, sometimes expressing sympathy for them, sometimes drawing attention to the perceived threat they posed, but almost always emphasizing their difference from "homeland" Japanese. On November 26, 1946, the *Asahi shinbun* published a submission from a Dr. Fujii who warned readers about Manchurian typhus. He described it at length and then offered an epidemiological analysis with a social subtext that was not difficult to discern.

Recently many people have returned from Manchuria and more are on the way. The people returning from Manchuria have immunities to Manchurian typhus and do not develop it—they only bring the infected fleas back with them. That is why the disease is spreading among the people of *naichi*. In the past, Manchurian typhus has not been treated as a communicable disease, but clearly it presents our society with a serious social problem. One gets fleas, like lice, in lodgings, baths, in trains, and at the movie theaters. We need to come up with a strategy at once.[54]

Dr. Fujii's anxieties about the threat of contamination posed by repatriates appeared in print just after a million civilians had been repatriated from Manchuria between May and October 1946, and characterizes the initial, uneasy encounter between the people of *naichi* and returnees.

In May 1949, the monthly magazine *Nippon shūhō* carried an article entitled "I was repatriated but . . ." in which the writer seeks to convey the troubles faced by repatriates.[55] The article begins by asserting that repatriates, having lost their belongings, assets, and homes, are the most tragic victims of the war. The reporter then goes on to depict them as self-interested, suspicious of others, prone to living in filth, and sexually promiscuous. Because they cannot get along with others, he notes, they always fail in cooperative ventures. Their traumatic experiences abroad during repatriation have robbed them of their moral orientation and rendered some of them "no longer human" (*ningen shikkaku* 人間失格), a reference, perhaps, to the popular Dazai Osamu novel of the same title

---

54. "Nomi taisaku kōzeyo," *Asahi shinbun*, November 26, 1946.
55. "Ruporutâju: hikiagete wa mita keredo," 8–13.

published less than a year before.[56] What kept them going, he continues, is a primal vitality, a strength for living, and as long as that will to live burns, he surmises, they would always be called repatriates.[57] The article illustrates how an ambivalent press both sympathized with and stigmatized returnees. Another example is an editorial from the July 28, 1948 *Asahi shinbun* arguing that the government is not doing enough to aid war victims and especially repatriates. Throughout the editorial, the author talks about "repatriates" (*hikiagesha*) and "general citizens" (*ippan kokumin* 一般国民), and the need to shrink the distance between the two. Moreover, he notes that citizens in general (*kokumin ippan* 国民一般) need to reflect on their cold response to the repatriates.[58] An article in the October 30, 1948 issue speculates that returnees must have welcomed the opportunity to come back to *naichi* but were probably surprised by the chilly reception of *hikiagesha* at home.[59]

People who had been tagged with the repatriate label had a keen ear for the kinds of characterizations that swirled around them, and they immediately began to challenge, modify, and in some cases accept the categorization of *hikiagesha*. The interaction between the official category of the repatriate, the social category as produced by the press, and the response by repatriates themselves generated and sustained the category across the postwar period, as different constituents used it for different ends.

In immediate postwar Japan, repatriates struggled alongside the domestic population for food, clothing, and shelter. While trying to fulfill their basic needs, they also sought to stabilize their lives by seeking jobs and creating community ties. Returnees formed self-help groups and political organizations and began to lobby for redress for their assets lost overseas. From the beginning, repatriates also sought to make sense, intellectually and spiritually, of their lives in the colonies, their ignominious return, and what they sometimes called "the cold wind of *naichi*," or

---

56. The novel *Ningen shikkaku*, translated as *No Longer Human* by Donald Keene in 1958, was originally published in two issues of the magazine *Tenbō* just before and after Dazai's suicide in June 1948. Dazai, *Shayō, Ningen shikkaku*, 390.

57. "Ruporutâju: hikiagete wa mita keredo," 13.

58. "Shasetsu: hikiagesha taisaku ni sekkyokusei o." *Asahi shinbun*, July 28, 1948.

59. "Haikyū mo moraenu ryō; hikiagesha ni tsumetai 'fuyu 2'," *Asahi shinbun*, October 30, 1948.

the less-than-hearty reception on the part of Japanese at home. So serious was their mission of making sense of themselves and their communities that they devoted scarce resources to publishing newspapers, magazines, and newsletters for their communities.

Beginning in 1946, repatriates throughout Japan began to use such publications as a means of communicating with each other. Many served as the newsletters of local repatriate organizations, some were the alumni magazines of schools in the former colonies, a few were the work of a single passionate individual.[60] Some were short-lived, such as the two-issue newspaper *Sensō giseisha*.[61] The most stable papers were the newsletters of semi-official repatriate organizations, such as the *Onshi zaidan dōhō engo kaihō* (formerly the *Dōhō engo*), newsletter of the repatriation organization supported by the imperial household, the Onshi zaidan dōhō engokai.[62] Publication records are not available for most of the papers, but a typical newsletter, the *Hikiage dōhō shinbun* in Gifu Prefecture had a circulation of 5,000 copies.[63]

Repatriate journalists, like all writers in postwar Japan, faced the challenge of Allied censorship. Liberated from the constraints of wartime Japanese military censorship, the Japanese publishing industry confronted a whole new set of restrictions imposed by the new authorities.[64] The Civil Censorship Detachment (CCD), under the Civil Intelligence Section of SCAP, oversaw the censorship operation.[65] From September 1945 through the fall of 1947, all newspapers, magazines, books, and pamphlets were subject to pre-publication censorship. The CCD re-

---

60. *Gojo kaihō* and *Shimane-ken gaichi hikiage minpō* were local newsletters; *Konpeki* was the alumni magazine of Seoul Imperial University; and *Hikiagesha no koe*, classified as neither left nor right but "merely radical" by Allied censors, was published by an individual.

61. The two issues of *Sensō giseisha* (War victims) were published in June and August 1946.

62. *Onshi zaidan engo kaihō* was published between 1945 and 1949 (and possibly beyond). Zenren (Hikiagesha dantai zenkoku rengōkai), the national organization for repatriates, reportedly published a newsletter called *Shinkensetsu* (Reconstruction) from 1946, and another publication, the *Hikiage zenren tsūshin*, from 1956.

63. "Newspaper Report," *Hikiage dōhō shinbun*.

64. Dower, *Embracing Defeat*, especially "Censored Democracy: Policing the New Taboos," 405–40.

65. Marlene Mayo, "The War of Words Continues," 52.

quired publishers to submit two copies of each publication. Censors vetted the material, marked any required deletions or suppressions, and kept track of other violations, such as mentioning Allied censorship or substituting symbols for deleted words. CCD kept one copy and returned the other to the publisher.[66] During the autumn of 1947, the CCD moved most publications to post-publication censorship and checked for transgressions only after the works had already gone to press. They kept 26 left-leaning and 2 nationalist magazines on pre-publication censorship until the entire censorship apparatus was dismantled in October 1949.[67]

The initial goal of Allied censorship was to guard against the publication of information concerning troop movements and to eliminate propaganda, but soon censors began to use media surveillance as a means to reeducate the Japanese public and install SCAP's vision of a free and objective press.[68] Censors sought to combat the promotion of militarism, expansionism, and ultra-nationalism by deleting any mention of them, as well as suppressing any criticism of the Allied forces. Occupation officials knew with some precision the topics they believed to be unacceptable, a body of offenses that changed over time. They kept these lists of taboo subjects in secret "key logs," the contents of which scholars have since verified.[69] Censors chose not to share the specifics with Japanese publishers and writers. Instead they provided only a vague press code that exhorted writers to "adhere strictly to the truth" and publish nothing that might "disturb the public tranquility."[70] Editors submitted publications to censors only to have them returned heavily marked up with deletions and suppressions for reasons that were not always self-evident. As John Dower has pointed out, this

---

66. The CCD retained copies of most of the books, magazines, newspapers, and other publications that passed through their office, which included most of the works published in 1945 and 1946. These materials were shipped to the University of Maryland in 1950 and now make up the Gordon W. Prange Collection.

67. Okuizumi, ed., *User's Guide to the Microfilm Edition of Censored Periodicals*, 512–25.

68. Coughlin, *Conquered Press*, 30.

69. Dower, *Embracing Defeat*, 411; Furukawa, "Kenkyū shiryō," 136–37.

70. The press code is reproduced in Coughlin, *Conquered Press*, 149–50.

forced writers to guess at what might be censored and to learn by trial and error.[71]

The striking overlap between information unacceptable to the censors and issues surrounding repatriation created special problems for repatriate publications. This is not to suggest that Allied censors sought to suppress discussions of the return in particular. Rather, because repatriation involved overseas Japanese nationals passing through newly liberated territories under the auspices of the Allies, the very nature of the topic led to trouble with the censors. Nearly all of the 31 taboo subjects listed in a key log of June 1946, the peak of the arrival of civilians from Manchuria, could be applied to any discussion of repatriation; of these, nine are particularly relevant. They include criticizing Russia, criticizing Korea (and Koreans), criticizing China, criticizing other Allies, criticizing Japanese activities in Manchuria, employing "Greater East Asia" propaganda, describing black market activities, overplaying starvation, and inciting violence or unrest. It was difficult for repatriates to publish accounts of their postwar experiences without violating these taboo subjects, and we cannot know how the media would have covered repatriation had there been no censorship. By looking at how articles on repatriation were censored, we can see the kinds of limits that were placed on the discussion.

As analyzed by Kimoto Itaru, the following paragraph appeared in the draft of an article entitled "How are our compatriots living under Soviet Rule?" in a 1946 issue of the left-leaning monthly magazine *Shinsō*: "Many repatriates [in North Korea under Soviet rule] report unpleasant experiences during the period of confusion following the war, such as the theft of wristwatches and pens, expulsion from their homes, and a lack of food, forcing them to live off Soviets leftovers." CCD ordered this passage to be deleted because it was critical of an Allied power.[72] The censoring of this relatively mild description from 1946 of the "unpleasantness" experienced under Soviet rule suggests that more graphic depictions of violence or forced labor would not be allowed.

Another example of the censorship of repatriate-related issues, as analyzed by Furukawa Atsushi, is a story in the January 1947 issue of

---

71. Dower, *Embracing Defeat*, 410.
72. Kimoto, *Zasshi de yomu sengoshi*, 40.

the magazine *Kaizō*.[73] The protagonist of the story "A Spectacular Scandal" by Satomi Ton is a Manchurian repatriate. Censors ordered the magazine to delete the phrase, "the inspections, insults and looting by foreign people" as "critical of Chinese." Also ordered deleted was the phrase "frightening nighttime, when even the daughters of high officials were carted away" as it was deemed "critical of Chinese or Russians." The phrase "robbed along the way" was seen as critical of Chinese, and a description of hiding one's watch to protect it from theft was deemed "critical of Chinese actions to repatriates." The phrase "the loyalty of a Japanese military man" was deemed "militaristic" and ordered deleted. Although censorship was reduced in 1947 and ended in 1949, repatriation remained under the auspices of the Occupation until 1952 and coverage of it also remained somewhat under the Allies' control. As late as March 1949, the Occupation still continued to issue restrictions on journalists covering repatriation.[74]

Nevertheless, returnees persevered in publishing their views. Reflecting the outpouring of new voices in the immediate postwar period, discussions of the repatriation problem provided an array of political views and suggestions on how repatriates should make their way in postwar society. Some depictions reflect discourses of the time, but always with a repatriate emphasis. The newspaper *Senso giseisha* sought to unite all of the (Japanese) victims of the war, from widows to bereaved families, to domestic bombing victims and repatriates. The first, uncensored issue contained an inexplicable combination of fiery, anti-government, anti-Occupation Marxist rhetoric and reverence for the spirits at Yasukuni Shrine, the controversial site designated to house the spirits of all of Japan's war dead. The draft of the second issue, vetted by CCD censors, is marked up with the words "suppress" and "delete." Censors did not respond to the anti-government or Marxist rhetoric, but indicated deep concern at the appearance of Yasukuni. The publisher of *Senso giseisha* managed to produce a second issue satisfactory to

---

73. Furukawa, "Kenkyū shiryō," 150–53.
74. Maizuru chihō engokyoku, *Maizuru chihō hikiage engokyoku shi*, 272–76.

the censors, but no third issue was printed.[75] Other newspapers follow a similar publishing pattern.[76]

Discussions of repatriates intersected with the heated debates of the day, including Marxism and democracy. In "Kaigai hikiagesha wa uttae-ru" (Protests of overseas repatriates), Tokuda Tsuneo offers a fresh interpretation of the end of the war in Asia, arguing that it forced the "working masses abroad" out of their jobs and robbed them of their one final possession, their strength to labor.[77] The solution, according to Tokuda, was to replace the current government, which represented only capitalists and landlords, with a true people's government (*jinmin seifu*). Tokuda pointed out that repatriates were perhaps the ultimate victims of the war, but only the "repatriate laborers" (*hikiage kinrōsha* 引揚勤労者) were the most deserving of sympathy. They were forced to return to Japan against their will, and once they arrived there were no jobs and the government did nothing to help them.

A year later, a more staid writer explained the difference between repatriates and the proletariat to his readers. On November 10, 1947, Kawaguchi Tadatoku, the president of the *Reishi shinbun*, published an editorial in which he argued against growing ties between repatriate groups and unions.[78] Although he had nothing against the existence of unions, he believed that closer ties with them would cause repatriate groups to lose sight of their mission, which was the rehabilitation of the repatriate community. Moreover, he insisted, there was a fundamental difference between the proletariat and poor repatriates. The proletariat, and the unions that supported their rights, were parts of a class system. Spiritually and in practice, repatriates who had held secure positions overseas before the war were not part of a class system. Their current dire situation, therefore, was due not to class but rather to the circumstances of defeat.[79]

---

75. *Sensō giseisha*, August 1946.

76. *Dōhō kōsei shinbun*. The two issues appeared in November and December 1946.

77. "Kaigai ni atta kinrō taishū" (Working masses abroad), in Tokuda, "Kaigai hiki-agesha wa uttaeru."

78. *Reishi shinbun*, November 19, 1947.

79. The 48-year-old Kawaguchi had apparently made the best of a bad situation. During his repatriation from a communist-controlled part of Manchuria, he networked among the other repatriates on the voyage to Hakata. His fellow deportees and he had

A Kumamoto newspaper shows the efforts of one man to link repatriate concerns with political representation. The *Hikiage minpō* served as the newsletter for the Kumamoto repatriate self-help organization, the Kumamoto-ken gaichi hikiage gojokai. This handwritten tabloid, a labor of love by an individual with the surname Hamada, sought to educate and inspire the local repatriate community. Instead of merely editorializing on the government's responsibility to treat overseas Japanese assets in the same manner as domestic assets, Hamada made the connection between lobbying for overseas assets and political representation. In the April 1, 1946 edition, Hamada informed his readers that anyone with a stable address who was repatriated by March 20 was eligible to vote in the first major postwar national election of April 1946.[80] (Later, repatriates had to be at the same address for three months in order to be eligible to vote.) The paper then promoted three repatriate candidates, one of whom, Nanjō Akira, had been a politician, lawyer, and representative in the colonial government in Seoul.

Hamada of the *Hikiage minpō* was not the only person to link repatriates and potential political power through voting. On March 19, 1947, an *Asahi shinbun* article stressed the potential power of the repatriate voting block by pointing out that the 5.3 million repatriates significantly outnumbered other groups, including the 4.42 million members of labor unions and the 1.3 million members of the farmer's union. The article conceded that repatriates lacked political organization but as a discrete "social stratum" (*shakai sō*), they shared political interests. The article gave voice to apprehension that communist ideology might play a role in the voting patterns of repatriates.[81]

Although Hamada tried to gain political power by promoting repatriate candidates, his efforts were in vain. A year after his first attempt to get out the vote, in the April 1947 issue of the paper, he conceded defeat in that repatriates did not succeed in sending a single repatriate represen-

---

made a pact to work for the rehabilitation of repatriates and the reconstruction of a new, peaceful Japan. Upon arrival, the repatriates all returned to their hometowns, creating a nationwide network for Kawaguchi's organization, the Overseas Repatriates Self-Help Organization (Kaigai hikiagesha jijo dantai).

80. *Gojo kaihō*, April 1, 1946, 2.

81. "Naichi no genkyō ni fuman—iro koi kakushin taibō," *Asahi shinbun*, March 19, 1947.

tative to the National Diet from his district. The political resolve of the repatriates, he lamented, had fallen short. Repatriates came from all different classes and factions, he noted, but were tied together by similar interests, including seeking compensation for overseas assets. Representation on key committees, such as the economic rehabilitation committees, was therefore critical to their recovery.[82]

Although the papers were published in disparate places—as far north as Otaru in Hokkaido and as far south as Kagoshima in Kyushu—they tell of similar concerns of repatriates throughout Japan.[83] Regardless of geographic location or political slant, the newspapers advocated three things: they encouraged the government to put more effort into bringing the remaining overseas Japanese back home; they asked repeatedly for resources from the government in order to recover on their own; and they asked for assurances that their overseas assets would be protected, or that they would be reimbursed for them in some way. Additionally, nearly all of the papers included practical information (job retraining, remarriage services) aimed specifically at returnees.

Repatriates frequently reported on slights that people at home used against them. Sometimes they sought commiseration, but in other cases the complaints segued into a more positive interpretation of the repatriate experience. One reporter told of a confrontation he had with people from the local community, who shouted at him, "Repatriates, repatriates, that's all any one ever talks about, but isn't it true that all of you were accomplices to the provocateurs of the war? If you hadn't gone out to the colonies, there wouldn't have been a war."[84] A second person reported an incident in which an unsympathetic metropolitan Japanese used the new rhetoric of democracy to cajole repatriates on their way home. According to this account, one day during the summer of 1946, the ferry office in Kagoshima was selling tickets to the island of Tanegashima. Of the 200 people in line, only 70 were able to purchase tickets. Fewer tickets than usual were available because people who had just been repatriated from overseas had been given priority. An ignorant person had said, "I thought democracy meant that we and

---

82. *Hikiage minpō*, April 1, 1947.
83. *Sensaisha jihō*, Otaru; *Hikiage dōhō*, Kagoshima.
84. *Hikiage minpō*, October 10, 1946, 2.

the repatriates were all the same citizens. That's not democratic."[85] (The passage is also instructive for the emphasis on the distinction between "we" (*ware ware*) and "repatriates" (*hikiagesha*), at least as reported by the repatriate.) A third lamented that repatriates had been branded as "the running dogs of imperialism" (*teikoku shugi shinryaku no sōku* 帝国主義侵略の走狗) but then offered another interpretation of their experiences. Their knowledge of foreign countries was a plus (*purasu*). With their many years, sometimes decades, of business experience overseas, repatriates were in a terrific position to be the leaders of Japan's future international trade. They had learned their lesson and would stop viewing Asia as merely a large source of cheap labor. Instead, they would become more culturally polished and interact with other countries based on respect and understanding.[86] The same publication, the newsletter of the Repatriate Benefit Group of Shizuoka Prefecture (Shizuoka-ken gaichi hikiagesha gojokai), indicated its overall optimism of the future role of repatriates by naming their magazine *Kokusaijin* (Internationalists). A commentary in the same issue argues that returnees needed to shed the label "repatriate" as quickly as possible.[87] "Internationalist," the paper suggested, was an appropriate substitution. The June 1947 issue of *Shimane-ken gaichi hikiage minpō* tells of an organization called the Overseas Conditions Investigation Group (Kaigai jijō konwakai 海外事情懇話会) devoted to planning for repatriate-centered international trade after Japan regained sovereignty. Their goal was the reconstruction of a peaceful Japan.[88] The magazine *Minato* (Harbor), in promoting itself as "the magazine of culture for continentals" (*tairikujin bunka zasshi* 大陸人文化雑誌), demonstrates a similar impulse to put a positive spin on "overseas experience" by renaming repatriates as continentals and explicitly associating them with culture.[89]

In addition to advocating new names and concepts for themselves, the early repatriate community re-narrated negative stories or highlighted positive ones to diffuse the flow of negative press. One example

---

85. *Hikiage dōhō*, September 16, 1946.

86. Yamada Seiji, "Sōkan no kotoba," *Kokusaijin*, September 10, 1947.

87. Kawahara Iwao, "Makoto no teikei," *Kokusaijin*, September 10, 1947.

88. *Shimane-ken gaichi hikiage minpō*, June 1, 1947, 2

89. *Minato*, vol. 2, no. 2, February 1947. The subtitle "the magazine of culture for continentals" (*tairikujin bunka zasshi*) appears from this issue.

is a retelling of the story of demobilized Japanese men who rejected their repatriated Manchurian wives. The story appeared in the relentlessly cheerful *Kaigai hikiage shinbun* (Overseas repatriate newspaper). The cover story of the single extant issue tells a "beautiful Manchurian repatriation tale":

> Embracing his weeping wife, their everlasting love lives on,
> a beautiful Manchuria repatriation tale;
> Female victims of the war need help.

There are many men who upon demobilization have returned to Japan to find that their wives have not yet been repatriated. They wait for a while, but then take another wife. They tire of waiting and perhaps the bonds of love were not that strong to begin with. When the first wife eventually does return to Japan, it causes all sorts of pain for everyone.

But let us tell you a beautiful story of everlasting love. Mr. X was a South Manchuria Railway Company employee drafted during the last stages of the war. At the end of the war, he was demobilized and repatriated to Japan but had no news of his wife, whom he had last seen in Fengtian in 1944. His friends told him to give up on her. Even if she did return, she would not be the same woman he married. But the young man was not dissuaded. When he heard of her arrival at her parents' home in Miyazaki, Kyushu, he traveled all the way from Ibaragi to fetch her.

Upon seeing her husband, "Ito" burst into tears and said, "Forgive me and this terrible broken down body." Her parents said, "We assumed you had taken another bride." The young man rejected these sentiments and took his wife back to Ibaragi to nurse her back to health. They are now farming happily together. "I'm her husband," he said. "If I don't take care of her, who will?"[90]

This story celebrating Mr. X's actions implies that perhaps other men were not as devoted to their wives repatriated from Manchuria. And the ominous "not the same woman he married" speaks to people's fears of possible sexual violence against Japanese women in postwar Manchuria. The need to tell a "beautiful Manchurian repatriation tale" suggests that the reality, in contrast, was troubled.

Repatriate self-help groups appear to have been torn on the issue of the troublemakers among them. On the one hand, they understood how poverty, loss, and the cold reception at home could turn a person to

---

90. *Kaigai hikiage shinbun.* September 8, 1946.

crime and prostitution. On the other hand, they recognized that these were precisely the people who gave repatriates a bad name. Repatriate press coverage of two incidents shows some of the ambivalence within the local community. The *Hikiage dōhō shinbun* covered the story of a defiant shantytown of Manchurian repatriates who had occupied the public plaza in front of the Gifu City train station.[91] In 1946, a group of returnees from Manchuria had received tickets to their home prefecture of Gifu, but, because they had no place else to go, set up temporary homes in Gifu City. A charismatic repatriate leader by the name of Takai Isamu set up a booth in the public plaza in front of the station to welcome the repatriates home. They stayed and built a community that came to be known as "Harbin Town."

Harbin Town grew to accommodate open-air stalls and makeshift housing for hundreds of people. In December 1948, Harbin Town had enough civic pride to advertise itself as the best place for holiday shopping. Crisis was looming, though, as Takai Isamu was indicted for selling rationed goods on the black market that had been earmarked for his repatriate constituency. He was also caught up in a repatriate housing scandal: he had collected funds and promised housing to 3,000 people, but succeeded in building only 500 spots. Moreover, the people of Gifu wanted their plaza back. Hesitant to crack down on the repatriate community, city and prefectural authorities pressured the repatriates to disband on their own. By 1949, over a hundred families lived and operated black market stalls there. The issue had finally come to a head with the prefectural and local authorities, and had even become an issue in the national news. The newsletter of the organization, which advocated for repatriates, urged the squatters to resolve the dispute as smoothly and quickly as possible, lest it reflect badly on the rest of the repatriate community.

In another case, a newspaper surveyed repatriate opinion on a tragedy in their community. A woman and her six children had made it back to Japan from Manchuria only to find conditions equally dire. Desperate, she committed *shinjū*, or murder-suicide, with her children.[92]

---

91. *Hikiage dōhō shinbun*, no. 46, December 22, 1948, 2; no. 51, May 5, 1949, 1; no. 55, September 5, 1949, 2.

92. *Hikiage dōhō* (Kagoshima), September 16, 1946.

Opinion was split. One group felt it reflected a failure of society at large and the repatriate community in particular. But another group felt that since the woman had been given the gift of making it home alive, she should have persevered.

In the end, on a practical level, repatriates could do little to promote their first and third goals, of encouraging the government to repatriate remaining overseas Japanese and to guarantee their assets abroad. As we have seen, SCAP took over Japan's foreign relations, including negotiations for overseas Japanese, until the end of the Occupation in 1952. As for overseas assets, with Japan's defeat, there was little possibility or sympathy for trying to retrieve colonial possessions or assets from Korea or Taiwan. The Chinese mainland was rent by civil war from 1946 to 1949, and with the establishment of the PRC, people abandoned attempts to retrieve assets from China. Chaos accompanying the war on the Korean peninsula in 1950 put an end to the attempts to lay claim to assets. Repatriates did succeed in getting rehabilitation loans and other aid from the government, and the momentum in trying to secure their overseas assets was channeled into a more general effort at securing compensation from the Japanese government.

From 1946 to 1949, repatriates actively responded to how the homeland society depicted them, in the MHW camps and then in the popular press, by attempting to place repatriate issues into the discourses of the day, by analyzing the nature of the slights and charges against them, and by promoting alternative versions of the meaning of the word "repatriate." Some advocated shedding the label as quickly as possible, but others sought new beginnings in postwar Japan *as* repatriates. Others, especially youth repatriated from Manchuria, hung on to the label, or at least the maverick identity associated with it. It was in these ways—during the immediate postwar years, in broadsheets and handwritten newsletters, in repatriate communities throughout Japan, and in response to the mainstream press—that the early *hikiagesha* were co-produced.

From Imperial Subject into Foreigner: The Allied Deportation of "Third Country Nationals" from Japan

In 1945 and 1946, Occupation authorities and Japanese government officials were busy with another group of dislocated people—former colonial subjects in Japan. Roughly 2 million Koreans, 56,000 people from mainland China and 35,000 people from Taiwan were in Japan at the end of the war.[93] Both the Occupation authorities and the Japanese government assumed that all former colonial peoples would leave Japan. How the Japanese government, under instructions from SCAP, handled this population during the Occupation set the tone for the future of former colonial subjects in Japan throughout the postwar period.

During the last few months of the war and the first few months after the Japanese surrender, Koreans streamed to southern Honshu and Kyushu and returned to Korea by any possible means. During this period of unregulated migration, Koreans were able to take money and

---

93. Estimates of the number of Koreans, Chinese, other Asian foreigners, and Okinawans in Japan at the end of the war vary widely. The MHW estimated that the number of Koreans in Japan at the end of 1944 was 1,936,843, but this may not include tens of thousands of Koreans transported to Japan as forced laborers in the final year of the war. Kōseishō hikiage engokyoku, *Zoku zoku hikiage engo no kiroku*, 271. Using U.S. military numbers, Edward Wagner estimates that the number of Koreans in Japan was 2.4 million as of March 1945, but that 400,000 left Japan before the end of the war, resulting in a population of approximately 2 million Koreans as of August 1945 (Wagner, *The Korean Minority in Japan*, 96). Yukiko Koshiro concurs with this number (Koshiro, *Trans-Pacific Racisms*, 113). Takemae Eiji puts the number of Koreans in Japan at the time of defeat at 2.4 million. He also gives a 2000 Foreign Ministry estimate of 2.16 million Koreans in Japan as of October 1945 (Takemae, *Inside GHQ*, 447). The MHW figures for the numbers of Koreans at the end of the war are quite low at an estimated 1,561,358, but this figure is based on adding the number of Koreans officially deported from Japan from the end of the war through February 18, 1946 to the number of Koreans registered for future deportation on a survey conducted on February 18, 1946. In other words, it does not include Koreans who reached home by unofficial means or those who were not counted in the February 18 survey (Kōseishō engokyoku, *Hikiage to engo 30-nen no ayumi*, 151). For ease of discussion, I use the figure of 2 million Koreans in Japan at the end of the war, 600,000 of whom decided to remain permanently. A number of secondary sources use the figure of 30,000 when talking about the number of Chinese and Taiwanese in Japan at the end of the war. MHW records suggest that these figures are too low. According to their figures, again based on adding the numbers of people officially deported and those counted in the February 18 survey, 56,051 people from mainland China and 34,368 people from Taiwan were in Japan at the end of the war (Kōseishō hikiage engokyoku. *Zoku zoku hikiage engo no kiroku*, 151). All but a few thousand accepted deportation. The estimated number of people deported by February 18, 1946 are as follows: Koreans, 914,352; Chinese, 41,110; Taiwanese, 18,462; Greater Ryūkyūans (南西諸島民), 13,675. Kōseishō engokyoku, *Hikiage to engo sanjūnen no ayumi*, 151–52.

possessions home with them.[94] Approximately 950,000 Koreans returned to Korea outside official channels between March and the end of
November 1945.[95]

A number of factors came together at the end of 1945 and slowed
the pace of repatriation for the remaining 775,000 Koreans in Japan.
Although SCAP was eager to be rid of a group of people they saw
as having "created many annoying complications for the American occupation forces"[96] and as "an unwelcome additional administrative burden,"[97] it was SCAP that instituted the monetary restrictions and other
obstacles that slowed the departure of Koreans from Japan. SCAP set
strict quarantine procedures and limits for the amount of money and
valuables Koreans could take home with them. The cash limit was set
at 1,000 yen per person plus whatever he or she could carry, the same
limits placed on defeated Japanese nationals. The prospect of leaving
everything behind and starting from scratch in Korea apparently made
some Koreans decide to remain in Japan, at least temporarily. Moreover,
reports from Korea about bad economic conditions, floods, and a chilly
reception for returnees made repatriation even less appealing for some.[98]

SCAP instructed the MHW to administer the deportation of former
colonial subjects. According to MHW accounts, Koreans and other
Asian foreigners were housed, fed, and processed in the same manner
as Japanese repatriates.[99] In that sense, the repatriation centers served
as two-way valves in the social dismantling of empire. One participant,

---

94. Wagner, *The Korean Minority in Japan*, 41–46.

95. Ibid.

96. The phrase comes from Edwin O. Reischauer's "Foreword" in Wagner, *The Korean Minority in Japan*, i. (Reischauer's "Foreword" is analyzed further in Fujitani, "The Reischauer Memo.") The language is instructive and I include the relevant portions here:
"The Koreans in post-war Japan have created many annoying complications for the
American occupation forces, and the seemingly insoluble problem of their presence in
Japan as an unassimilable minority will continue to cause bitterness between certain
elements among the Japanese and Korean peoples, if not between their respective governments. . . . the Koreans in Japan, meanwhile, have remained a source of irritation and
embarrassment to American groups in Japan and to the United Nations forces in Korea."

97. Wagner, *The Korean Minority in Japan*, 2.

98. Ibid., 43–46.

99. Kōseishō engokyoku. *Hikiage to engo 30-nen no ayumi*, 149–68.

Table 4
Number of People Deported from Japan as of December 31, 1950

National origin	Number deported	Deported against their will
Korean	1,014,541	37,215
Chinese	43,736	66
Taiwanese	24,406	103
Greater Ryukyu (Nansei shotōmin)	180,016	249
Germans	1,968	0
Italians	158	0
Others	266	0
TOTAL	1,265,091	37,633

SOURCE: Kōseishō engokyoku, *Hikiage to engo 30-nen no ayumi*, 152.

however, reported that "in its conduct of the repatriation program the Japanese Government repeatedly violated the spirit, and often the letter, of the instructions from SCAP. Unsatisfactory conditions at reception centers and on repatriation vessels were repeatedly noted by SCAP in directives ordering corrective action."[100] He went on to suggest that the Japanese saved their supplies for Japanese returnees and confiscated belongings from returning Koreans. The most egregious behavior on the part of Japanese officials was that they deliberately did not inform Koreans of the rules, regulations, and options facing them in repatriation, such as relaxed restrictions on assets or the legal option of remaining in Japan.[101] By 1949, only 600,000 of the approximately 2 million Koreans in Japan at the end of the war remained. (For numbers of people deported, see Table 4.)

The deportation of former colonials and the treatment of those who remained behind over the course of the Occupation were critical elements in the transformation of "imperial subjects" (*teikoku shinmin* 帝国臣民) into the postwar categories of "third country nationals" (*sangokujin*) and "resident foreigners" (*zainichi gaikokujin* 在日外国人). From the annexation of Korea in 1910 until the end of the war, Koreans had been classified as "Japanese subjects of the Korean race." They did not receive

100. Wagner, *The Korean Minority in Japan*, 49.
101. Ibid., 60.

the full benefits of Japanese citizenship but in some cases were considered Japanese nationals.[102] As imperial subjects, some Taiwanese and Korean men who resided in metropolitan Japan had the right to vote and to be elected to public office. Before the war, eleven such men stood for office and two were elected.[103]

When Allied officials arrived in Japan, they sorted everyone into groups: United Nations, neutral, and enemy nationals, but they did not include resident Koreans in any of those categories.[104] Eventually, SCAP placed Korea into a group of "Special Status Nations," but Koreans received none of the benefits (such as special foreigner rations) and all of the burdens (such as taxes) of being foreigners in Japan.[105] At some point during this process, Occupation authorities began to refer to former colonials as "third country nationals." That term was translated into Japanese as _daisangokujin_ or _sangokujin_ (literally "person from a third country"), and easily became part of the Japanese vernacular. In Japanese repatriation materials from 1945 to 1952, three categories appear: Japanese (_hōjin_ 邦人); foreigners (_gaikokujin_ 外国人); and "non-Japanese" (_hi-Nihonjin_ 非日本人), sometimes rendered as "third country nationals." Foreigners and others (_gaikokujin sonota_) were "foreigners, detained fishermen, postwar travelers, temporary returnees, etc." "Non-Japanese" were glossed as "Koreans, Taiwanese and those from Greater Ryukyu," that is, people from former Japanese colonies and Okinawa.[106] _Sangokujin_ became the technically correct but disparaging referent for former colonials. In his memoir about his work repatriating civilians from Manchuria, Hirashima Toshio complained about the violent and arrogant "third country nationals" he encountered upon repatriation to

---

102. Wagner, _The Korean Minority in Japan_, 9.

103. Tanaka, _Zainichi gaikokujin_. 63–64.

104. Wagner, _The Korean Minority in Japan_, 58; "Definition of 'United Nations,' 'Neutral Nations,' and 'Enemy Nations.'" SCAPIN 217, October 31, 1945, in Takemae, ed., _GHQ shirei sōshūsei_, vol. 2, 331–33.

105. Wagner, _The Korean Minority in Japan_, 58; "Rations for United Nations' Nationals, Neutral Nationals and Stateless Persons." SCAPIN 1094, July 30, 1946, in Takemae, ed., _GHQ shirei sōshūsei_, vol. 5, 2153–54; "Definition of United, Neutral, Enemy, Special Status and Undetermined Status Nations." SCAPIN 1912, June 21, 1948 (later rescinded by SCAPIN 1951 and 2136) in Takemae, ed., _GHQ shirei sōshūsei_, vol. 13, 6128–29.

106. Maizuru chihō engokyoku, _Maizuru chihō hikiage engokyoku shi_, 541; the rendering "third country national" is discussed in Wagner, _The Korean Minority in Japan_, 61.

Sasebo in the fall of 1947, and called their presence in postwar Japan unbearable.[107] There is no question that he was referring to Koreans.

Like the Occupation officials, the Japanese government busied itself with new categorizations for former imperial subjects—the 600,000 Koreans and few thousand Taiwanese and Chinese who remained in Japan. In December 1945, election laws were changed to give women the right to vote. At the same time, some bylaws were added stating that the right to vote and to run for election would be terminated for people who did not qualify under the terms of the registry (*koseki* 戸籍) laws. Because Koreans and Taiwanese had not been allowed to transfer their home registries from the colonies to *naichi*, most of them—except for those exempt because of marriage or adoption—were disqualified under the terms of the *koseki* laws and lost the right to vote. Home Minister Horikiri Zenjirō justified this decision by explaining that Koreans and Taiwanese had lost their Japanese nationality with Japan's acceptance of the Potsdam Declaration and therefore it was not appropriate for them to retain the right to vote. Technically, they would retain Japanese nationality until the Peace Treaty went into effect and therefore their voting rights were not yet "prohibited" (*kinshi* 禁止); rather, they had been "terminated" (*teishi* 停止).[108]

The next change in the status of former colonials was new legislation requiring foreigners to register. On the day before the new constitution went into effect in 1947, the final imperial edict issued in Japan stipulated that Koreans and Taiwanese would, from that point on, be treated as foreigners (*gaikokujin*) and required to comply with the law requiring foreigners to register. Although they had been designated foreigners, in 1948 Korean children were ordered to attend Japanese schools and they were treated as Japanese nationals.[109]

Another change came at the time the San Francisco Peace Treaty came into effect in 1952. Although the treaty was not explicit about the change in nationality of former colonials, on April 19, 1952, the Justice Ministry issued a notice clarifying their status. It included four main points:

---

107. Hirashima, *Rakudo kara naraku e*, 288.
108. Tanaka, *Zainichi gaikokujin*, 64–65.
109. Ibid., 66.

1. All Koreans and Taiwanese, even those on the home islands, lose their Japanese nationality.

2. If before the Peace Treaty went into effect, these people had become Japanese by marriage or adoption, they remain Japanese.

3. People who had been removed from family registers before the Treaty have lost their Japanese nationality.

4. In order for a Korean or Taiwanese person to become Japanese, he will need to undergo the same naturalization process as any other foreigner. The fact that he used to be a Japanese subject or is a person who had lost his Japanese citizenship makes no difference. [110]

At this point, former colonials who for seven years had been in the gray area of "third country nationals" or "non-Japanese" became foreigners (*gaikokujin*), but the coded words used to describe them lived on.[111]

Conclusion

As discussed above, during the colonial period the homeland and the colonies had sustained and defined each other. Metropolitan and colonial Japanese were also categories defined by geography and that functioned as a pair in tension. With the loss of the colonies, the tension that held the defining constructs of the homeland and the colonies, and the homeland Japanese and the colonists, went slack. Use of the word *naichi* or "homeland" to describe the home islands of Japan became less relevant and fell out of fashion, in official discourse at least, during the first few years after the war. The reworking of the home islands from the metropole of an empire into a nation with clear national borders was relatively straightforward, although Japan's deferment of establishing a new relationship with its former colonies would come back to haunt East Asian relations in the last decades of the twentieth century.

The transformation of the relationship between the people of the homeland and the people of the colonies into something that made

---

110. Ibid., 66–67.

111. In *Exodus to North Korea*, Morris-Suzuki provides an overview of how Koreans in Japan were transformed from imperial subjects into foreigners, and then goes on to show how their status as foreigners made them vulnerable to a scheme in the late 1950s to move them to the Democratic People's Republic of Korea (North Korea). In all, nearly 100,000 ethnic Koreans were moved. Morris-Suzuki, *Exodus to North Korea*.

sense in post-imperial Japan was more complicated. The tension that sustained the dichotomy remained and took on new forms. The formerly colonial Japanese served as useful foils for re-inventing the formerly metropolitan Japanese who were rendered as the peace-loving citizens of the postwar nation of Japan. Defining oneself as a metropolitan Japanese in contrast to a person from the colonies meant that one had spent the war within the home islands, allowing one to dip into the new streams of discourse that provided the means for Japanese people, in the first few decades after the end of the war, to see themselves as victims and not perpetrators of World War II. These include highlighting the fact that people in Japan had suffered conventional and atomic bombings, and the idea that it was Japanese leaders and soldiers abroad who had committed wrongs, but that ordinary people at home were less culpable.[112] Defining oneself as a homeland Japanese, and not a repatriate, was a way to place a buffer between one's self and the imperial project.

As for the colonial Japanese, as long as they remained abroad, and in appropriate tension with people at home, their compatriots expressed concern about their welfare. Once they arrived back in Japan and passed through a repatriation center, however, they were handed a set of papers providing them with their new official identity as repatriates. Soon after the war, because Japan was no longer an empire, the term "homeland Japanese" became less relevant, and in contrast to colonial Japanese, they became "ordinary people" (*ippan no hito*). Returnees were stuck with the moniker "repatriate" (*hikiagesha*), excluding them from the category of ordinary Japanese. This was one of the ways in which the tensions of empire took on new life in different forms, and in which repatriates, tainted with foreign experience, continued to be marginalized in new guises in postwar Japan.

---

112. Dower, *Embracing Defeat*, 486–96.

THREE

"The Future of the Japanese Race" and

"Argumentative Types": Women from Manchuria

and Men from Siberia

In Hani Susumu's 1963 film *Kanojo to kare* (She and he), the protagonist Naoko, repatriated as a child from Manchuria, causes discord in her marriage to her "ordinary" husband Eichi, with whom she lives in a middle-class housing complex.[1] What sets Naoko apart from her neighbors is not her class or ethnicity, but rather her history as a Manchurian repatriate, even though she was just a child at the time of her return. Although that history is not specifically the cause of her marital problems, the filmmaker's decision to make Naoko a Manchurian repatriate provides just the right amount of difference between the other characters and her. In Yamasaki Toyoko's 1976 novel *Fumō chitai* (translated as *The Barren Zone*), a well-meaning couple tries to arrange a marriage between a woman repatriated from Manchuria and a former soldier who had been detained in the Soviet Union.[2] The matchmakers speculate that the experiences of the repatriate and the detainee in postwar

---

1. Hani, *Kanojo to kare*, 1963. The neighborhood women, while gossiping among themselves, identify Naoko as a Manchurian repatriate and say, "She must have had a terrible time."

2. Yamasaki, *The Barren Zone*, 272–73.

Manchuria might make the two compatible. One possible interpretation of their rationale is that the appropriate mate for a female Manchurian repatriate is another repatriate, perhaps a Siberian detainee. How did it come to be, in the popular imagination, that repatriates were perhaps best suited for each other, instead of as mates for ordinary Japanese? An examination of the historical circumstances that produced these people, and subsequent representations of the female Manchurian repatriate and the Soviet detainee, both rendered as *hikiagesha*, will illuminate further the uses and meanings of the word in the transitions of the postwar period.

As discussed in the previous chapter, during the first few years after the war, people at home and the returnees coproduced the category of *hikiagesha*. For many repatriates, especially those who were willing and able to disassociate themselves from the label, it never took, or faded with time. But women in postwar Manchuria and men detained in the Soviet Union faced particularly difficult situations, raising concern at home. Their usefulness as foils helped to create and sustain a special stigma for these two groups. Their stigmatization was solidified first in official discourse, then in the press, and eventually taken up in novels, films, and social criticism, where it continues to be useful into the twenty-first century. This chapter shows how the word *hikiagesha* acquired layers of meanings, often gendered, that encapsulated postwar anxieties, and how the word traveled across time, first as a device to reinterpret the end of the empire and then serving as a lightening rod for anxieties about communism.

"For the Sake of the Future of the Japanese Race": Female Repatriates from Manchuria

One of the most enduring images of the repatriate in Japan is a bedraggled woman from Manchuria, sometimes with children in tow, with a rucksack on her back. An early representation of this image, on the cover of this book, is the artist Yamana Ayao's 1945 Repatriate Relief poster for Shiseidō encouraging people to donate clothing to repatriates, especially women and children, who, as the poster explains, were especially hard pressed. (The word *hikiagesha* is prominent, in the center of the poster in bold.) A cartoon by Akatsuka Fujio, is another representation.[3] Published in the 1990s, Akatsuka's drawing shows his mother, rucksack on her back, her mouth set with determination, leading four small children to Fengtian for repatriation.[4] Although this depiction may reflect the afterlife of the image, immediate postwar representations of the women, including the poster on the cover, exist as well.

The comic strip *Sazae* (often compared to and perhaps inspired by *Blondie*) devoted a few episodes to repatriation, one of which provides an image of a woman from Manchuria, with a twist. In a cartoon that appeared in the Fukuoka newspaper the *Yūkan Fukunichi* in the summer of 1946, the main character Sazae staffs a table bearing a sign that reads "Manchurian Repatriate Reception Center" and provides tea and a greeting to a family of Manchurian repatriates.[5] The father wears parts of a tattered military uniform and a necktie. The mother wears clothes worn by most women during the war, simple trousers (*monpei*) and a Japanese-style blouse. Her heavy backpack and children in tow serve as markers that the woman is a Manchurian repatriate. The joke is that the parents are cross-dressed—the person with the necktie is the mother. She shaved her head and dressed like a man "because it was dangerous." That is, she tried to disguise the fact that she was female to escape sexual assault. The father is dressed in women's clothes because nothing else was available. Readers had to be familiar with the image of repatriates in postwar Japan in order for the joke to work. Another cartoon shows Sazae offering to a woman repatriated from Manchuria toys and clothes for her children, only to discover that the "children" are middle-aged men, lazing about with their belongings in a cramped room.[6] These

---

3. Akatsuka Fujio, in Chūgoku hikiage mangaka no kai, ed., *Boku no Manshū*, 37.

4. Akatsuka discussed his parents' history in the context of "Manshū rōnin" (満州浪人), adventurers who went to Manchuria to escape the confines of Japanese society. His father was a colonial policeman. His mother had been an entertainer in Japan and decided to take her chances in Manchuria. While working in a restaurant there she met Akatsuka's future father, with whom she had four children. Chūgoku hikiage mangaka no kai, ed., *Boku no Manshū*, 29–32.

5. *Sazaesan*, *Yūkan Fukunichi*, May 17, 1946. (Prange Collection Newspapers and Newsletters, Reel Y-65 (April 8, 1946–Sep. 30, 1946), frame 235.) Also available in Hasegawa, *Sazaesan*, 10–11.

6. *Sazaesan*, *Yūkan Fukunichi*, July 12, 1946. (Prange Collection Newspapers and Newsletters, Reel Y-65 (April 8, 1946–Sep. 30, 1946), frame 337.) Also available in Hasegawa, *Sazaesan*, 4.

depictions reveal the homeland perception that repatriates were not always able to conform to social norms in terms of gender and the life cycle. Somewhere in between the experiences of repatriation from Manchuria and the stories that followed them, the image of the female Manchurian repatriate emerged.

Prewar and wartime metropolitan perceptions of Japanese women abroad conditioned the ambivalent reception of them from Manchuria in the postwar period. Suspicion toward Japanese women abroad, especially those outside official enclaves, had a long history. Some of the first to go overseas were *karayukisan*, migrant prostitutes who moved throughout the Asia and Asia-Pacific region in the first half of the twentieth century. Nurses working with the military abroad suffered suspicions that they no longer met domestic standards of chastity. Houses of prostitution, including establishments using Japanese as well as local women, flourished in the colonies, where prostitution was legal just as it was in the homeland.[7] Japanese businessmen and women ran hotels, restaurants, and taverns in the colonies, establishments that sometimes intersected with prostitution. It was not hard for people at home to associate women abroad, especially in Manchuria where social mores were less constrained than at home, with sexual availability.

The Soviet invasion and occupation in northeast Asia created violent circumstances for Japanese nationals. On August 8, 1945, the Soviet Union joined the war against Japan, and just after midnight, the Soviet military launched attacks against Japanese territories that bordered the Soviet Union. In some instances, the Kwantung Army engaged the Soviets in battle, but for the most part the Army collapsed without a fight. The military had evacuated its personnel and their families from the cities of Changchun, Shenyang, and elsewhere. Some employees from the Manchukuo government and semi-governmental companies were evacuated as well, but all of the Japanese people in the countryside and most of the private citizens in the cities were left behind.[8] Settlers

---

7. For a history of licensed prostitution in Japan, see Garon, "The World's Oldest Debate?"

8. Young, *Japan's Total Empire*, 407–9. The Japanese military claimed that it issued evacuation orders to everyone but that the civilians failed to show up for the evacuation trains on time.

CARL A. RUDISILL LIBRARY
LENOIR-RHYNE UNIVERSITY

reported that when the Kwantung Army retreated, it destroyed bridges and other transportation infrastructure, making it even more difficult for settlers to make their way to safety.[9] Civilians throughout Manchuria, especially those in the settlements, were exposed to the Soviet onslaught.

The stories of the last days of the Japanese settlers in Manchuria appear as a collage of nightmares—a combination of flight, hunger, terror, sickness, and death. Accounts by residents of the Senzan Sarashinagō agricultural settlement (discussed in Chapter 1) bring the story into focus. Tsukada Asae, the elementary school teacher who went to Manchuria in 1941, devoted herself to preserving the history of the end of the settlement.[10] In 1944, the Japanese military drafted only a few men from the village, but during the summer of 1945, in violation of promises made to them when they went to Manchuria, the military commandeered almost all able-bodied men and by the end of the war, only 407 women, children, and the elderly remained in the isolated Senzan community in a region that jutted up into the Soviet Union (see Map 1).[11]

On August 9, 1945, following last-minute evacuation orders issued by the Kwantung Army, the villagers set out for the nearby village of Baoqing. They expected that Japanese troops would be there to protect them, but with the exception of a few sick and injured soldiers, the military had already withdrawn. The settlers from Senzan wandered around for days, joining with other groups of Japanese civilians on the run. Toward the end of August, an assortment of the remnants of the villagers, Youth Corps Brigades, and other Japanese stragglers, a group of approximately a thousand people, settled temporarily in the remains of the abandoned Sawatari agricultural settlement. They were lost, with no

---

9. NHK, *Saikai*. The companion volume to this documentary is Yamamoto and Hara, *Saikai*.

10. Tsukada, "Haisen zengo no Senzan Sarashinagō kaitakudan hinan jōkyō kiroku"; Tsukada, "Kaitakudan gakkō no omoide." A similar telling of the incident at the remains of the Sawatari settlement, which may be based on Tsukada's report, appears in the history of the participation of the residents of Nagano Prefecture in the colonization of Manchuria: Nagano-ken kaitaku jikōkai Manshū kaitaku shi kankōkai, ed., *Nagano-ken Manshū kaitaku shi*, vol. 2, 332–34.

11. Towards the end of the war, able-bodied men from the agricultural settlements were drafted into the Kwantung Army and many of those units, with their equipment, were sent to the Philippines or other battlefronts in Southeast Asia. Suzuki, *Nihon teikokushugi to Manshū*, 401–5.

CARL A. RUDISILL LIBRARY
LENOIR-RHYNE UNIVERSITY

food or water, and vulnerable to reprisals. Leaders of the various groups met to decide upon a course of action but could not reach a consensus. On August 27, the Soviet military attacked the settlement. Some of the groups decided to commit suicide—the adults killed the children and then themselves. According to Tsukada, the Senzan villagers decided to go down fighting and most of them, including children older than twelve, and armed with sticks and rocks, charged the Soviet soldiers in battle. Others, including the schoolteacher Tsukada Asae, drank poison in an attempt to commit suicide. The Soviet troops responded, and 337 of the 387 people from Senzan present at Sawatari were killed.

Tsukada lost consciousness and was revived later by some of her surviving students. A Soviet hand grenade had blinded her in one eye, and caused her to lose her hearing in one ear. While begging for food from Chinese villagers, the women and children made their way to the city of Boli by September 1, 1945. There, with her one good eye, and fifteen days after capitulation, Tsukada first saw a flyer announcing that Japan had surrendered.[12] In Boli, the women and children were moved from camp to camp. In one such camp, Tsukada was reunited with 20 children from her settlement who had miraculously survived the battle at the end of August. At this point, 67 of the original 407 who had fled from Senzan were still alive.

The refugees were placed with Chinese farm families for the winter of 1945–46. Some died of illness or injury and a few reported violence at the hands of their Chinese host families, leading some to commit suicide. Tsukada, though, reported that she was treated the same as the other people in the household and was provided with the same quality and amount of food.

In April 1946, rumors of repatriation reached the city of Boli. The 48 members of the Senzan community who had survived the winter were placed into a repatriation unit of 500 people. Three orphaned Japanese boys remained behind with Chinese families. The repatriation unit moved from Boli to Harbin to wait for instructions and was placed in a former Japanese school, the Hanazono kokumin gakkō, now a PRC military training facility. The refugees maintained good health throughout most of May, but because of disease, starvation, and maltreatment

---

12. Tsukada, "Kaitakudan gakkō no omoide," 332–39.

at the hands of the Soviets, they began to die off. By the time their turn for repatriation came at the end of August, of the 48 people from Senzan who had made it to Harbin, only seven children and one adult, Tsukada, were alive. Of those, one child was sick and two others stayed behind. On August 23, 1946, Tsukada and four seven-year-old girls left Harbin with their repatriation unit. One child died along the way; a second, Hayashibe Rie, died while the ship was held up off the shore of Japan in quarantine for cholera. Tsukada and the two others arrived in Hakata in September.[13] Nineteen other people who had split off from the group before the battle at Sawatari eventually made it back to Japan by other means, but only three of the 67 survivors of Sawatari returned to Japan in the immediate postwar period.

While the settlers were exposed to the worst of the Soviet violence and other hardships, city-dwelling Japanese civilians in Manchuria faced difficulties as well. Contemporary sources offer a glimpse of the problems faced by Japanese in the major cities of Shenyang and Changchun, which served as refugee processing centers and key transportation hubs in the deportation process. In the spring of 1946, Chiang Kai-shek's Nationalists replaced the retreating Soviet military as the reigning authority in most of the Manchurian cities. In cooperation with the U.S. military in China, and relying heavily on Japanese civilian groups, the Nationalists established the Management Office for Japanese Civilians and Prisoners of War and began to deport the million remaining Japanese civilians.[14] Partly as a means to spread pro-Nationalist propaganda but also to provide deportation information to the Japanese community, the Nationalists sponsored a Japanese-language newspaper, the *Tōhoku dōhō*, or "Gazette of the Northeast." The title of the newspaper contains a pun: the characters for gazette (*dōhō* 導報) are homonymous with those for "compatriot" (*dōhō* 同胞), the word most frequently used to describe Japanese nationals overseas. Read phonetically, *Tōhoku dōhō* could mean

---

13. Tsukada, "Haisen zengo no Senzan Sarashinagō kaitakudan hinan jōkyō kiroku."

14. The civilian groups included the Nikkyō zengo renraku sōsho 日僑善後連絡総処 and Nichiren zen kyūsai 日連前救済. In order to process the remaining Japanese in China, the Nationalists established the Management Office for Japanese Civilians and Prisoners of War (Nikkyōfu kanrisho 日僑俘管理所), abbreviated as Nikkan 日管.

"our compatriots in the Northeast."[15] Published in Shenyang from May 1946 through at least September 1947, and in Changchun from July 1946 through at least April 1947, the *Tōhoku dōhō* was produced by Japanese journalists formerly of the *Manshū Nichinichi shinbun* and other colonial Japanese-language newspapers.[16] Each issue was only a single, tabloid-sized, double-sided page, but the daily paper gives a fascinating glimpse into the uprooted lives of postwar Manchurian Japanese and the transformation of the formerly Japanese cities into Chinese ones.

Demonstrating and retaining one's national identity, keeping families together, and negotiating the breakdown of the Japanese community were three problems faced by the Japanese in Manchuria. One of the most intriguing figures in postwar Manchuria is the "stateless person" (*musekisha* 無籍者). During Japanese rule in Manchuria, "stateless persons" usually referred to refugees from pre-revolutionary Russia, but after the Japanese government lost its ability to govern, the word appears more and more frequently in terms of describing Japanese people. In some cases, being contracted to a foreign organization deprived one of one's Japanese registration; in other cases, Japanese women who married foreign men were removed from their family registers and lost their claim on Japanese citizenship. These situations obstructed the efforts of people to return home. The daily column on local affairs in the Changchun edition of the *Tōhoku dōhō* gave an overview of the kinds of "stateless persons" in postwar Changchun.

From September 4 to 7 [1946], the Japanese Deportation Consultation Office received 283 applications from "stateless persons" [*musekisha*] for a spot in a

---

15. The issues of the *Tōhoku dōhō* referenced here are held in the Foreign Language Newspaper Reading Room of the National Library of China, formerly the Beijing Library. The National Diet Library of Japan holds a copy of the Shenyang edition, but it does not appear in the catalogue. In 2002, under the direction of Katō Kiyofumi, Yumani shobō published 35 volumes and two CD-ROMs of primary sources related to repatriation. Issues of the Changchun edition of the *Tōhoku dōhō* from the summer of 1946 are available on "Supplement 3" (*hoi dai 3 kan* 補遺第 3 巻), the first CD in this series. Katō Kiyofumi, ed., *Kaigai hikiage kankei shiryō shūsei*, supplement 3.

16. Names of the journalists rarely appear but there is evidence that Yamamoto Noritsugu, and the father of Ishiko Jun, both formerly of the *Manshū Nichinichi*, worked for the paper. Hirashima, *Rakudo kara naraku e*, 262–63 and Chūgoku hikiage mangaka no kai, ed., *Boku no Manshū*, 237.

deportation group. 60 percent were people who had lived within the walls of the old city and had fallen through the cracks of the registration process; 20 percent were people who worked in Chinese restaurants and bars; 10 percent were people who had had a spot in a deportation group but due to illness had been excluded and become stateless; 5 percent were women who had been married to Chinese men and then ran away; 3 percent were people who did not have enough money for deportation and have remained behind; and 2 percent, if you can believe it, included people who before deportation went around to say farewell to all of their acquaintances and missed their trains.[17]

This article indicates the variety of Japanese residents in the former capital of Manchukuo, and the myriad ways in which a person could get separated from the repatriation process. No one in the Japanese community seemed to doubt that these "stateless persons" were Japanese. Nevertheless, it was their failure to register for repatriation and acquire the necessary papers that caused them to lose their official identity.

The passage indicated another route to losing one's national identity: being separated from one's deportation group. Even without papers, it was possible in most cases for Japanese to register for deportation, but once a person had been assigned to a deportation unit (部隊 *butai*, the military expression for "unit"), that became his or her primary means of official identification. Being able to prove one was Japanese was necessary for the ticket home, and once one became part of a deportation group, separation from it meant the loss of identity. News coverage of one such unfortunate man appeared in the daily column on local affairs in the Shenyang edition of the *Tōhoku dōhō*:

We were finishing up the deportation paperwork after having sent off nine trains of 15,000 people on the 12th of this month [September 1946] when an odd fellow showed up, showed up, wandered around, and appeared to be looking for something. When asked "What's wrong?" he replied, "The train I'm supposed to be on is not here." He had gone off to find something to eat and in his absence the train had departed. He had no idea what deportation unit or battalion he belonged to, only that he had come from the direction of Tonghua. To make matters worse, his two children were on the train.[18]

---

17. "Korō" (The Watchtower), *Tōhoku dōhō*, Changchun edition, September 11, 1946.
18. "Sōmatō" (Kaleidoscope), *Tōhoku dōhō*, Shenyang edition, September 14, 1946.

This man managed to lose his identity and his children at the same time. Later, people explored the existential crisis of what it had meant to be a Japanese person in postwar Manchuria, but at the time the ability to prove one's national identity was a more pressing concern.

In another case, the writer Sawachi Hisae recalls her journey as a fourteen-year-old refugee from Changchun to Jinzhou via Shenyang, as she witnessed one of the many ways to get separated from a deportation group.

In August 1946, my family had been living as refugees since defeat. We moved south from Jilin and ended up in a refugee camp in a place called "Kin-ken." We rode on a freight train that had no side walls and only a single plank between the wheels and us. On the way, a child fell off. The repatriate train backed up to retrieve the child. The child was fine. Later, a youth who was riding in between two cars fell off. They left him behind.[19]

Sometimes families had to entertain the possibility of leaving a family member behind in order to depart with their assigned deportation group, as illustrated by these two personal advertisements in the *Tōhoku dōhō*.

- Missing Children:
   Hashimoto Kōtarō (older brother, age 11)
   Hashimoto Mutsumi (younger sister, age 9)

   These siblings have a tendency to wander. They left the house on about the third of this month [the ad appeared on June 11, 1946] and we have not heard from them since. Our departure is imminent. Please contact us if you have any information on these children.

   Tetsunishi-ku Kumodani, No. 15, Manchuria Lacquerware Company Employees' Dormitory
   Hashimoto Michitsugu (Father)[20]

- Miyoko: I left the things at Mr. Liu's and departed.—Toshio.[21]

On October 10, 1946, the Shenyang edition published a full page ad warning all remaining Japanese to register for repatriation as soon as

---

19. Sawachi, *Mō hitotsu no Manshū*, 23.

20. "Tazuneko" (Missing children), *Tōhoku dōhō*, Shenyang edition, no. 51, June 11, 1946.

21. *Tōhoku dōhō*, Changchun edition, no. 82, September 12, 1946.

possible or lose forever the opportunity to return to Japan.[22] These bits of evidence mesh with the fragments of memories of orphans left behind in China. In 1980, one woman recalled that her parents left her and their belongings with a Chinese neighbor and departed. She never saw them again.[23]

The *Tōhoku dōhō* provides some evidence of conflict within the Japanese community. One news story about the Kin-ken refugee camp tells of one camp for wealthy deportees, where they used up all of their extra money drinking beer and listening to jazz records, in contrast to another camp, where deportees subsisted on two meals of sorghum a day.[24] The Allies overseeing repatriation saw the Japanese as a monolithic group, but this report indicates that the class divisions in colonial Manchuria continued to reverberate through the repatriation process.

It is not clear how many people in Changchun, Shenyang, Jinzhou, and Huludao had access to the *Tōhoku dōhō*. One documentary film reports that it circulated in the refugee camps.[25] As one of the few Japanese-language sources of information on deportation and conditions back in Japan, those who had access to copies of it reportedly read it voraciously. A few stories indicated that Manchurian returnees already had a bad reputation in Japan and that the return to their "homeland," which so many people had lived for, promised to be fraught with unanticipated problems. One told of a repatriation ship worker who reported an incident in Kyoto. A person there, seeing the long line of repatriates returning to Japan, remarked that "even more potential armed robbers have returned." The investigation of these comments reached as high as the mayor's office and the person who uttered these remarks apologized.[26] Another warned future returnees that upon arrival in Japan, nearly all of them were forced to work in open air stalls—in other

---

22. "Hitori mo moreru na" (Don't leave even one behind), *Tōhoku dōhō*, Shenyang edition, no. 172, October 10, 1946.

23. NHK, *Saikai*.

24. "Kono tokoro mo kane no yo no naka: shūyōjo meian nijū sō" (This place, too, is governed by money: the two dimensions of light and dark in the refugee camp), *Tōhoku dōhō*, Shenyang edition, no. 133, September 1, 1946.

25. Kunihiro, *Korotō daikenhen*.

26. "Kōro," *Tōhoku dōhō*, Changchun edition, no. 65, August 26, 1946.

words, the black market—in order to survive.[27] Another article reported that a repatriate housing project was described as a "den of criminals."[28] All these reports appeared in the newspaper in Manchuria even before deportees had been repatriated. Having just experienced a radical change in what it meant to be Japanese in Manchuria, the articles foreshadowed that they were about to experience another change: what it meant to be a Manchurian repatriate back in Japan.

The memoir of Dalian-born Kazuko Kuramoto details her family's humiliation in the village of Pulandian where her father served as an official, at the hands of the Chinese communist guerillas at the end of the war, and their sorrow at seeing boys in the military youth corps massacred by the Chinese.[29] Kuramoto's account describes how, as people with financial and spiritual resources, her family lived in relative safety and comfort in postwar Dalian, especially when compared to the settlers. Nevertheless, Kuramoto wrote of not being able to move about for fear of Soviet assault, and mentioned rumors that abortions were performed in the Dalian hospital on women who had become pregnant during sexual assaults.[30]

The writers Fujiwara Tei, Itsuki Hiroyuki, and others all describe difficulties faced by their families in postwar Manchuria and North Korea, also occupied by the Soviets. Fujiwara wrote of evacuating from Manchuria in early August, traveling with children, ages six, three, and one month old. They crossed the border into North Korea, and lived in a camp there, but faced problems when the Soviets came to occupy the region.[31] In 2003, the prolific and well-known essayist Itsuki Hiroyuki published an account of his memories of the problems his family faced in postwar Pyongyang, where his father worked as a schoolteacher. When the Soviets arrived at their home in employee housing of the school, his father was in the bath. His mother, who had fallen ill after

---

27. "Kikokugo no shinseikatsu wa hotondo rotensho kara sai shuppatsu" (Nearly everyone begins their new life back in Japan at an open air stall), *Tōhoku dōhō*, Changchun edition, no. 36, July 28, 1946.

28. "Hikiagesha bakari no chōnaikai" (A local government made up solely of repatriates), *Tōhoku dōhō*, Shenyang edition, no. 131, August 30, 1946.

29. Pulandian (普蘭店), Furanten in Japanese.

30. Kuramoto, *Manchurian Legacy*, 118.

31. Fujiwara, *Nagareru hoshi wa ikiteiru*, 20–33.

childbirth six months before, lay on a futon on the floor. The soldiers burst in, and held his naked father and the thirteen-year-old Hiroyuki against the wall with guns. Then one of the soldiers went to his mother. He pulled off the covers, and tore open her kimono. Laughing, he pressed down on her chest with his boot. At that point, blood began to pour out of her mouth. Itsuki did not know whether the blood was because of her illness, or whether she had bitten the inside of her own mouth. The soldiers realized she was sick. They picked up both sides of the futon, and, as if she were a bag of cement, tossed her from the hallway into the yard. After the Soviets had looted the house and left, Itsuki and his father carried his mother back into the house. The Soviets came back a few days later to requisition the house, turning the family out onto the street. His mother died a few days after that, on September 20, 1945.[32]

In these recollections, the writers do not speak directly to the issue of the rapes of Japanese women by Soviet soldiers, although Itsuki indicates that he feared that had his mother not been ill and bleeding from the mouth, "something even worse" would have happened.[33] Other accounts are more explicit. The worst period of sexual violence perpetrated on Japanese women by the Soviets was during the first few weeks after the Soviet attack, when soldiers described as undisciplined "prisoner-troops" raped in a chaotic atmosphere. To give just one report, according to a history of the end of the war in Manchuria, *Man-Mō shūsen shi*, on August 22, 1945, the Soviet military occupied the Dunhua Nichiman Pulp Factory in Jilin Province. More than 300 Soviet troops removed all of the Japanese men from the company dormitory but held the remaining 170 Japanese women and their children and used the women for sex. Several other sources and contemporary reports emphasize the brutality of the first Soviet troops to arrive in Asia.[34] The sexual

---

32. Itsuki, *Unmei no ashioto*, 17–23.

33. Ibid., 21.

34. Man-Mō dōhō engokai, ed., *Man-Mō shūsen shi*, 543; Gane, "Foreign Affairs of South Korea"; Nimmo, *Behind a Curtain of Silence*. Another example of the raping of Japanese women occurred in late August, when Soviet troops stopped a train full of civilians at the Gongzhuling station (between Changchun and Shenyang), pulled off all of the Japanese women, and assaulted each of them on the platform in view of their families. Wakatsuki, *Sengo hikiage no kiroku*, 125.

violence subsided after the Soviet military established their occupation apparatus, but women remained vulnerable for the entire period under Soviet jurisdiction. Some women sought ways to make themselves and their children less vulnerable. One particularly vivid example comes from an interview conducted by the historian Greg Guelcher with Kirihara Sadako. An agricultural settler pregnant at the end of the war, she ended up in a Chinese Nationalist camp, where Soviet soldiers came at night hunting for Japanese women. When a Chinese man proposed marriage, Kirihara guessed that the chances for survival, for herself and her unborn child, were higher with a Chinese family than in a refugee camp, so she married the man.[35] Yamamoto Tokuko recalled finding a job as a hostess in postwar Dalian, dancing with Chinese and Korean men for tips, in order to survive and to save money to reclaim her infant daughter from the Chinese foster family where she had placed the child for safekeeping.[36] These situations led to the stranding of thousands of women and children in postwar Manchuria, the "women and orphans left behind in China" (*Chūgoku zanryū fujin koji*).

It is difficult to get a sense of the numbers of Japanese women assaulted at the end of the war. In 1984, Takeda Shigetarō, a medical doctor, estimated that 30,000 to 40,000 Japanese women were sexually assaulted in Soviet-controlled zones following the defeat, but he does so in the context of a fictionalized account.[37] Whatever the numbers, these women faced special challenges when they returned to Japan.

Reception at Home

The arrival of a million overseas Japanese, people who had spent a year in Allied jurisdiction, onto the shores of Japan in the summer of 1946 provoked a variety of responses, ranging from sympathy to anxiety. An article in the *Asahi shinbun* captures the tendency both to express concern for the women and to make use of them to address other issues. The article appeared on April 24, 1946, a few weeks before the first boatload of repatriates arrived from Manchuria on May 14.

---

35. Guelcher, "Dreams of Empire," 252.
36. Yomiuri shinbunsha Ōsaka shakaibu, *Chūgoku koji*, 119.
37. Takeda, *Chinmoku no 40-nen*, 196.

In addition to developing measures to promote repatriation, we need to develop humane policies with a woman's touch that will address the problem of
mixed race children who will be born as a result of defeat in war. . . . War and
venereal diseases have a relationship that is impossible to sever. For the sake
of the future of the Japanese race, some measures need to be taken. According
to people who have escaped from Manchuria, 40 percent of the women there
have been given the burden of bearing a mixed-race child.[38]

This passage lays out many of the domestic concerns about women
from Manchuria. The author advocates for positive, practical matters:
promoting repatriation and taking care of the women. The passage also
reveals the nature of the concern about the women, that the venereal
disease and mixed race children they might be bringing with them had
the potential to threaten "the future of the Japanese race."[39]

Practically speaking, women who conceived babies during the worst
period of sexual assaults, August and September 1945, would have been
nearly nine months pregnant at repatriation, the summer of 1946. These
women had probably either received abortions or given birth before
their arrival in Japan. Anecdotal evidence suggests that abortions were
performed in Manchuria before repatriation, and on the repatriation
ships home. Pregnant women returning to Japan may have conceived
children in ways other than assault at the hands of Soviet troops. Nevertheless, the discourse at the time expresses concerns in terms of the

---

38. "Hikiage ni mo josei no chikara" (Women's strength is needed for repatriation,
too), *Asahi shinbun*, April 24, 1946. The word for mixed race child here is literally
"mixed-blood child" (*konketsuji*; 混血児).

39. At least two sources discuss an overlap between repatriation and postwar prostitution. In an overview of desperate lives in immediate postwar Tokyo, Ōtani Susumu wrote
that repatriates were the second most numerous kind of woman who fell into prostitution. They followed domestic bombing victims, but supplied more than runaways,
dancers, bad girls, former geishas, and secretaries (Ōtani, *Ikiteiru*, 66–67). According to
an article in the magazine *Shinsō*, 50 women were repatriated from Karafuto in July 1949.
Classified as "people with no relatives" the repatriation authorities placed them in the
Iwashio dormitory, a facility that had been converted from soldiers barracks about 30
miles outside of the northern city of Morioka in Iwate Prefecture. Unemployed, the
women traveled door to door to peddle their personal belongings. The young men who
ran the local black market recognized it as a business opportunity and transformed the
dormitory into a brothel ("Hikiagete wa mita keredo," 56).

possibility of mixed-race children and "foreign" venereal disease.[40] The passage above, which does not identify the perpetrators (the Soviet soldiers and other men who inflicted violence upon Japanese women) perhaps in order to avoid the attention of the censors, foreshadows both the system that emerged to care for the women and the association of Japanese women from Manchuria with bodily contamination.

Although some of the attention paid to the issue of women from Manchuria was out of genuine concern for their well-being, returnees sensed that people at home expressed an almost pornographic interest in the stories of sexual violence at the end of the war. Fujiwara Tei, in her fictionalized memoir of her harrowing return from Manchuria and North Korea, recalls an encounter her children and she experienced on a train back home. A man boarded their train and gave her children pears, but then began to question Fujiwara intensely, pressing her for details on the violence against Japanese women.[41] Another example includes a key scene in the 1947 short story "Rira saku gogatsu to nareba" (When May arrives and the lilacs bloom). A lecherous man from metropolitan Japan encourages two women to reminisce about the sexual violence in Manchuria, only then to accuse them of being unchaste.[42] In proscribing the telling of explicit stories of the violence, censorship may have contributed to curiosity about the history. The lurid interest in the fate of Japanese women exposed to foreign troops abroad, perhaps as a projection of concerns about domestic fraternization, helped keep the fires of the story alive.

The MHW worked with local citizens' groups to prepare for the arrival of the Manchurian repatriates. The issue of unwanted pregnancies was particularly worrisome for the government. Before and during the war, the Japanese government promoted a number of pro-natalist policies, and performing abortions was criminal. Abortion remained illegal

---

40. A newspaper reporter investigating the abortions used words that, because of the choice of characters, conveyed this sense more viscerally: "the children of people from different countries in the shelter of one's womb" (jibun no tainai ni yadotteiru ihōjin no kodomo 自分の胎内に宿っている異邦人の子供). "Hokuman hikiage fujin no shūdan ninpu chūzetsu shimatsuki," 8.

41. Fujiwara, *Nagareru hoshi wa ikiteiru*, 300.

42. Imai, "Rira saku gogatsu to nareba."

until a change in the eugenics law was implemented in 1948.[43] In the spring of 1946, officials at the MHW perceived their choice to be providing abortions in violation of their own laws or living with the potential consequences of as many as several hundred mixed-race children, conceived in some cases without the consent of the mother. In the end, two sets of medical workers emerged to care for the women repatriated from Manchuria. The Seoul Group, composed of medical workers, activists, and the photographer Iiyama Tatsuo from the former Imperial University in Keijō (Seoul), worked as private citizens to care for the later returnees. The Kyushu University Group, composed of former military doctors, emerged to treat female repatriates as well.

Evidence concerning the treatment of the repatriated women at the ports of Maizuru, Sasebo, and Hakata is uneven and fragmentary. Records of the abortions may yet surface, but at present the story rests on ambiguous statements in the official records of the regional repatriation centers, testimony of medical workers, documentaries based on that testimony, newspaper articles, and a few other bits of evidence. It has been suggested that women in need of treatment who passed through Maizuru were sent to the national hospital in Niigata for treatment.[44]

There is more evidence concerning the treatment of women who passed through Sasebo, a port city on the island of Kyushu not far from Nagasaki. Saitō Sōichi, the head of the Repatriate Relief Authority, went on record in a 1953 newspaper article outlining the system for treating pregnant returnees.[45] According to this article, volunteers from Tomo no Kai, the women's service organization affiliated with the magazine *Fujin no tomo*, worked with the staff at the Sasebo Regional Repatriation Center to screen all of the women who passed through. The volunteers asked three questions: Have you been subjected to violence? Are you feeling any discomfort? Is your menstrual cycle unusual? Women who answered yes to these questions were examined further. Those in need of treatment were sent to a special medical facility in Hario where medi-

---

43. Norgren, *Abortion Before Birth Control*, 28–44.

44. Hikiagekō Hakata o kangaeru tsudoi, *Sengo 50-nen hikiage o omou (zoku)*, 25.

45. Details of Saitō's tenure appear in Kōseishō engokyoku, *Hikiage to engo 30-nen no ayumi*, 501. The article in which he described the treatment of pregnant returnees is "Hokuman hikiage fujin no shūdan ninpu chūzetsu shimatsu ki," 8.

cal staff under the direction of former Navy doctor Shimabara Bango provided abortions and treatment.[46]

Published in 1949, the official government record of the Sasebo Regional Repatriation Center does not include an explicit discussion of the abortions, but refers to the problem euphemistically. According to that document, 62,929 women made use of the women's consultation office, with 2,400 patients treated locally and 1,148 women sent to other facilities. There were 66 women who had already traveled to their homes within Japan but returned to the facility for treatment, apparently to get abortions they could not get elsewhere. A table indicates that 473 pregnant women returned from North Korea and Manchuria between May 1946 and April 1947. Another entry lists 214 women "in need of an artificial miscarriage."[47]

The Hakata Regional Repatriation Center's treatment of female returnees is the best documented case. The Seoul Group began their outreach work even before the women arrived in Japan, by establishing a medical relief unit in Korea,[48] offering information and treatment on the repatriation ship home, and creating a women's health facility in Japan for more thorough treatment and abortions. They also established a facility at the Shōfukuji temple for children who had become orphaned in Manchuria and had no means of survival upon return to Japan.[49] In many ways, they were treating their own. One story that appears in a few sources is that of a former female student of Dr. Yamamoto Yoshitake, the pediatrician who cared for the repatriate orphans at Shōfukuji. In colonial Korea, Dr. Yamamoto had taught at the Women's Normal University. While working at the repatriation center after the war, he encountered a nineteen-year-old former student who had just been repatriated from North Korea. Later, her parents came to him, explained that she had been raped by Soviet soldiers and was now pregnant. Yamamoto arranged for an illegal abortion but the young woman died during the procedure. The story of her death, and the sui-

---

46. "Hokuman hikiage fujin no shūdan ninpu chūzetsu shimatsu ki," 7.
47. Sasebo hikiage engokyoku jōhōka, *Sasebo hikiage engokyoku shi*, vol. 1, 102–4.
48. Ibid., 41–47.
49. Kamitsubo, *Mizuko no uta: hikiage koji to okasareta onnatachi no kiroku*, 17–38; 168–85.

cide of another pregnant repatriate, were credited with motivating the Seoul Group to address the problem systematically.[50]

The history of the Hakata Regional Repatriation Center, published in 1947, meshes with the accounts of the Seoul Group and is more explicit than the Sasebo record. It includes references to the treatment provided to the women by naming the special facility where the abortions were performed—the Futsuka'ichi Sanatorium—and providing more anecdotal evidence. The Hakata record points out that the Futsuka'ichi facility placed carefully worded advertisements in the local paper in an effort to inform women that abortions and treatment for sexually transmitted diseases were available.[51] The ad provided the name and location of the facility and listed the names of the sponsors, the Hakata Regional Repatriation Center and the Repatriate Aid Society.

During the Occupation, frank discussions of the women were not possible, in part because of censorship. In 1953, however, a year after the end of the Occupation, a popular weekly magazine affiliated with one of Japan's three major national daily newspapers, the *Mainichi*, published an article that provided names, numbers, and other details on the medical treatment of the Manchurian repatriates. The interpretation of events in the article by an unnamed female journalist was spelled out in the subtitle: "The reason no children of Red soldiers were born in Japan" (*akai heitai no ko ga umarenu wake*). The article depicted the screening and abortions as a humane solution to an awful but perhaps unavoidable situation, the violence of war.[52]

In the mid-1970s, another investigative journalist, Kamitsubo Takashi, inadvertently unearthed the story again. Repatriated as an eleven-year-old boy from Manchuria in 1946, Kamitsubo began the project as a documentary on a tragedy he had barely avoided: becoming a "repatriate orphan" (*hikiage koji*). In tracking down a few dozen people who had been cared for as children in the Shōfukuji temple repatriate orphanage in Hakata, Kamitsubo found that the orphans and the pregnant women

---

50. Ibid., 174–76.

51. Hakata hikiage engokyoku (Kōseishō hikiage engoin), *Kyoku shi*, 100–102, 108–10. On July 17, 1946 the *Nishi Nihon shinbun* carried the ad, reproduced in Kamitsubo, *Mizuko no uta: hikiage koji to okasareta onnatachi no kiroku* and Hikiagekō Hakata o kangaeru tsudoi, *Sengo 50-nen hikiage o omou (zoku)*, 23.

52. "Hokuman hikiage fujin no shūdan ninpu chūzetsu shimatsu ki."

had much in common. They had been repatriated in the same deportation process and had been cared for by the same group of medical workers, the Seoul Group. Kamitsubo proceeded to interview as many of them as possible. At first he asked about the orphans but then the conversation led to the women. When interviewed by Kamitsubo, the medical doctor Hashizume Hiroshi, who performed the abortions at the Futsuka'ichi Sanatorium in Hakata, remarked that he had not spoken of that period to anyone since a journalist had interviewed him more than 20 years before, presumably for the *Mainichi* article.[53]

Kamitsubo's research led to a documentary film and a monograph about the women and orphans repatriated to Fukuoka.[54] It generated a good deal of press in the local papers as well.[55] Whereas the 1953 article had focused primarily on Japanese women victimized by war, the 1978 documentary by Kamitsubo attempted to place the episode in the context of the violence that militaries inflict upon civilians. He did so by including a few pieces of evidence about the actions of Japanese military men during the 1937 Nanjing Atrocity, perhaps as part of the nationwide discussion of the event in 1970s Japan.[56] Despite Kamitsubo's good faith attempt to lift the issue out of the realm of Japanese victimization, his research ignited an unexpected debate—a controversy about infanticide. Kamitsubo based his documentary and book mainly on the testimony of the adult orphans and the people who cared for them, but he also included some 1946 photographs taken by the photographer Iiyama Tatsuo. After repatriation from Korea, Iiyama felt that something needed to be done about those left behind in Manchuria. Disguised as a Red Cross worker, he snuck back into Manchuria to photograph Japanese women and children who had been abandoned by their government. He submitted those photographs to the Japanese government and the Occupation authorities. It is not clear whether his photos prompted any action, but after his submission, repatriation swung into high gear. Iiyama took almost all of the extant photographs of Manchu-

---

53. Kamitsubo, *Mizuko no uta: hikiage koji to okasareta onnatachi no kiroku*, 188.
54. *Hikiagekō Hakata wan*. This 44-minute, made-for-television documentary was broadcast in Kyushu on June 28, 1978.
55. Hikiagekō Hakata o kangaeru tsudoi, *Sengo 50-nen hikiage o omou (zoku)*, 23.
56. Yoshida, *The Making of the "Rape of Nanking."*

rian repatriation, including the now canonical photo of a young girl with a shaved head and a box of ashes around her neck.[57] He also took photographs of his friends caring for the returned orphans and women.

Iiyama had published many of the repatriation-related photographs, but out of concern for the secrecy of the medical center and his friends in the Seoul Group, he had never published photos he had taken of the abortion procedures. In the late 1970s, Iiyama allowed Kamitsubo to use the graphic photos of doctors performing abortions.[58] The photos showed what the doctors and nurses knew all along—some of the women were in the early stages of pregnancy, but others were six, seven, or eight months pregnant. Staff induced labor and when the baby was born, they disposed of it, either by letting it die or with an injection. According to a nurse identified by the name "Ikue," the staff would put in a call to one of the custodians, who would then bury the remains on the edge of the property.[59] Japanese society in 1946, grappling with the stringent postwar conditions, had little room to fret over the killing of unwanted infants. By the mid-1970s, however, Japan had reached a level of affluence and was about to be lauded by Harvard sociologist Ezra Vogel as "Number One" in social and economic terms. Less of an issue in 1946 or 1953, by 1977 the fate of the infants, as much as that of the women, became a source of concern. Most of the doctors and nurses who participated in the abortions went on to have successful careers, but at least one of the doctors suffered public censure after this history came to light.[60]

---

57. Kamitsubo, *Mizuko no uta: hikiage koji to okasareta onnatachi no kiroku*, 168–72; Iiyama, *Haisen, hikiage no dōkoku*; "Ano kodomotachi no 36-nen no ima!" *Sandē mainichi*, November 30, 1986, 32–33. The husband of the woman pictured as a girl wrote to Iiyama to ask him to stop using her photo as an emblem of repatriation, and Iiyama complied with their wishes.

58. The photos appear in the 1979 edition of the book but were deleted from the 1993 edition. In the later edition, pseudonyms replaced real names, graphic photographs were removed, and the subtitle was toned down from "the record of repatriate orphans and violated women" to "a documentary look at repatriate orphans and women."

59. Kamitsubo, *Mizuko no uta: hikiage koji to okasareta onnatachi no kiroku*, 196.

60. Takeda, *Chinmoku no 40-nen*, 197. Some doctors were named in newspaper articles nonetheless. "Shin ningen no jōken," *Tōkyō shinbun*, January 7, 1980, 14.

The issue surfaced again in a 1980 newspaper series on the history of the legalization of abortion in Japan.[61] The series pointed out that Japan bore the ambiguous legacy of being the first country after the Soviet Union to legalize abortion, and then explored a number of possible explanations for that history. In pointing out the dire conditions of postwar Japan—the return of millions from overseas, the worst harvest since the famine of 1904, and government predictions that ten million people would starve without food aid—the article said the only things that did exist were "a shiny new democracy, blues skies, and illegally aborted fetuses."[62] In seeking to solve the mystery of why abortion was legalized so quickly with little input from women's groups, the MHW, or religious groups, the journalist then proffered a number of possible explanations. Perhaps the Occupation officials supported legalizing abortion? This was not the case: although SCAP hoped that the Japanese would embrace family planning, they apparently tried to avoid this issue of abortion.[63] How, then, did this come about? According to the 1980 article, repatriation provides the answer.

The article discusses the case of Dr. Ishihama Atsumi, who, in 1979, published an account of his role performing illegal abortions on repatriates.[64] According to Ishihama, sometime in 1945, his senior colleague Kihara Yukio, Assistant Professor of Medicine at Kyushu Imperial University, informed him that the MHW had ordered them to treat female repatriates for sexually transmitted diseases and "unlawful" pregnancies. "For the sake of the future of the Japanese race," he said, it was important to stop these problems "at water's edge." Abortion was a criminal act, he continued, but the government would assume all responsibility. For about a year, female repatriates were sent to tuberculosis wards in national hospitals in Fukuoka (the Koga facility) and Saga (the Nakahara facility). Doctors who had no experience performed the abortions, reading the textbook as they went along. Records were forbidden, but Ishihama estimates that more than 1,000 abortions were

---

61. "Shin ningen no jōken," *Tōkyō shinbun*, January 7, 1980.
62. "Shin ningen no jōken," *Tōkyō shinbun*, January 6, 1980, 14.
63. "41-nen no shōgen: hikiage josei no higeki," *Mainichi shinbun*, August 18, 1987, in Hikiagekō Hakata o kangaeru tsudoi, *Sengo 50-nen hikiage o omou (zoku)*, 63.
64. Amemiya, "The Road to Pro-Choice Ideology in Japan," 160–64.

performed in his jurisdiction. Similar procedures took place at national hospitals in Nagasaki and Kumamoto as well. Kihara's attitude was so firm that Ishihama believed the orders came from the government. Based on this information Ishihama concluded that not SCAP but someone in the Japanese government decided to authorize the abortions.

The article was not particularly persuasive in arguing that abortion was legalized in 1948 to cover the tracks of the government-sponsored illegal abortions in 1946, but it did result in one of the first public tellings of the government's role in sponsoring the work of the Kyushu University Group. A decade later, a second doctor published a similar report in a medical journal.[65]

There is not enough evidence to give a definitive number of illegal abortions performed on repatriates. Moreover, the language in the official records tends to be euphemistic. Investigative journalists and participants from the time, however, have reached a consensus on a number: 1,200 to 1,300 abortions provided in Sasebo, and 400 to 500 at the Futsuka'ichi Sanitorium in Hakata.[66]

Although journalists, with the cooperation of the participants and local history groups, tried to initiate a discussion of the fate of thousands of overseas Japanese women, the issue never received a full public hearing in the national press or the government. A handful of people came forward to testify that they participated in providing the abortions. One anonymous woman left a message for a journalist who was trying to argue that the abortions were forced, saying that the women were grateful that the procedure was available to them.[67]

---

65. Iwasaki Tadasu reportedly published a similar account in August 1987. A newspaper article profiling Dr. Iwasaki states that he claimed that the government ordered doctors to perform abortions. "41-nen no shōgen: hikiage josei no higeki," *Mainichi shinbun*, August 15, 1987, reproduced in Hikiagekō Hakata o kangaeru tsudoi, *Sengo 50-nen hikiage o omou (zoku)*, 60. Iwasaki's testimony is corroborated by Tenko Miyako, another Kyushu University obstetrician, in Hikiagekō Hakata o kangaeru tsudoi, *Sengo 50-nen hikiage o omou (zoku)*, 26.

66. The Sasebo figures are given in "Hokuman hikiage fujin no shūdan ninpu chūzetsu shimatsu ki," 4; the Hakata figures appear in Kamitsubo, *Mizuko no uta: hikiage koji to okasareta onnatachi no kiroku*, 209 and "Hokuman hikiage fujin no shūdan ninpu chūzetsu shimatsu ki," 10.

67. "41-nen no shōgen: hikiage josei no higeki," *Mainichi shinbun*, August 19, 1987; reproduced in Hikiagekō Hakata o kangaeru tsudoi, *Sengo 50-nen hikiage o omou (zoku)*, 64.

These periodic and sketchy forays into the history of the treatment of female Manchurian repatriates have generated a number of interpretations. Historians of the Seoul Group valorize the efforts of the young, idealistic people who bravely broke the law to care for the women. The fact that they cared for orphans whom everyone else was willing to discard lends credence to the story. The Seoul Group stands in contrast to the Kyushu University Group, former military men who later claimed that they were just following orders. One critic attributes the reticence of the Kyushu University Group to concerns about their careers and the need to deflect attention from their wartime history. The medical department there had been plagued by rumors that its staff had performed vivisections on Allied POWs in the spring of 1945.[68] In recounting their histories, each group said they had no knowledge of the other. Members of both groups also claimed that Prince Takamatsu, the brother of Emperor Hirohito, made unannounced visits to their facilities, an act that they interpreted as expressing the consent of the government.[69] In her 1993 dissertation, Kozy Kazuko Amemiya analyzes the incident to support her argument that the state sanctioned abortion when it was convenient with little regard to the law.[70]

Although all of these interpretations are plausible, the combination of the women in Manchuria, stories of rape, their reception back home, and the subsequent postwar silence invite further analysis in terms of what the incident meant for the end of the war and empire in Japan. Michael Molasky has written about the tendency of Japanese male writers to use the rape of Japanese women as a metaphor for their own victimization after the war:

With remarkable consistency, male writers from both mainland Japan and Okinawa have articulated their humiliating experience of the defeat and occupation in terms of the sexual violation of women. This propensity of male writers to appropriate rape's symbolic dimensions while ignoring its violent reality may be what prompted Kōno Taeko, an acclaimed female writer, to

---

68. Ibid.

69. The Seoul Group's claim that Prince Takamatsu visited its facility appears in Hikiagekō Hakata o kangaeru tsudoi, *Sengo 50-nen hikiage o omou*, 170.

70. Amemiya, "The Road to Pro-Choice Ideology in Japan," 64.

sardonically state that "it might have been best had the victors raped every woman in Japan." [71]

The women from Manchuria presented evidence of victors raping Japanese women, provoking questions as to how the episode was used.

In the case of Japanese women in Soviet zones, the government was unable to respond to the rapes at the time and has remained silent since. After all, some Japanese military men, sometimes with the knowledge of their leaders in the field and their government back home, inflicted sexual violence on civilian women in regions under Japanese military control. The 1937 Nanjing Atrocity and the so-called comfort women—a military brothel system in which women from the colonies (and some from Japan) were forced to serve as sexual partners for Japanese military men—are the best-known examples of the kinds of violence that occurred under Japanese military domination. In the context of that history, the Japanese government had little moral authority to condemn the assaults perpetrated by a different military force upon its own citizens. Moreover, its own policies, such as facilitating migration to dangerous areas of Manchuria, placed its citizens in danger. When that danger arrived, the state was not able to protect them. In the 1990s, the Prime Minister's Office instituted a program to commemorate the hardship faced by repatriates after the war but it did not address the sexual violence. The issue was not used in political interaction with the Soviet Union, which would have required some recognition of the government's contribution to the vulnerability of the women in Manchuria.

Although the issue of the sexual violation of Japanese women was not politicized by the government, it was a useful ingredient in the process of the social othering of repatriates in postwar Japan. The Manchurian repatriates were a burden on scarce resources back home. By custom, women in Japan enter the families of their husbands upon marriage, and repatriated women were supposed to return to their husbands' families upon arrival. In many cases, though, those husbands were dead or missing, or had taken on new wives in the absence of information on their first wives. The "beautiful Manchurian repatriate tale" in the previous chapter spoke directly to these issues, celebrating

---

71. Molasky, *The American Occupation of Japan and Okinawa*, 11–12.

the man who did not abandon his repatriated wife. In some cases, Manchurian wives and daughters-in-law, rendered contaminated, were easier to reject.

On a metaphorical level, Manchurian women suspected of contamination served as a foil for appropriate Japanese womanhood—women who remained "at home" in *naichi*, and who did not fraternize, willingly or not, with foreign men. Fujiwara Tei tells of her realization, prompted by an observation by her seven-year-old son Masahiro upon arrival at the Hakata Regional Repatriation Center, that as a Manchurian repatriate she stood outside the definition of a "Japanese woman." Fujiwara recounted the episode as follows:

"Look, Mother, there's a Japanese woman." There was a woman in a kimono, tied with a proper obi, walking by. I was as mystified as Masahiro. I had thought that women in Japan, as people from a defeated nation, would look as pitiful as the rest of us. I was a Japanese woman and the young woman in line in front of me with a rucksack on her back was a Japanese woman, but as dirty repatriates we were like different people [*betsujin no yō ni*] from the Japanese woman Masahiro saw.[72]

The women from Manchuria were useful, therefore, in the recasting of the colonial project as its history was rewritten in the postwar period. From the beginning, the empire had been depicted as masculine, with Japanese men dominating Asian women, and a masculine Japan conquering a feminized Asia. The historian Stewart Lone noticed this tendency of a "masculine Japan united with feminine China," as reflected in the diary of a soldier stationed there.[73] Yoshikuni Igarashi and others have argued that Japan experienced a gender change at the end of the war, from a place depicted as masculine and military to a feminized nation occupied by American soldiers.[74] The face of Japan went from the image of Japanese military men taming fierce native women (as depicted in the film *China Night*), to Japanese civilian women fraternizing with American military men.[75] In a parallel process, the empire, especially Manchuria, was feminized, made into a victim, and made irrelevant to

---

72. Fujiwara, *Nagareru hoshi wa ikiteiru*, 292.
73. Lone, *Japan's First Modern War*, 68.
74. Igarashi, *Bodies of Memory*, 35–36.
75. Shibusawa, *America's Geisha Ally*.

"ordinary people" within Japan. The empire left Japan masculine and military, but when empire came home in 1946, it was feminine, victimized, treated for foreign contaminants, and hopefully never heard from again. This provided little relief for the women themselves, but proved useful in Japan's disengagement from its colonies and contributed to the occlusion of the history of empire in postwar Japan.

It is illuminating to consider analyses of other wartime violations of a "nation's women"—and the responses to such violations. Chung-moo Choi shows how the fact of the bodily violation of the "comfort women" disrupts the process of rendering colonial Korea female in order to remasculinize it in the post-colonial period. As Choi explains, "Precisely because the bodily experience of the comfort women is that of sexual violation, the comfort women issue directly assaults the masculine desire of the Korean nation to overcome the symbolic emasculinization that Japanese colonialism has left on the Korean male psyche."[76] The women served the nation's project of remasculinization as long as they remained on the metaphorical level, as sites of discourse, but that precluded addressing the actual pain experienced by the women themselves. Being forced to remain as metaphors, in the face of the violent history of sexual slavery, had a silencing and damaging impact on the women. Reflecting upon the nature of reconciliation for comfort women, Choi suggests that the right question is not about compensation or apologies, but rather, how to heal the wound. She argues that "we also need to pursue a way of bringing the women themselves to center stage in an effort to heal their wounds by transforming their own subjectivities," and suggests that some of the comfort women she wrote about did find some relief, some ability to process their trauma, in being able to express themselves verbally and through art.[77]

Women in other settings have apparently found some relief in discussing wartime rapes in private with their families or in public. In her research on German women raped by Soviet soldiers at the end of World War II, Atina Grossmann asserts that they discussed their ex-

---

76. Choi, "The Politics of War Memories toward Healing," 398.
77. Ibid., 404.

periences among themselves, if not in public.[78] For CNN's 1998 documentary *The Cold War*, Elfriede von Assel, identified as a resident of Berlin, calmly narrated her experience of being raped by Soviet soldiers in Berlin in 1945.[79] Von Assel's testimony was remarkable for her matter-of-fact manner and the apparent lack of stigma in identifying herself publicly as a rape victim. Jan Ruff-O'Herne was living in the Dutch East Indies with family when the Japanese military invaded and incorporated her into their military brothel system. Although her experiences as a Japanese war rape victim were no doubt horrific, she was able, at some level, to process what happened through speaking about it privately and then in a documentary, *50 Years of Silence*.[80] In 1991, in the face of tremendous stigmatization, several Korean comfort women came forward to tell of their wartime violations.

Most striking about the women assaulted by Soviet soldiers in Manchuria after World War II is their collective silence. As Ueno Chizuko has pointed out, there has been no room for Japanese comfort women to come forward to discuss their experiences, when obviously they suffered as well.[81] This appears to be true also for women assaulted in Manchuria. Socially, the women had nothing to gain and a great deal to lose by confirming suspicions of the violation. Although there was a compelling discourse of the Japanese people as the victims of World War II, the story of the rapes of the Japanese women in Manchuria did not contribute to it—people within Japan did not point to the rapes of Japanese women by the Soviets and say, "Our nation, too, suffered in the war." Any possible political uses—"sacrificed for our nation"—were not pursued. People did not identify with the women; rather, they worked hard to distance themselves from them. Even for people who had supported Japanese colonization in Manchuria, and most people did, it was easy to step away from these women, and to disassociate oneself from the imperial project.

---

78. "Gendered Defeat: Rape, Motherhood, and Fraternization," Chapter 2 of Grossmann, *Jews, Germans, and Allies*. This chapter overlaps in some ways with a previous article, Grossmann, "A Question of Silence."

79. CNN Presents. *The Cold War*, vol. 1, episode 2. Transcripts of the series are available at http://www.cnn.com/SPECIALS/cold.war/.

80. Choi, "The Politics of War Memories toward Healing," 402–4.

81. Ueno, "The Politics of Memory," 141.

The Return of the *"Red Repatriates,"* 1949

The figure of the female Manchurian repatriate emerged in the summer of 1946. Three summers later, another set of returnees arrived and sent the discussion of the *hikiagesha* in a new direction.

When the fighting in Manchuria ended, the Soviets accepted the surrender of Japanese soldiers. Instead of sending them back home, however, they formed them into groups of 1,000 men, loaded them onto trains, and sent them to Siberia as a captive labor force. When there were not enough soldiers to meet the requirement for the thousand-person units, the Soviets rounded up whomever else they could find—Japanese civilian men, former Korean soldiers and civilians, and a few Japanese women—and inserted them into units. The Soviet military dragooned approximately 575,000 men, 450,000 military personnel and 125,000 civilians, and transported them to camps, mainly in Siberia, but also as far west as Kazakhstan and the vicinity of Moscow. Thousands of people died during the journey and the first year of captivity. Others labored in the camps from one to seven years, and men sentenced as war criminals served lengthier sentences.[82] Survivors were released over the course of a decade beginning in 1946. According to the numbers in Japanese government sources, of the 575,000 men in Soviet custody, 473,000 eventually returned to Japan.[83] The Soviets claimed they held far fewer men, and do not accept the figure of 100,000 men dead or missing.

During the first two years after the war, the men in Soviet captivity were exploited simply for their labor, as loggers, farmers, and manual laborers. All accounts indicate that their lives were hard, physically and psychologically. They were forced to live and work in the extreme cold with almost nothing to eat and little medical care. Soviet guards were indifferent to little except whether the men were able to work. Most Japanese accounts go out of their way to point out that Soviet citizens, especially in 1946, lived and worked in nearly the same conditions, with very little food, heat, or clothing in a world of equal opportunity suffering. By 1947 or 1948, the Soviets realized that they had an opportunity to influence politics in Japan, even though they had been excluded

---

82. Nimmo, *Behind a Curtain of Silence*, 39–44.
83. Kōseishō shakai engokyoku, *Engo 50-nen shi*, 456.

from what became an American Occupation. They began to indoc-
trinate Japanese detainees with socialist ideology, with plans to release
them into Japanese society.[84]

Because of the near-subsistence level of existence, some men suc-
cumbed relatively easily to the ideological manipulation. Among themselves, detainees had preserved the military hierarchy of the Imperial
Japanese Army in the camps as a way of maintaining order. That meant
that men who had been low-ranking and mistreated soldiers in the military remained low-ranking, and often mistreated, prisoners within the
camps. Soviet operatives selected these dissatisfied men, explained to
them that the emperor, for whom they had been fighting and suffering,
was still reigning, unpunished, in Japan (true), that no one in Japan had
expressed any interest in their well-being (false), and that the only real
solution for Japan was socialist revolution. The Soviets gave privileges
and power to these men within the camps. The only reading material
available in the Japanese camps was the Soviet-produced Japanese-
language newspaper, *Nihon shinbun*, suffused with Soviet propaganda.[85]
Starved for anything to read, the men reportedly read it religiously.
Moreover, it became clear that professing communist beliefs was necessary in order to secure passage home.

The Soviet Union began to release some of the men in the first year
after they detained them, and in the summers of 1946, 1947, and 1948,
tens of thousands of men returned home without incident. But by 1949,
the effects of the indoctrination campaign had begun to take hold. On
June 27, 1949, a boatload of 2,000 Japanese men arrived in Maizuru—
a port town in Kyoto Prefecture located on the Sea of Japan—from
Nakhodka in the Soviet Far East (see Map 1).[86] As described in the history of the Maizuru Regional Repatriation Center, family members, local
schoolchildren, and citizens roused by repatriate support groups gathered on the pier. They waved flags and banners, and waited for their

---

84. Kuznetsov, "The Ideological Indoctrination of Japanese Prisoners of War in the
Stalinist Camps of the Soviet Union"; Kuznetsov, "The Situation of Japanese Prisoners
of War in Soviet Camps (1945–1956)."

85. Asahi shinbunsha, *Nihon shinbun fukkokuban.*

86. The men included 1,941 former Army men, 37 Navy, 9 civilians, 5 "non-Japanese"
(*hi-Nihonjin*) military, and 1 "non-Japanese" civilian. Maizuru chihō hikiage engokyoku,
Maizuru chihō hikiage engokyoku shi, 531.

husbands, fathers, sons, and countrymen.[87] In the spring and early summer of 1949, the press reported on MHW plans to welcome the men by providing nostalgic food on the ships home and offering flowers and entertainment during their stay in Maizuru. The MHW also organized "the love movement" (*ai no undō*), during which student and women's groups and "ordinary citizens" (*ippan kokumin*) would be called upon to greet the returnees.[88] Another story in May 1949 profiled a group of wives and children of Soviet detainees.[89] Living in poverty in a gloomy repatriate dormitory, they welcomed the announcement that the men detained in the Soviet Union would be arriving home soon, with the children asking their mothers if their fathers were really coming home. These plans for warmly receiving the men were thwarted, though, when the men who were finally released by the Soviets arrived in Maizuru. At the pier, they linked arms and executed a "landing in the face of the enemy" (*tekizen jōriku*), that enemy being "the land of the emperor." Without greeting even their mothers, they sang the *Internationale*, danced collective farm dances, and clamored to join the Japan Communist Party. A reporter for the *New York Times*, filing his story from Maizuru, described the men as "thoroughly indoctrinated with Communist theory and, according to their own statement, sworn to joining the Japanese Communist party with the object of Sovietizing Japan."[90]

During their four-day stay in Maizuru, the men continued to act collectively, and presented a list of demands to surprised repatriation officials, who expected the men to be grateful to be back home.[91] After four years of captivity, during which the Soviets convinced the men that they were willing to release them if only the Japanese government would send a ship or express any interest in their welfare, they were prepared to spread revolution in the country they believed had betrayed and then

---

87. Ibid., 531. A similar description can be found in "Nani ga kare o sō saseta ka!" *Nippon keizai shinbun*, July 8, 1949. This article depicts frightened women, children, and well-meaning members of the "love movement" in contrast to strident masses of men in the communist party or labor movements.

88. "Hikiage saikai chikashi," *Jiji shinpō*, March 7, 1949.

89. "Hikiage yōyaku saikai," *Asahi shinbun*, May 22, 1949.

90. Parrott, "Japanese Repatriated by Soviet Sworn to Communize Homeland."

91. Maizuru chihō hikiage engokyoku, *Maizuru chihō hikiage engokyoku shi*, 69.

Figure 1 Repatriates from Siberia, 1949. Men indoctrinated with socialist ideology during their captivity in the Soviet Union arrive in Maizuru and ignore a poster, featuring the image of a wife and children, designed to welcome them home. The photograph appeared with the title "Brainwashed repatriates from Siberia return to Japan" (*sennō sareta Shiberia kara no hikiagesha ga kikoku*). Used by permission of Mainichi shinbunsha.

forgotten them. Figure 1 is a photograph of a group of the indoctrinated men, fiercely ignoring a poster with an image of a woman with two children, pleased at the return of their husband and father.

The timing of their return could not have been worse. During the first two years the Americans dismantled the Japanese military and promoted democracy in several arenas, including enfranchising women and producing a new constitution. Occupation officials also supported strong labor unions as an expression of a healthy democracy, and did not, at first, object to people in unions promoting socialism, or to ties between unions and the Japan Communist Party.[92] Then, on February 1, 1947, General Douglas MacArthur cancelled a strike planned by labor unions throughout Japan. The cancellation of the strike serves as a symbolic marker for a change in mood and policies of the Occupation, in particular, less tolerance for socialists and communists. From that point on, communists, socialists, and union members faced more and more challenges from the Americans and their conservative collaborators.

---

92. Gordon, *The Wages of Affluence*, 9–10.

More active persecution of communists began in 1949. Early that year, the conservative Japanese government, with support from Occupation officials, began a campaign against the far left.[93] On July 4, 1949, a few days after the first group of indoctrinated men arrived from the Soviet Union, MacArthur stoked the fires of anti-communism by deeming communism a "national and international outlawry," a comment carried in the Japanese press. During the same period, Occupation officials ordered the largest news agency in Japan, Kyōdō, to clean house of all communists.[94] By the following summer, the "red purge" in the media and other industries began in earnest. Occupation forces and the Japan Newspaper Association announced the purge of communists from the press. People with communist affiliations began to be fired from newspapers, wire services, broadcasting, and other media. Communists in other industries including electronics, industry, and mining were fired from their jobs, and by December 1950, over 10,000 people in 24 industries had been dismissed.[95] The ideological battles being fought in Japan took place in the context of Mao Zedong's victory in China, and growing tensions between the United States and the Soviet Union that culminated in the outbreak of the Korean War in June 1950. The indoctrinated returnees unwittingly walked into this hostile atmosphere.

The response to the chaos created by the landing of the indoctrinated returnees in the summer of 1949 was swift. An editorial in the business-oriented daily *Nihon keizai shinbun* blamed the growing communist movement for exacerbating the problems surrounding the return of the detainees. It went on to point out that only four years before, people in Japan were preparing to defend the nation with bamboo spears, and that part of the problem was that these men had gone from one oppressive environment, the Imperial Japanese Army, into another, Soviet camps.[96] While arguing for a sympathetic response to the men, the article, with its word choice, emphasizes a gap between "us" (*ware ware*) and "them" (*karera*) or "repatriates" (*hikiagesha*). On August 11, the government passed a cabinet ordinance that gave repatriation officials some

93. Coughlin, *Conquered Press*, 30, 69–70.
94. Ibid., 106–9.
95. Iwanami shoten henshūbu, ed., *Kindai Nihon sōgō nenpyō*, 378–80.
96. "Shasetsu: Soren hikiagesha no kōdō," *Nihon keizai shinbun*, July 7, 1949.

extra authority for managing the departure of the detainees from Maizuru and back to their homes.[97] The ordinance indicated that returnees
should follow the instructions of the repatriation center staff and tried
to limit interaction between members of the Japan Communist Party
and other political groups by allowing only designated family members
to greet the detainees at their points of arrival.[98] Clashes continued into
the fall of 1949, with members of one student group devoted to aiding
repatriates reporting an uncomfortable encounter with the returnees.
The students were on the train to welcome home the men and pass out
surveys in an attempt to establish communication between the men
and their relatives at home. The men cornered the students, and, using
techniques they had learned in Soviet custody, subjected them to a
people's court (*tsurushiage*), demanding to know for whom they worked.
When the students insisted that as an aid organization they were politically neutral, the former detainees responded, "Neutrality is our enemy."[99] During the summer and fall of 1949, in legal documents and in
press coverage, these men were labeled *hikiagesha* and were depicted as
unruly, possibly communist, and in need of special rules to govern them.

Problems at Home

Most of the Siberian detainees shed their socialist rhetoric upon arrival
in Japan when provided with evidence, in the form of newspaper coverage, of American and Japanese attempts to free them from captivity.
Nevertheless, by autumn of 1949, with extensive newspaper coverage
of the obstreperous returnees, the damage had been done.[100] To be a

----

97. "Hikiagesha no chitsujo hoji ni kansuru seirei." Regional repatriation centers were
apparently staffed by former officers of the Imperial Japanese Army and Navy, a fact that
offended some of the Siberian detainees who no longer wanted to take orders from the
Japanese military.

98. "Ronsetsu: jiyū o mamoru yūki," *Tōkyō nichinichi shinbun*, August 13, 1949. This
editorial also laments that the Siberian detainees tried to appropriate the word "democracy" for the system in the Soviet Union, an attempt that offended those who had embraced Japan's postwar version of democracy.

99. "Engo gakusei o tsurushiage," *Nihon keizai shinbun*, August 4, 1949.

100. An example of that coverage in English is Parrott, "Japan to Punish Red Repatriates." The article describes administrative ordinances in response to the men who

Soviet detainee was to be suspected of communism. This was compounded by other problems, including the stigma of being a defeated Japanese soldier who had been on the continent, a place associated with atrocities. The economic "gift from the gods" in the form of the Korean War had not yet been proffered, and people still struggled to secure food, shelter, clothing, and medical care.

Having been released from wretched conditions in the Soviet Union, Siberian detainees faced a new set of problems at home: securing housing, finding work, and trying to support families who had gone without military pensions or any steady source of income since the end of the war. Three monthly magazines carried articles titled "I was Repatriated, But . . ."—a phrase evocative of director Ozu Yasujirō's films *I was Born, But . . .* and *I Graduated, But . . .*—indicating that coming back to Japan did not live up to their initial expectations.[101]

One source detailed the problems encountered by the detainees, especially in terms of finding work. Encouraged by the MHW, detainees tried to make use of employment agencies to aid repatriates and others. Bureaucrats boasted that they had a good record of matching men with their former, prewar professions. They cited the example of Ōkoshi Chūichi, a civil engineer and director of a special construction unit in Manchuria for whom they found a job related to his former profession. Ōkoshi found himself digging ditches for a road construction crew for 230 yen a day.[102] By the time Saitō Noboru had arrived, a month after the first boatload of indoctrinated men, employment offices no longer served Soviet detainees, saying that employers had asked them not to send any more of the "argumentative [*rikutsu*] types."[103]

The press also criticized how major companies including Mitsubishi, Mitsui, and Hitachi and their affiliates treated the returnees, suggesting that they had a policy of refusing to rehire employees who had been

---

refused to debark from ships or complete paperwork, who staged sit-ins at railway stations, and who held "people's trials" of repatriation officials.

101. "Ruporutāju: hikiagete wa mita keredo." Two other magazines, *Chūō kōron* and *Shinsō*, carried similar articles of nearly the same title within twelve months of the *Nihon shūhō* article: "Rupo: hikiagete wa kita keredo" and "Hikiagete wa mita keredo."

102. "Hikiagete wa mita keredo," 54. The names in the article were pseudonyms.

103. Ibid., 53.

interned and returned in 1949 or after. Some of the men who returned to Japan in 1948 were taken back to their old jobs, but those who returned in 1949 were refused. Two such men, ages 38 and 40, had five family members each to support. In some cases, the policy was retroactive. Ōishi Kōichi worked for Mitsubishi Heavy Industries before he was drafted. After the war, he was interned in the Soviet Union and returned to Japan in December 1948. In February 1949, he got his old job back at Mitsubishi. In April, however, Ōishi and 67 other men were fired, allegedly due to "overstaffing," though all 68 men who were laid off were Soviet detainees. Unions within these companies, eager to distance themselves from the taint of communism and wary that Soviet detainees were willing to work for any wage, treated repatriates with similar disdain.[104]

Other companies practiced different kinds of discrimination. After repatriation in 1948, Kurosaki Kenji received notice that he could return to his prewar job as a machinist for a company that constructed trains. There was a problem, however, and he was called into the office. On his résumé he had written, "July: returned from the Soviet Union." People at the company scolded him because calling them "the Soviet Union" amounts to praise; they insisted that the country should be called "Russia" and the people there "Ruskies" (*rosuke*). Another person, a mechanical engineer who had worked for a Mitsubishi affiliate, was required to submit forms, which had been stamped by the head of police, testifying that he would not join the Japan Communist Party.[105]

In the midst of the "red purge" of 1949–50, it was easy to dismiss all Soviet detainees as potentially tainted with communism, and, as a result, many of the men were unable to find work and support their families. Their return, instead of rescuing their families from poverty, often exacerbated problems. A new image of a repatriate emerged: a man, possibly ideologically contaminated, whose masculinity in terms of being able to support his family had been compromised. From 1949, for male repatriates, "possibly communist" was layered on top of the previous associations of "supporter of empire," increasing the negative emanation of the word—all the more reason for earlier repatriates, both male and female, to disassociate themselves from the category.

---

104. Ibid., 54–55.
105. Ibid., 55.

Soviet Detainees as "Repatriates"

A few scholars have addressed the issue of the Soviet detainees. William Nimmo, author of a monograph on the Soviet detention of Japanese men, discusses the event in terms of trying to understand Soviet motives. He concludes that Soviet actions revealed that they subscribed to the notion that the people go with the territory, and that a need for labor, more than an articulated vision of revenge or compensation, lay behind the capture and forced labor of more than half a million men.[106] The Soviets already had a system in place for transporting and detaining domestic prisoners—extending that system to include Japanese and German POWs was relatively easy.[107]

Until recently, the potential political usefulness of the Soviet detainee issue has received scant attention in Japan from politicians, ideologues, or historians. Yoshikuni Igarashi has addressed the question of the relative silence concerning these men in an essay showing that in the immediate postwar period, various leftist intellectuals turned to socialism in general and to the Soviet Union's version in particular as possible alternatives to "the semi-colonial condition under American hegemony."[108] The detainees, obvious victims of Soviet mistreatment and living proof of the failure of state socialism, presented evidence contrary to the idea of a Soviet utopia. The most likely supporter of the men, the Japan Communist Party, at times denied the stories of hardship at the hands of the Soviet Union, calling some of the men liars. On the other hand, detainees who provided more nuanced accounts of their time in detention, or those who had expressed sympathy for the Russian people, who suffered along with them, provided ammunition for people on the right to criticize the detainees as pro-Soviet and communist. The image of the indoctrinated men was overwhelmingly negative: strident, gaunt, unhappy, disruptive men who spurned their families and nation for the sake of communism. These images were useful to the Americans and conservative Japanese politicians, who used them to represent the ugly face of communism. No group found any political use for the detainees, except as negative publicity.

---

106. Nimmo, *Behind a Curtain of Silence*, 20.
107. Ibid., 44.
108. Igarashi, "Belated Homecomings," 118.

Igarashi's analysis of the Soviet detainees as liabilities for all parties during a time of growing concern about communism—an interpretation in the context of the cold war—makes an important contribution to understanding the relative lack of political and scholarly attention paid to the men. Contemporary sources show that the men were also folded into the supple discourse of repatriation. Although the men are now referred to as "Soviet detainees," (*Shiberiya yokuryūsha*), in 1949 and the early 1950s the press categorized them as *hikiagesha*, referring to the indoctrinated ones as *akai hikiagesha* or "red repatriates." As former military men, they did not qualify technically as repatriates, but the press overlooked that fact. An editorial from 1949 captures the application of the word "repatriate" to describe Soviet detainees. Titled "Repatriates—Reflect on Your Behavior," the article scolds *hikiagesha* for their disruptive behavior by reasoning that "because repatriates are, after all, Japanese, one would think that their return to Japan would be smooth. It saddens us that this is not the case."[109] This criticism of repatriates has the dual purpose of using common Japaneseness to discipline the behavior of the returnees, and to cast doubt on whether they are truly Japanese. In this way, returnees, political and personal disruptive behavior, and communism were all reiterated as un-Japanese. The men served as foils to define what postwar Japanese men should not be: defeated and captured soldiers, contaminated with foreign ideologies, and "argumentative." As unwelcome remnants of the Imperial Japanese Army, as pawns in the early cold war, as victims with no apparent political utility for the right or the left, and as unlikely "repatriates," few people in Japan found use for the Siberian detainees and their stories.

Repatriation from China, 1948–1972

For the Japanese who remained in China after 1948, the possibility of returning to Japan depended on a constellation of factors, including the political relationship between Japan and the PRC. Over a million Japanese people had been repatriated during the initial effort during the summer of 1946, and people continued to move back to Japan in fits and starts over the subsequent two years. By 1948, most of the esti-

---

109. "Hikiagesha wa hansei seyo," *Tōkyō shinbun*, August 2, 1949.

mated 3.5 million Japanese nationals who had been on the continent had been repatriated, but tens of thousands remained unaccounted for. Some had died during the war and postwar chaos; others had slipped through the cracks. A few had stayed behind deliberately because of work opportunities, family ties, or an aversion to returning to Japan. In October 1949, Mao Zedong declared the establishment of the People's Republic of China. The fate of the remaining Japanese nationals was uncertain, and many resigned themselves to remaining in China indefinitely.

Early in 1952, however, the state-run radio station in Beijing suddenly announced that the Chinese government would support the deportation of the remaining Japanese nationals in China. The PRC and Japan had no diplomatic relations. Although Japanese businessmen and others were enthusiastic about the prospect of stronger ties with the mainland, the government, whose foreign policy was dominated by the United States, played at best a passive role in relations with China. As a result, three non-governmental organizations within Japan took on the role of negotiating the repatriation of the remaining Japanese nationals: the Japanese Red Cross Society (Nihon sekijūjisha), the Japan-China Friendship Association (Nitchū yūkō kyōkai), and the Peace Liaison Society (Nihon heiwa renrakukai), known as Heiren. These three organizations negotiated with the Chinese Red Cross, and in 1953, the first group of official repatriates from China since 1948 arrived in Maizuru. Over 20,000 people returned that year in an event that caused a media frenzy.[110]

For the next six years, Japanese trickled back from China. Between 1953 and 1958, a total of 32,506 people were repatriated by the PRC to Japan through semi-official channels.[111] This included the 1956 repatriation of approximately 1,000 men convicted by the Soviet Union and the PRC as war criminals, men who had spent long years in Soviet and Chinese re-education camps.[112] The uncertain diplomatic relationship

---

110. "Kikokusen o meguru shinbun gassen."

111. Kōseishō engokyoku, *Hikiage to engo 30-nen no ayumi*, 109–14. K. W. Radtke puts the figure at 34,998 (Radtke, "Negotiations between the PRC and Japan," 198).

112. The Soviets held 969 men whom they had identified as war criminals. They turned them over to the Chinese at Suifenhe on July 17, 1950. This group included the men who fought for the Nationalists against the CCP. Kōseishō shakai engokyoku, *Engo 50-nen shi*, 88–89. On the Group of Returnees from China (Chūgoku kikansha

between Japan and the PRC took a turn for the worse in 1958 when a combination of political factors, including the election of Kishi Nobusuke, a suspected Class A war criminal as prime minister, and domestic Chinese politics, in the form of Mao's Great Leap Forward, led to a breakdown of the relationship and end of the repatriation. Formal repatriation did not begin again until after the PRC and Japan normalized relations in 1972.[113] As one of the few open channels between the PRC and Japan between 1953 and 1958, repatriation was for the Chinese government one means of establishing ties with Japan that could be put to use in the future.[114]

Conclusion

In the immediate postwar period, the word *hikiagesha* was used to identify almost all overseas returnees. In the summer of 1946, *hikiagesha* became most closely associated with women repatriated from Manchuria. From 1949, *hikiagesha* referred to disruptive Siberian detainees, with a negative connotation that spread to other returnees. Whereas female repatriates were suspected of physical contamination, the men, as potential carriers of the "alien" doctrine of communism, posed an ideological threat. From 1953 to 1958, *hikiagesha* referred to the later returnees from the PRC, although eventually, as it did in 1946, *hikiagesha* evoked a poor woman from Manchuria. The object of the *hikiagesha* discourse moved from women to men, and from bodies to minds, and it adapted itself to new political circumstances. What remained the same was the process of othering those who had been outside of the home islands at the end of the war, in ways that were useful for people at home in making the transition from war and empire into postwar Japan.

---

renrakukai 中国帰還者連絡会, or Chūkiren) see Yoshida, *The Making of the "Rape of Nanking"*, 56–57.

113. Kōseishō engokyoku, *Chūgoku zanryū koji.*

114. Radtke, "Negotiations between the PRC and Japan," 210–11; Seraphim, *War Memory and Social Politics in Japan.*

FOUR

"In the End, It Was the Japanese Who Got Us":

Repatriates in Literature, Songs, and Film

Across the postwar period, writers, lyricists, and filmmakers took up the issue of the end of the war in the colonies and the role of repatriates in postwar Japan. They began as soon as the war ended, but for a number of reasons, including Allied censorship and temporal proximity, the fictional figure of the repatriate did not appear in force in literary and filmic sources until the late 1950s. Representations of *hikiagesha* in cultural works at times continued the process of stigmatization, but also provided ways to imagine other meanings of what it meant to be a repatriate. This manifested itself in rewriting parts of the end of the war in ways that deviated from the usual storyline, or in using repatriates as an internal other only to empower them over "ordinary" Japanese. Fictional representations of the end of the war in the colonies gave full play to the various meanings of those who lived through it.

As we saw in Chapter 2, the government and the press facilitated the official and social image of the repatriate, an image that was challenged, modified, rejected, and in some cases, co-opted by repatriates themselves. By the late 1950s, the government announced the "end" of the issue of repatriation. The Repatriate Benefits Law, intended to bring closure to the issue, was passed in 1957.[1] The PRC and the Soviet Union

---

1. Kōseishō shakai engokyoku, *Engo 50-nen shi*, 99–101.

deported the last of the convicted war criminals in 1956 and the only remaining regional repatriation center, at Maizuru, was closed in 1958.[2] By this time, organized repatriation was over. The MHW then set about writing the history of repatriation. In these published volumes, the story is one of dedicated bureaucrats with few resources doing their best to resettle the overseas Japanese back home. As if to challenge the bureaucratic and social attempts to contain, neutralize, and perhaps move beyond the history of the end of the colonies, repatriation-related short stories and novels, songs, and films embraced that history and explored many of the issues that had been censored, suppressed, or elided by other accounts of the process. The association of sexual contamination with Japanese women in Manchuria, confusion about identity, and explorations of the fates of those left behind are three persistent themes in repatriate-related popular culture. A look at how those sources made sense of—or at least used—repatriates reveals the lively afterlife of the *hikiagesha* in the later decades of postwar Japan.

Repatriates and Popular Culture

Repatriate-related cultural products fall into four loose categories. The first category includes novels, short stories, films, and *manga* (comic strips) about repatriation by repatriates. Examples include Gomikawa Junpei's novel, *Ningen no jōken* (*The Human Condition*, 1956–58), made into a three-part film of the same title by director Kobayashi Masaki. Born and raised in Manchuria and repatriated in 1948, Gomikawa refers to himself as a "second generation Manchurian Japanese" (*Manshū nisei* 満州二世).[3] Drafted in 1942 and sent to Manchuria, Shōchiku director Kobayashi Masaki experienced war's end in Okinawa and became a POW. He remained in American custody until his demobilization in November 1946.[4] The second category includes works produced by artists raised in the colonies that do not directly address repatriate issues, but whose authors may still concern themselves with repatriation in other ways. The well-known essayist Itsuki Hiroyuki did not write about

---

2. Ibid., 771.

3. Gomikawa, "Genten toshite no waga *Sensō to ningen*," 191. Biographical information on Gomikawa is from *Ningen no jōken*, copyright page.

4. Kinema junpōsha, ed., *Nihon eiga terebi kantoku zenshū*, 160–62.

his family's traumatic experience in Korea until 2003, but he did direct attention to Kamitsubo Takashi's little-known 1979 book on a repatriate orphanage in Hakata.[5] That attention resulted in a reprint of the out-of-print book in a 1993 paperback edition that received much wider circulation.

Third, there are works produced by writers and film directors who were not repatriates but addressed repatriation. This group includes Ōshima Nagisa, the director of the film *Gishiki* (*Ceremony*, 1971), and the best-selling novelist Yamasaki Toyoko, author of the novels *Fumō chitai* (*The Barren Zone*) and *Daichi no ko* (*Child of the Continent*). Fourth, there were non-repatriate writers whose works did not directly address the issue of repatriation but used repatriates as a device, either to establish alterity in one of the characters—as in Hani Susumu's film *Kanojo to kare* (1963)—or as a link between postwar Japanese society and its imperial past, as in Murakami Haruki's novel *Nejimakidori kuronikuru* (*The Wind-Up Bird Chronicle*, 1993–95).

The complexity of cultural production sometimes spills out of these four loose categories. The *manga* artist Kitami Ken'ichi returned to Japan from Manchuria when he was just five or six years old. Barely old enough to remember his repatriate experience, he was still classified as a "repatriate artist" and he traveled back to China with a group of "China-born" *manga* artists.[6] In other cases, repatriates may have influenced cultural products behind the scenes. Gosho Heinosuke, director of the repatriate-themed film *Kiiroi karasu* (*The Yellow Crow*, 1957) was not a repatriate, but the screenwriter, Tateoka Kennosuke, was.[7] Although Ōshima Nagisa was not a repatriate, he demonstrated his engagement with the issue of repatriation in the film *Gishiki* and an investigative article in a popular magazine recounting the violent end of a Manchurian agricultural settlement from Nagano.[8] On the other hand, Yamada Yōji, who was repatriated as a boy from Dalian in 1947 and entered the Shōchiku studio in the same class as Ōshima in 1954, found

---

5. Itsuki, *Unmei no ashioto*; Kamitsubo, *Mizuko no uta: hikiage koji to okasareta onnatachi no kiroku*; and Kamitsubo, *Mizuko no uta: dokyumento hikiage koji to onnatachi*.

6. Chūgoku hikiage mangaka no kai, *Boku no Manshū*, 230.

7. "Hikiage o motomete," 90; Kawamoto, "Sarai shinema rebyū nozoku," 116–17.

8. Ōshima, "Kieta Nagano-ken no Yomikaki-mura."

commercial success as the director of the "Tora-san" series of come-
dies.[9] Novelist Yamasaki Toyoko did not grow up overseas, but her
younger brother was a graduate of the East Asian Common Culture
Institute (Tōa dōbun shoin 東亜同文書院) in Shanghai and was reportedly fluent in Chinese.[10]

Repatriate artists who did not explicitly address repatriate themes
sometimes point out the ties between a colonial past and art, in their
own work and that of others. After playfully speculating that American
filmmaker John Ford must have been raised in Manchuria—as Yamada
Yōji was—to have such a dramatic sense of horizon in his films, *manga*
artist Morita Kenji links his own appreciation of horizon to his childhood in Manchuria.[11] In one of his cartoons, Morita depicts an open
freight train, packed with hundreds of Japanese deportees, dwarfed by
the vast Manchurian horizon. Someone holds the seven-year-old Morita
up to urinate over the edge of the car. Words within the cartoon read
"Pissing on the big red sun, this is the horizon in my soul."[12] Morita at-
tributed the violence in his manga to his childhood in which he witnessed casual violence on a daily basis. In another scene, the boy, again
packed in with a group of terrified Japanese civilians in postwar China,
recalls a scene of bored Japanese military men executing Chinese peasants. Words within the cartoon read, "You wonder why there are so
many execution scenes in my *manga*?"[13] The conductor Ozawa Seiji
provides another example of a Japanese cultural figure publicly claiming
his continental roots. In order to salute the international audience of
the 2002 New Years' Day concert by the Vienna State Opera, participants were encouraged to deliver a greeting in their native language.

---

9. Born in 1932, Ōshima Nagisa graduated from Kyoto University and joined the
Shōchiku studio as an assistant in 1954, began to direct in 1959, and left Shōchiku circa
1961. Born in 1931, University of Tokyo graduate Yamada Yōji joined the Shōchiku studio in 1954 in the same class as Ōshima. He began directing in 1963 and struck gold in
1969 with the first "Tora-san" movie *Otoko wa tsurai yo* starring Atsumi Kiyoshi. He
made two episodes a year for twenty years. Kinema junpōsha, ed., *Nihon eiga terebi kantoku zenshū*, 63–66, 444–46.

10. Yamasaki, *"Daichi no ko" to watashi*, 14.

11. Chūgoku hikiage mangaka no kai, ed., *Boku no Manshū*, 98.

12. Ibid., 111.

13. Ibid., 109.

The newly appointed music director, Manchurian-born and raised conductor Seiji Ozawa, spoke in Chinese.[14]

Early Fictional Treatment of Repatriation

Fictional depictions of repatriates in novels, short stories, poems, plays, and songs began to appear in 1945, especially in publications by and for repatriates. Originally published from within the Hakata Regional Repatriation Center, the monthly magazine *Minato* (Harbor) frequently carried stories about repatriation-related problems. The first issue of *Minato* appeared in June 1946, just as the impact of the million-person repatriation was making itself felt. As explained in the inaugural issue, the goal of the magazine was to provide guidance for aid to repatriates, and the editors stated that any profits from the magazine would be donated to the effort to rehabilitate them. The first few issues of the magazine included a pastiche of submissions from MHW bureaucrats, idealistic journalists who exhorted repatriates to "brighten up," and ads from the local shipping cooperative, arguing that the key to the recovery of Hakata and Japan at large was the revitalization of the shipping industry.[15]

By February 1947, *Minato* had settled on an identity for itself as the "magazine of culture for continentals" (*tairikujin bunka zasshi* 大陸人文化雑誌).[16] The editors made an effort to include Chinese and Korean people in the definition of cultured continentals and carried at least one submission from a Chinese national, one Ō Shinshō (王振聲), who argued that the Japanese people (*minzoku*) were a race without substance that needed to raise its level of intellect and culture.[17] In one instance, however, the magazine satisfied the "continental" part of its mission by putting the image of a beautiful Chinese woman on the cover.

In June 1947, *Minato* carried a short story called "Rira saku gogatsu to nareba" (When May arrives and the lilacs bloom). It tells the story of

---

14. "Ozawa's Vienna Debut Will Be a Waltz Worth the Wait," *Boston Globe*, January 1, 2002. Seiji Ozawa was music director of the Boston Symphony Orchestra for 29 years before his move to the Vienna State Opera.

15. One pullout tells readers to stop submitting gloomy pieces and send in brighter, more interesting ones. "Dokusha no minasama e," *Minato*, June 1946, 45.

16. *Minato*, February 1947.

17. Ō Shinshō, "Nihonjin no yokogao," *Minato*, November 1946, 10.

a young widow Chiyoko and her beloved 20-year-old sister-in-law Katsue, both of whom escaped the violence of postwar Manchuria to arrive safely in Japan. Chiyoko had been away from Japan for more than eight years, but for Manchurian-born Katsue, repatriation was her first encounter with "the homeland." Buffeted by the cold winds of the home islands (*naichi no kaze no tsumetasa*; 内地の風の冷たさ), they find it difficult to make sense of the unsympathetic people of Japan.[18]

A few months after settling in Kumamoto, Chiyoko and Katsue meet up with Takayama, an old friend from Manchuria, who begins to court Katsue. One evening, Chiyoko's boss Hirota pays an evening visit to Chiyoko, Katsue, and Takayama. At Hirota's urging, the three begin to reminisce about the end of the war in Manchuria. Chiyoko recalls how Japanese women fell victim to indiscriminate sexual violence. Chiyoko and Katsue agree that it was a miracle they got out alive. Hirota, a *naichi* person with little sympathy for the Manchurian-Japanese, responds with lewd interest, doubting out loud that they escaped with their virtue. Chiyoko protests, but the damage is done. The chastity of the prospective bride has been called into doubt in the presence of her suitor Takayama, who then disappears.

Some weeks later, a representative from the local repatriation citizens group calls Chiyoko to ask for help. A desperately ill woman from Harbin had recently arrived. The woman's Japan-side relatives had refused to give blood, but perhaps as a repatriate, Chiyoko would be more sympathetic. Chiyoko immediately departs to the hospital to get tested but her blood type is incompatible. But Katsue has accompanied Chiyoko. She has the right kind of blood, which she willingly donates to her fellow repatriate. Woozy from the loss of blood, Katsue slips in and out of consciousness and mumbles, "my blood is pure!" (*atashi no chi wa kirei nano yo!*).[19] Chiyoko's tears of sympathy splash down onto Katsue's face, reviving her.

Through a blood-giving relay, the repatriate community saves the returnee from Harbin. The local paper carried this moving human-interest story on the front page, but the repatriate community did not let the flattering portrayal sway them. One character shakes his head at the fick-

---

18. Imai, "Rira saku gogatsu to nareba," 28.
19. Ibid., 28–29.

leness of the press, wryly noting that today they might be heroes, but tomorrow the paper would revert to stories of repatriate crime. Katsue's suitor Takayama sees the article and is moved by her selflessness. He immediately realizes that it was wrong for him to entertain any doubt about her chastity and seeks her forgiveness. In the final scene, with Kyushu engulfed in the yellow sands blown from the continent, Chiyoko plans to bring lilacs to the May wedding of Katsue and Takayama.

This simple story nevertheless invites interpretation. In the first place, it contains an early representation of the issue of *naichi* suspicions of the sexual impurity of women from Manchuria, one that casts the homeland Japanese person as an unsympathetic lecher. What is noteworthy about the depiction is how the author Imai Shūji naturalizes this new category of a potentially compromised woman by placing it in an old system of discrimination: the disqualification of a young woman as a suitable marriage partner because of a stigma. The plot of Tanizaki Jun'ichirō's *Sasameyuki* (*The Makioka Sisters*) revolves around the family's attempts to arrange a marriage for the third Makioka daughter, Yukiko. In most cases, the prospective suitor fails in some small way to meet the high standards of the Makioka family. In one case, however, a promising suitor discovers a history of tuberculosis in the family and unceremoniously withdraws from the negotiations.[20] Imai's story shows that although "repatriates" were a new category, it was easy to place them in old patterns of stigmatization and discrimination.

It is safe to say that people in Japan were not moved by the melodrama of "Rira saku gogatsu to nareba," at least in its original form. The Allied censors deleted the section critical to the plot—the discussion of the rape of Japanese women in Manchuria—on the grounds that it was "critical of Russia" at a time when the Soviet Union was still an Allied power.[21]

Machi Jurō's short story "Kin-ken shūchūei" (The Kin-ken refugee camp), also published in *Minato*, highlights another repatriate problem: the difficulty of preserving one's identity.[22] The story begins one rainy

---

20. William Johnston's analysis of *Sasameyuki* in his research on the history of tuberculosis in Japanese society is instructive here (Johnston, *The Modern Epidemic*, 151–54).

21. Censorship documents, *Minato,* June 1946.

22. Machi, "Kin-ken shūchūei."

night in the summer of 1946 with the protagonist Toyo and her companion Ryūzō crowded onto an open deportation train, on a journey from Changchun through Shenyang to the deportation staging camp at Jinzhou (錦州; in Japanese, Kinshū Prefecture, abbreviated as "Kin-ken" 錦県). From there, they will board the repatriation ship back to Japan. Toyo, a lovely young country woman, had moved to Manchuria as part of an agricultural settlement. Her husband was drafted just before the end of the war and she had not heard from him since. As a single woman in postwar Manchuria she found herself vulnerable. She made her way to a refugee camp in Changchun and then secured a position as a maid for Ryūzō, an older, wealthy man whose wife had died of cholera at the end of the war. Soon Ryūzō and Toyo were living as husband and wife.

Upon arrival at the Kin-ken refugee camp, Toyo learns that Ryūzō has registered her as his wife, destined for his home town of Yamaguchi. The prospect of arriving in Japan registered as another man's wife is distressing to her. She confronts Ryūzō, and tells him it was wrong for him to register her without her knowledge and that she wanted to go to her own home. He argues that he feels responsible for her, and that they will work everything out after they make it home. She approaches an official and asks him to change the paperwork but is refused. On the next day, though, the official informs Toyo that there is a job available at the camp preparing sorghum to feed the stream of deportees. The refugee camp was a terrible disease-ridden place, and the opportunity to return to Japan was standing right in front of her. Nevertheless, Toyo remains behind.

Several readings of this story are possible. It highlights the overlapping power of paternalism and paperwork in the processes of repatriation. The author Machi may be giving Toyo agency for deciding under what terms she will return to Japan in a situation where destitute and unattached women had few choices. Women in Manchuria probably knew that returning to *naichi* meant facing stricter social codes and additional scrutiny. But it also shows how easily, in the chaos of postwar Manchuria, identities were lost and reassigned. Given the opportunity to return to Japan, but only with a new identity, Toyo chooses to remain in Manchuria. The story suggests that in Toyo's case, hanging on to one's old self and returning to Japan are incompatible.

Popular songs about repatriation expressed sentimental aspects of the episode. The first of three songs often associated with repatriation, "Kaeribune" (The ship home), was singer Tabata Yoshio's first postwar hit in 1946. It is a sentimental song about the poignant journey back to Japan. The second song, "Ikoku no oka" (Hills of a foreign land), about the tragic lives of the men still held in Soviet detention, had a dramatic history. It was introduced to Japan on August 1, 1948, when a demobilized soldier recently returned from detention in the Soviet Union stepped up to the microphone of the NHK radio program "Shirōto nodo jiman" (Amateur hour) and mesmerized the nation with the darkly moving song. Siberian detainee Yoshida Tadashi, the author of the song, arrived home in 1949 to discover that the song he had written was already well-known, carried home by one of his war buddies.[23] Officials sought to make use of the song during the tense repatriation process of the Siberian detainees, and, thinking it would provide comfort, played the song on the ship home. Detainees indoctrinated by the Soviets objected, complaining that the melody, apparently borrowed from an old Russian folk song, was "bourgeois." In January 1950, a boatload of Soviet detainees pinned Japanese national flags to their chests and upon arrival in Maizuru broke out, in chorus, into "Ikoku no oka." The gesture effectively communicated their patriotism and rejection of communism, redeeming them in the eyes of a nation suspicious of the detainees.[24]

"Ganpeki no haha" (The mother who waits by the wharf), a third, popular repatriation-related song, first appeared in 1954, and became a nation-wide hit upon re-release in 1972.[25] The song and subsequent film were based on the life of Hatano Ise, a woman who reportedly waited daily on the dock at Maizuru from January 1950 for the return of her only son.[26] Even after she received the official notice of his death in 1956,

---

23. Maizuru-shi, ed., *Hikiagekō Maizuru no kiroku*, 79; Ishikawa et al., eds., *Taishū bunka jiten*, 670, 819.

24. Maizuru-shi, ed., *Hikiagekō Maizuru no kiroku*, 80.

25. Ibid., 80; 1954 recording by Kikuchi Shōko, Tei Records; 1972 recording by Futaba Yuriko, King Records.

26. Information on Hatano Ise in Maizuru hikiage kinenkan, *Haha naru minato Maizuru*, 38.

she continued to wait, believing that he would return.[27] In 1978, officials at the Maizuru Repatriation Museum inscribed the lyrics to "Ikoku no oka" and "Ganpeki no haha" into a stone monument, explicitly tying the songs to the site devoted to memorializing repatriation, and perhaps facilitating ties in the minds of visitors between the popular songs and the history of repatriation.[28] Moreover, "Ganpeki no haha" became a kind of shorthand for the tragic aspects of repatriation. In 1995, to commemorate the fiftieth anniversary of the end of the war, the popular weekly men's magazine *SPA!* published a list of the ten most important happenings in postwar Japan, with repatriation and deportation at the top of the list.[29] It characterized the event as the return of 9 percent of the population, accompanied by the tears of "the mother who waits by the wharf." Upon hearing of my research interest in postwar repatriation, two non-repatriate Japanese burst into "Ganpeki no haha."[30] The songs, simple and sentimental, provide an emotional connection to the issues of returning, or failing to return, to Japan after the war.

The End of Colonial Manchuria in 1950s Fiction

Although the government announced the end of repatriation in 1958, a divergent trend was also apparent: a graphic re-visitation of the circumstances of the end of the war in popular and literary culture. The government's moves in 1957 and 1958 were measured and bureaucratic. Artistic depictions of overseas Japanese at the end of the war were messy and violent, tarnishing the veneer of an industrious, peaceful, and harmonious postwar Japanese society.

---

27. Of the 7,264 items displayed at the Maizuru Repatriation Museum as of 1995, 836—11 percent—were related to Hatano Ise, who died in 1981, at the age of 88. Maizuru hikiage kinenkan, *Haha naru minato Maizuru*, 53.

28. Ibid., 60.

29. Saraki, "ZOOMUP." Another example of the use of the song "Ganpeki no haha" as a link to the history of repatriation is a review of the Maizuru Repatriation Museum, the title of which suggests that if you close your eyes, you will hear the song. Hashikaku, "Hōmon omoshirokan."

30. During a research trip to Yamaguchi Prefecture in May 1999, colleagues who knew of my interest in repatriation took me to an old-fashioned karaoke bar and, accompanied by the bar hostess, sang "Ikoku no oka" and "Ganpeki no haha."

In 1956 and 1957, Gomikawa Junpei published his epic six-volume novel *Ningen no jōken*, which went on to sell over 2.4 million copies in less than three years.[31] Director Kobayashi Masaki then turned the book into a nine-hour, three-part film on life in Manchuria during and after the war, starring the well-known actor Nakadai Tatsuya as the protagonist Kaji.[32] The response to the novel and the film indicates that a story about the end of the colonies in Manchuria could be of wide interest in Japan.

Ningen no jōken is the story of Kaji, an idealistic young man who takes a job in Manchuria during the 1930s. He is determined to demonstrate the effectiveness of kindness to Koreans and Chinese as well as Japanese in the administration of the large, semi-governmental industrial company where he works. Over the course of the war, circumstances grow worse and worse, and Kaji is repeatedly faced with terrible choices. Even, or especially, when he makes the right moral choice, Kaji finds that the consequences are bad for him and everyone else. Against the terms of his contract, he is drafted from his civilian post and then exposed to the extreme brutality of the Japanese military. His life spirals downward. By the beginning of the fifth volume, published in 1957, the war is over. Kaji becomes the leader of a ragtag bunch of Japanese bandits, trying to elude capture at the hands of the Soviets. Few in postwar Manchuria are sympathetic to these defeated Japanese soldiers. At one point, a female Japanese refugee informs Kaji that the brutal Soviet soldiers are not as bad as the Japanese military men. Her words sting Kaji, as he wonders in disbelief: "A reputation worse than the Red Army?"[33] All Kaji wants to do is return to his home, not in Japan but in southern Manchuria, and to see his wife Michiko. His love for her is what sustains him throughout.

Ningen no jōken invites a number of interpretations. James Orr analyzes *Ningen no jōken* in the context of an exploration of war guilt.[34] Some of Gomikawa's own writings show that he intended to explore that theme. Kaji's love for his wife, the complete absence of other family members, or any other kind of allegiance—to nation, military unit, company, or

---

31. Takahashi, *"Senki mono" o yomu*, 53.

32. Kobayashi, *Ningen no jōken*. For a brief review of the film, see Gluck, "The Human Condition."

33. Gomikawa, *Ningen no jōken*, vol. 6, 97–98.

34. Orr, *The Victim as Hero*, 106–36.

village—is striking. For that reason, the novel could be interpreted as promoting the romantic couple as the ideal social unit in postwar Japan.

Ningen no jōken is also provocative in terms of the transformation of colonial identities in the midst of the unmaking of the Japanese empire. Many of Kaji's troubles are due to his position as a soldier in the Japanese army and for that reason it appears that war and defeat shape him. In the last two volumes, however, Kaji frequently encounters remnants of the Japanese empire, including lost Japanese children from an agricultural settlement, liberated Koreans on their way home,[35] Chinese people seeking retribution, and Japanese women in a refugee camp.[36] The Japanese women still call the men "Mr. Soldier" (*heitaisan* 兵隊 さ ん), but Kaji dispenses with pleasantries and refers to himself and his men as "defeated, left-behind soldiers" (*haizanhei* 敗残兵). Ultimately, Kaji is defined by the end of the colony in Manchuria.

Ningen no jōken contains themes in common with earlier stories about repatriation. Like the short story "Rira saku gogatsu to nareba," *Ningen no jōken* addresses the problem of Japanese women in Manchuria and their perceived sexual availability. But Gomikawa's treatment of sex, rape, perpetrators, and contamination is more explicit than in the earlier works. In one scene, Kaji's band of bandits encounters an eighteen-year-old Japanese girl and her mute younger brother.[37] The girl is dirty and her clothes have been ripped apart, but her youth and beauty are still evident. Kaji's devoted follower, the naïve youth Teruda, asks, "Nothing happened to you?" Uncomfortable, the girl says, "Some Japanese female entertainers sacrificed themselves for us." "What happened to them?" Teruda asked. "The Russians took them away," she replied.[38]

The girl asks Kaji to allow her brother and her to travel with them. Kaji wants to refuse—the civilians will slow them down—but in the end he relents. After a day or so, a man named Kirihara and his two subordinates offer to escort the siblings to the border. Kaji is puzzled as to why the evil Kirihara has suddenly become a humanitarian, but assumes that something in the fresh beauty of the girl has touched a

---

35. Gomikawa, *Ningen no jōken*, vol. 5, 240–41.

36. Gomikawa, *Ningen no jōken*, vol. 6, 96–125.

37. Gomikawa, *Ningen no jōken*, vol. 5, 230–52; vol. 6, 30–38, 55–60.

38. Gomikawa, *Ningen no jōken*, vol. 5, 232.

soft spot within him. Kirihara, his men, and the two siblings then depart from the group.

A day later, Kirihara and his men return to Kaji's band. Seeking information about the distance to the border, Kaji asks one of Kirihara's men about the girl and her brother and how far they took them. The men are evasive so Kaji confronts Kirihara.

"What did you do with her?"
"I treated her appropriately, appropriately."
"What do you mean, 'appropriately'?"
"Do you really want to know? I purified her of that Russian contamination."[39]

The narrator informs us that the girl put up a violent resistance to Kirihara and his men when they attacked her, but that she was still able to hear one of them yell, "A girl like you who didn't kill herself after being attacked by the Russians—who are you to refuse a Japanese man?"[40] After the rape, Kirihara and his men dispose of the girl and her brother, who witnessed the attack, by killing them. This passage is significant because it is a rare depiction in which a representation of the sexual violence of Japanese military men and sexual attacks on Japanese civilian women intersect. In other accounts, the two are presented separately. *Ningen no jōken* forces the reader to consider Japanese-on-Japanese violence and possible links between the actions of Japanese soldiers in China during the war with the victimization of Japanese women.

Gomikawa's use of the language of sexual contamination, with Kirihara claiming to have "purified" the girl by raping her, resonates with discussions about the return of women from Manchuria in 1946. As discussed in Chapter 3, some medical personnel worked to provide care for the women; however, reports discussed the women in terms of the possible venereal diseases and "foreign fetuses" they carried and the need to stop those problems "at water's edge." The passage expresses the idea that there were some who believed that the problem with the rape of Japanese women by Soviet troops was not the violence perpetrated against the women but rather the threat of the contamination of Japanese bodies by foreign elements.

---

39. Gomikawa, *Ningen no jōken*, vol. 6, 58.
40. Ibid., 59.

Kaji and his men encounter more Japanese civilian women when they come upon a refugee camp of women. Their husbands had been drafted long ago, and most of the children and elderly had died. Kaji and his men help the women raid a nearby field for food and the two groups share a meal. In the evening, an orgy ensues. The women are depicted as willing, motivated by loneliness and the desire to have a man in their lives, if only for a night. The mutual assuagement between these groups comes to an abrupt end the next morning as the men are preparing to depart. The Soviets arrive and demand the surrender of the Japanese troops with the threat of death for everyone if they resist.

Throughout the overnight encounter, Kaji remains aloof, rejecting one of the women's advances. The woman then directs her attentions to the youth Teruda, who experiences his first sexual encounter. The scene says more about the relationship between the two men than it does about the anonymous woman. More importantly for our purposes, the scene in which the Japanese male soldiers give themselves up to the Soviets serves as a means for Gomikawa to rewrite the behavior of Japanese men into one in which they sacrifice themselves in order to save the lives of Japanese civilian women.

Kaji is clearly a fictional creation of Gomikawa, but their histories have some parallels. Gomikawa, born and raised in Manchuria, went to Japan for higher education but then returned to Manchuria to take a job at the Anshan Ironworks Company in Manchuria.[41] Later, he reflected that the economic conditions for a Japanese person in Manchuria were quite attractive, compared to Koreans and Chinese in Manchuria or even recent college graduates in Japan. He was drafted at the end of the war and miraculously survived a battle with Soviet tanks—of the 158 men in his unit, only 4 lived. He was repatriated to Japan in 1948.

At the same time Gomikawa published *Ningen no jōken*, Abe Kōbō's *Kemonotachi wa kokyō o mezasu* (*Wild Beasts Seek Home*) appeared in the literary magazine *Gunzō*. In the novel, a hapless Manchurian-born youth named Kuki Kyūzō (久木久三) escapes from his semi-captive position as a house boy for Soviet military officers in Harbin and heads south in an attempt to reach Japan. Unable to navigate the unforgiving geographical and political terrain of Manchuria in 1948, the naïve Kyūzō

---

41. Gomikawa, "Genten toshite no waga *Sensō to ningen.*"

is both aided and exploited by a crafty Korean heroin dealer, Kō Sekitō (高石塔). Born of a Japanese mother, Kō speaks Japanese and Chinese and is savvy to the complexities of post-colonial society in the throes of the Chinese civil war. During the journey, Kō robs Kyūzō and then leaves him for dead in the city of Shenyang. Kyūzō survives and with help is able to find the compound where a few remaining Japanese skilled workers and their families continue to live. When Kyūzō pleads with the Japanese guard, saying all he wants is to go home, the guard says, "The deportation camps are all closed, the repatriation ships are all gone . . . nothing can be done [*shōganai*]." After being turned away, Kyūzō approaches the house of a Japanese family. "I'm Japanese," he tells the children. They jeer at him. "You're a beggar! No Japanese could be that dark!" the children cry. Their mother calls the children inside and closes the door.[42]

Chased away by a Chinese guard, the starving and desperate Kyūzō meets up with some Japanese smugglers. When Kyūzō gives his name, the smugglers react first with surprise—a Kuki Kyūzō from Harbin has already negotiated with them for passage back to Japan—and then with wicked amusement at the prospect of two Kuki Kyūzō's. The smugglers take Kyūzō with them and arrange a confrontation between their two Kyūzō's on the ship back to Japan. Kō, who has stolen Kyūzō's identity, is revealed as the imposter. But Kō slips over into insanity, and, bound in chains, believes himself to be the true Kuki Kyūzō. The novel ends with Kyūzō and Kō, Manchurian Japanese and Manchurian Korean, imprisoned together in the hold of the ship, never reaching Japan.

Soon after his birth in Tokyo in 1924, the novelist Abe Kōbō moved to the Manchurian city of Fengtian (Shenyang) where his father Asakichi taught at the Manchurian Medical University.[43] In 1940, at age 16, he returned to Tokyo for high school, and then moved back and forth between Fengtian and Tokyo. In 1943, at age 19, Abe entered medical school at Tokyo Imperial University. In 1944 he began to believe the rumors that Japan was about to be defeated. He forged his identity pa-

---

42. Abe, *Kemonotachi wa kokyō o mezasu*, 204–5.

43. This biographical portrait is based on a 1960 chronology submitted by Abe to accompany a publication. Abe, *Abe Kōbō zenshū*, 464–65. Originally published as "Nenpu," *Shin'ei bungaku sōsho II Abe Kōbō shū*.

pers and returned to Manchuria. When the war ended, Abe was with his family in Fengtian, helping out at his father's medical clinic. He reported feeling a sense of elation after surrender but was soon confronted by the chaos of postwar Manchuria. The occupying Soviet forces turned the Abe family out of their home, after which point the family moved frequently to avoid them. Sometime late in 1945, Abe's father contracted typhus from the patients he had been treating and died. Abe supported himself (and perhaps his mother and siblings—he was the oldest of four) by making and peddling soft drinks on the streets. Sometime in the fall of 1946, the 22-year-old Abe boarded a repatriation ship with his family, bound for the Sasebo Regional Repatriation Center in Nagasaki Prefecture.[44] When cholera broke out on board, the ship remained anchored off the shore of Japan for more than ten days with all of the returnees quarantined on it. Forced to remain just off the shore on a squalid ship with limited supplies, some on board began to exhibit signs of madness. Abe wrote that this experience served as the foundation for the final scene aboard the ship in the novel *Kemonotachi wa kokyō o mezasu*.[45] Highlighting these parallels is not to suggest the novel is biographical. Nevertheless, Abe made creative use of his experience in and repatriation from postwar Manchuria.

Kemonotachi wa kokyō o mezasu occupies an odd place in Abe's oeuvre. An English-language translation of the novel has yet to be published, and critics of the novel were not especially impressed when it first appeared. By 1957 Abe had established a reputation for writing fantastical stories, and one disappointed critic said that is what he anticipated when he picked up *Kemonotachi wa kokyō o mezasu*. Another speculated that perhaps the young man had run out of ideas.[46] Although it is less celebrated than many of his other novels and plays, it is rich with many of the themes and tropes that define his work.

Literary scholars have identified the issues central to Abe's writings. E. Dale Saunders, the translator of Abe's *Suna no onna* (*Woman in the*

---

44. Abe, "Sakuhin nōto," 8. Abe was in Hokkaido by November 1946, indicating that his family and he probably boarded a repatriation ship in Huludao sometime during the summer or fall of 1946.

45. Abe, *Abe Kōbō zenshū*, vol. 12, 465.

46. Ozaki, Kanbayashi, and Tonomura, "Sōsaku gappyō."

Dunes) and other works, has summarized three strands prevalent in Abe's work: "the twin themes of alienation and the loss of identity"; "the stultifying effect of urban isolation on modern man"; and "the use of the literary device of the turnabout or inversion of roles in which the hunter becomes the hunted" or the aggressor becomes the victim.[47] William Currie has interpreted Abe's fiction as "searching for the roots of existence," symbolized by sand; "difficulty in communication," expressed by the use of masks; and "the discrepancy between the inner and outer reality," explored through the map and the city.[48] The literary critic Kawamura Minato has pointed out that the tensions in Abe's work, between chasing and being chased, the city and the wilderness, the hometown and the foreign country, appear to present opposite experiences but in fact are continuous and more like a Mobius strip.[49] Abe himself gives some hint to the underlying theme of *Kemonotachi wa kokyō o mezasu* by naming his protagonist Kuki Kyūzō, a play on the name of the philosopher Kuki Shūzō (九鬼周造), perhaps intended to invoke, with irony, the themes of authenticity, pluralism, and ties to the soil.[50]

In *Kemonotachi wa kokyō o mezasu*, Abe represented many of these dilemmas literally. Kyūzō lives the problems outlined by Saunders. First, he has lost his identity and is alienated from everyone around him. In urban Shenyang, he is physically near the Japanese compound but unable to find it by himself. When a Chinese youth offers to take him to "the place where the Japanese people are," Kyūzō wonders how it could be so simple, but when he arrives, the Japanese there reject him and he remains isolated. The premise of the book is an inversion of roles: a member of the formerly dominant nationality, Kyūzō is dependent on the Korean Kō for survival. The ambiguity of hunter and hunted appear when Kyūzō and Kō, starving and frozen on the Manchurian plains, encounter some wild dogs, also starving and frozen. The youths and the dogs assess each other as predator and prey.

---

47. Saunders, "Abe Kōbō."

48. Currie, "Metaphors of Alienation." A third scholar focuses on the fantastic in Abe's early work: Krieger, "The Fantastic Stories of Abe Kōbō."

49. Kawamura, *Ikyō no Shōwa bungaku*, 210.

50. Kuki Shūzō (1888-1941) is most notable as the author of *Iki no kōzō* (The Structure of *Iki*, 1930).

Kyūzō's inability to communicate with the Russians, Chinese, and Koreans around him renders him helpless and dependent on Kō. Maps play a key role. He steals one from his Russian benefactors, hoping in vain that it will show him the way home. As if to drive home the importance of maps, the original publication featured a hand-drawn map that accompanied the text. In *Kemonotachi wa kokyō o mezasu*, Kyūzō, a helpless foreigner in Manchuria, lives the alienation, isolation, and role inversion that appear in abstract forms in Abe's later works.[51] For Kyūzō, like Abe's other protagonists, home is always someplace else.

Some themes in *Kemonotachi wa kokyō o mezasu* resonate with those in other repatriate-related fiction. First, Kyūzō has problems maintaining his identity. The Soviets give him identity papers, but when he tries to use them, people ridicule him for his naïve belief that the papers, like maps, are meaningful. Later, after he has lost his papers, the Japanese community in Manchuria refuses to engage him because he cannot prove who he is. They do not doubt that he is Japanese, but because he does not have documentation, they find it easy to dismiss him. In the chaos of Manchuria in 1948, rejected by the remnants of the Japanese authorities and without papers, he has become a stateless person, a *musekisha*. Kyūzō loses his identity in another realm as well—it is stolen by the Korean Kō who uses it in his attempt to go to Japan. Kyūzō's inability to document his identity and the ease with which Kō steals it both go to show the precariousness of linking identity to a political state with mapped boundaries, both of which can dissolve.

Kyūzō's isolation from all of the other Japanese people around him is striking, given the social nature of Japanese communities, especially those abroad. His father died soon after he was born, and his mother and

---

51. Kawamura Minato suggests that Abe's repatriate experience is the foundation of much of his later work (*Ikyō no Shōwa bungaku*, 206, 209–17). Through an analysis of a different set of novels, Kawamura argues that a "repatriate spirit" (*hikiagesha seishin* 引揚者精神), which above all else prizes individuality, is manifested in "repatriate literature." This is a product of people who were children in Manchuria at the time of repatriation. They were discarded by the state and forced to leave the "foreign country" of their communities in Manchuria for their "hometowns" in Japan, when in fact Manchuria was home and Japan the foreign country. These experiences, he argues, created a class of artists who have a profoundly different understanding of the state, race, humanity, and the world.

he lived together in Harbin, where she managed a dormitory for Japanese workers. Just after the Soviet invasion, their community prepared to evacuate. But a random bullet struck Kyūzō's mother. The rest of the group continued with the evacuation, taking all of Kyūzō's money for safekeeping, while Kyūzō stayed behind to tend his dying mother. It is unclear who shot Kyūzō's mother, and in the linguistic confusion (in one of the darkly comic episodes of the book), the occupying Soviet soldiers hear that she was killed by unspecified fascists. In their worldview, any child orphaned by fascists deserved sympathy, which they express by making him into a kind of errand boy and providing for his care. After his flight from Harbin and arrival in Shenyang, Kyūzō finds Japanese people there, but after his separation from his Japanese community in Harbin, he is never reintegrated into one again. Kyūzō remains alone.

The Japanese-speaking Korean Kō Sekitō is a key figure in *Kemonotachi wa kokyō o mezasu*. Other works of fiction set in postwar Manchuria feature Japanese-speaking Koreans as well. In *Ningen no jōken* two versions of Japanese-speaking Koreans appear. The first is an evil purveyor of Chinese slave labor, and the second is a benign family who chat with Kaji on their way home. In *Daichi no ko*, discussed below, a Japanese-speaking Korean working for the Chinese People's Liberation Army threatens to expose the Japanese protagonist, who has been passing as Chinese, which would lead to certain death. The exposure does not occur, and the hero survives, but the threat posed by a Japanese-speaking Korean to a Japanese youth propels the plot forward. In *Kemonotachi wa kokyō o mezasu*, in an inversion of their colonial roles, Kyūzō finds himself dependent on Kō. In postwar literary treatments of repatriation, Koreans become a source of anxiety: a colonial creation that comes back to haunt Japanese in postwar Manchuria. Because *Kemonotachi wa kokyō o mezasu* ends with all of the characters in limbo, with uncertain identities, it highlights the ambiguous legacies of the colonial project. In the novel, at least, there is no resolution to the confusion.

Yet another work related to repatriation appeared in 1957: director Gosho Heinosuke's *Kiiroi karasu (The Yellow Crow)*.[52] The film opens with elementary school students practicing their drawing by sketching the Great Buddha in Kamakura, who looms above them. Nine-year-old

---

52. In 1958, *Kiiroi karasu* won a Golden Globe Award for best foreign film.

Kiyoshi has insisted on coloring his drawing yellow and black. Later, his teacher consults a male colleague with her concerns about Kiyoshi and his drawing. Formerly a well-adjusted boy, he had recently grown troubled and unruly. Her colleague authoritatively informs her that according to the latest psychological literature, war orphans and children from broken homes tend to color their drawings yellow and black. Kiyoshi's teacher responds brightly by telling him that Kiyoshi's family is intact—as a matter of fact, his father had been repatriated from China just the year before. "Ah," replied the male teacher with a knowing sigh. "A repatriate."[53]

In a series of flashbacks, the film tells of the father's return to Japan. Kiyoshi and his mother travel to Maizuru to welcome home the father Kiyoshi has never met. The father's prewar employer reluctantly hires him back, but in his long absence, the younger men have risen above him and treat him with condescension. He alienates his son, whom he has replaced in the bed that Kiyoshi had shared with his mother. The plot builds to a crisis in which the father chases Kiyoshi's pet crow away. Kiyoshi then draws the crow, in yellow and black.

After the crisis, Kiyoshi turns to a neighbor, a kindly war widow who already cares for one orphan. He asks her to take him in as well. His mother overhears the conversation and is heartbroken. The widow then delivers the message of the film: Kiyoshi's mother and father have been selfish in focusing on themselves instead of the boy who, after all, has been orphaned by the return of his father. Kiyoshi's mother confronts her husband and they resolve to live as a family, which they do, happily ever after.

A relatively straightforward drama, *Kiiroi karasu* reveals that the line "Ah, a repatriate," uttered near the beginning of the film, could serve to foreshadow for viewers the troublesome figure about to appear: a poorly socialized "argumentative" type, disruptive to society and home. Ultimately the family, with the help of the wise neighbor, is able to reintegrate "the repatriate," but only after his return stresses the family to the breaking point. Only through devotion and resilience, the film seems to say, will families be able to reincorporate their repatriated members.

---

53. "Aa, hikiagesha desu ka" (ああ、引揚者ですか).

Repatriates continued to appear in films and novels. In the 1963 film *Kanojo to kare*, the superficially ordinary housewife Naoko brings conflict into her marriage by caring for a homeless rag-picker, his dog, and an orphan. Naoko dresses, shops, and keeps house like the other housewives, but at the beginning of the film viewers learn from two middle-aged neighborhood women, gossiping with each other, that Naoko is a Manchurian repatriate. The women replicate the familiar pattern of expressing both sympathy ("she must have had a terrible time of it") and stigmatization. Naoko's repatriate past appears a second and final time in a conversation with the rag picker. She slips into a reverie, saying that as a child she walked for hundreds of miles in Manchuria before repatriation.

Kanojo to kare is the story of Naoko and her husband Ei'ichi and their lives in a new middle-class housing project (*danchi*). Midway through the film, Naoko's husband Ei'ichi declares that he is satisfied with *danchi* life. Towards the end, as Naoko becomes increasingly involved with the homeless family, the loving but exasperated Ei'ichi exclaims that he is just a regular person (*futsū no ningen da*) who wants a regular home (*futsū no katei*). This is, perhaps, in contrast to Naoko. Her experiences as a repatriate do not figure into the film, but she needed to be somehow different from her peers. Other tropes for difference in Japanese popular culture include foreigners, non-human characters, people changed by an experience (such as atomic bomb victims), and historical domestic minorities (such as *burakumin*). Sometimes being from Hokkaido or Okinawa is enough. In this case, the plot requires an internal other, someone Japanese enough to be married to an ordinary businessman and living in an ordinary neighborhood, but different enough to cause problems. Eighteen years after the end of the war, repatriates could still function as a domestic other, at least in fiction.

In 1971, another film was released that depicted Manchurian repatriates. Ōshima Nagisa's *Gishiki* is the story of Masuo, whose name is written with the characters "man of Manchuria" (満洲男). The film is structured around five gatherings of the Sakurada clan: a memorial service for Masuo's father in 1947; the funeral for Masuo's mother in 1952; the wedding of Masuo's uncle Isamu in 1956; Masuo's pointless wedding in 1961 (the bride has fled but the patriarch insists that Masuo go through the wedding by himself); and the funeral of the patriarch in 1970. Each of the ceremonies is entangled with important moments in the political and economic history of postwar Japan: the first anniversary in 1947 of the day that the emperor renounced his divinity; the end of the Occupation in 1952 and the patriarch's return to the public world after having been purged; the beginning of the "1955 system" of conservative LDP rule (in 1956); the revision of the U.S.-Japan Security Treaty in 1960; and preparations for the reversion of Okinawa in the early 1970s. By staging each ceremony at an important moment in postwar Japanese history, Ōshima uses the film as a critique of postwar society, which, in his depiction, was filled with war criminals, incest, and farce.

The film is also about the return of the colonial Japanese and the difficulties they faced in trying to reintegrate into metropolitan society. The second scene depicts a Japanese woman and child, dressed in rags with their meager possessions strapped on their backs, fleeing through the fields from unknown assailants. It is the canonical image of Japanese on the run in postwar Manchuria. But the irony is that the two are in Japan, on family property, fleeing from their relatives. After eighteen months as refugees in postwar Manchuria, the fourteen-year-old Masuo and his mother have been repatriated just in time to disrupt the memorial service for Masuo's father, who committed suicide a year before, on the day that the emperor renounced his divinity.

The initial confrontation between the patriarch and his daughter-in-law, Masuo's mother, presents all of the stereotypes associated with Japanese women in Manchuria at the end of the war. The patriarch interrogates her, asking why she ran away. She explains that she did not want to be a burden on the family, and that Masuo and she would make it on their own, just the two of them. He berates her, reminding her that now that her husband is dead, Masuo is the only heir. The patriarch continues:

> "People say that the Russians are devils. Was that your experience?"
> "It was terrifying."
> "Your eyes look yellow. Did the Russians use you as a prostitute?"
> "There were women who had the misfortune of such a fate."
> "You, you, I'm asking you."
> "If that had been the case, I would not have made it home."

But Masuo's mother remains under suspicion and Masuo is forced to participate in her vilification.

"Tell us about the Russians!"
"They gave me some black bread."
"Did they give your mother anything?"
[Silence]
"Were you ever separated from her?"
[Silence]

Masuo's mother never fully recovers, and her funeral, five years later, provides the reason for the next family gathering. The patriarch declares that she had a pathetic existence. The nineteen-year-old Masuo protests feebly that she was happy in Manchuria.

In the film, the Sakurada family has a problem with incest, leading to confusion about identity. The patriarch has abused most of the women in his family and it is not entirely clear who fathered three of the four grandchildren. In the past, he assaulted his niece Setsuko and then disposed of her by sending her to Manchuria to marry a Chinese collaborator, and in this way the film presents Manchuria as the appropriate place to send sullied women and the place from which sullied women return. The question of Masuo's paternity comes up only once, when Uncle Isamu, a Communist Party member, openly asks the patriarch whether he is Masuo's true father. Deflecting the question as trivial, he uses the occasion to lambaste the Japan Communist Party and squelch all challenges to his power. More than the question of paternity, it is having been born, raised, and then repatriated from Manchuria that contributes to Masuo's struggle with his identity. In the opening scene the adult Masuo and his cousin Ritsuko discuss their relationship. Masuo loves her, but she insists on calling him "a relative" (*shinseki no hito*). He unconvincingly asserts himself, saying he has a real name, the "Man of Manchuria," born in Manchuria. Although he tries to distance himself from the Sakurada family, he is unable to craft an independent identity of his own.

In addition to the linking of women in Manchuria to sexual contamination, and confusion about identity, *Gishiki* addresses a third theme common in repatriation-related works: problems surrounding the delayed return of fathers from China or the Soviet Union. This is the premise of *Kiiroi karasu* and the second half of Yamasaki Toyoko's novel *The Barren Zone*, discussed below. In *Gishiki*, Masuo's Uncle Susumu is repatriated in time to attend the 1956 wedding of Uncle Isamu. The mute

Susumu is barely human. A third uncle cajoles him, telling him to forget about the Chinese prison, and instead invites him to join him in singing "China Night," a song popular during colonial times. His son Takashi confronts Susumu, but it is not until the next day, after Setsuko is found dead, pinned to a tree with a sword through her chest, that Susumu speaks to his son. He braces his foot against the chest of the white kimono of Setsuko's corpse, yanks out the sword and then offers it to his son. "Hold this," he says. By 1961, however, Susumu has been domesticated into a docile, middle-aged salary man. It is his son who has become radicalized into a right-wing nationalist.

Things began to look up somewhat for fictional repatriates in Yamasaki Toyoko's novel *The Barren Zone*. Based loosely on the life of Kwantung Army officer and postwar backroom politician Sejima Ryūzō, *The Barren Zone* follows the protagonist Iki from his self-sacrificing move at the end of the war in Manchuria, to captivity in a Soviet labor camp, and then to the Siberian prison camp at Magadan. He survives the frigid wasteland of Siberia only to confront the spiritual wasteland of postwar Japanese society. His faithful and stoic wife accepts his return gratefully, but his son is unable to reconcile the image of his dashing young father with the toothless shell of a man who returned.

Nevertheless, Iki fares better than the previous characters, Kaji of *Ningen no jōken*, Kyūzō of *Kemonotachi wa kokyō o mezasu*, and Masuo of *Gishiki*. In the first place, he makes it home. Second, his masculinity is intact, made whole by his wife. Although he looks like a homeless beggar among the well-dressed and well-fed businessmen of postwar Japan, the perceptive president of a major trading company recognizes Iki's traditional values and insists on hiring him. Iki tries to refuse—he knows nothing about modern society, especially the business world. But by the end of the novel, Iki is in America on business, fighting the new, good war, the economic war. Iki has been redeemed.

The 1970s brought no similar redemption for fictional female repatriates from Manchuria. In *The Barren Zone*, Iki, his wife Yoshiko, and a friend Marucho try to find a wife for their friend, another Siberian detainee named Kaminori Takashi.

Kaminori Takashi had lost his wife and children in the turmoil following the Russian invasion of Manchuria. His parents, too, were dead, and he lived alone in Tokyo, kept busy with his work at the Defense Agency. In the exchange of letters, Iki had been urging him to remarry. Earlier he had arranged a formal meeting between Kaminori and a widowed classmate.

Yoshiko placed a photograph on the tea table. It was a snapshot of a well-dressed woman in her late thirties, a bit plump, with well-rounded features, and a nice smile that did not quite hide the air of sadness.

"She was in Manchuria when the war ended," Yoshiko explained. "Her husband, called into service in the last stage of the war, was killed in combat. They had two children, but the older one died during the evacuation. She and her son, now fourteen years old, are living in Semba with her brother's family."

"What do you think?" Marucho asked. "I went down to the pharmacy during my lunch hour and had a chat with her. She's a quiet woman, doesn't say much. I gathered that she was given very rough treatment by those Russian soldiers during the evacuation of Manchuria. She said she'd be agreeable to marrying as long as her husband is a man who knew hardship in Siberia. His job is not important to her. She has only one condition—that he be willing to adopt her son."

Iki, Yoshiko, and Marucho looked thoughtfully at the snapshot. They knew that two lives—perhaps three—hung in the balance. The raping of Japanese women in Manchuria by the invading Russians had been reported in Japan. Such unfortunate women were condemned forever. And everyone in Japan knew about young women who had been mere children when the war ended, but who were shunned as prospective brides simply because they had lived in Manchuria during that dreadful time of Russian presence.

"People who saw what happened to our Japanese in Manchuria would sympathize with those unfortunate women," Iki said soberly, expressing their common thought. "But I'm afraid most Japanese would not be so understanding. . . ."

"Mr. Kaminori would surely be understanding," Yoshiko said. "He would have great compassion for a woman who was subjected to the kind of cruelty his wife and children may have suffered before they died."[54]

This passage states in explicit terms the nature of the stigma that women in Manchuria suffered. It also gave voice to a sentiment common in postwar Japan, that the appropriate mate for a female Manchurian repatriate was a male Siberian detainee. There were circumstances in postwar Japan that may have made such marriages attractive. In some cases, female Manchurian repatriates and male Siberian detainees had been

---

54. Yamasaki, *The Barren Zone*, 272–73.

married couples before the end of the war. But some of the women in postwar Manchuria did not survive, and an estimated 60,000 of the men in Soviet detention died before returning to Japan. Some of the detainees arrived in Japan to find their families intact, but many, like the men from Senzan, found themselves widowers. Some women, like the writer Fujiwara Tei, were reunited with their husbands, but others waited in vain. One filmmaker who made a documentary about repatriation from Manchuria said that he could not have done it without the spiritual and material support of his wife, also a repatriate from Manchuria.[55] But many people in these groups saw no particular link—female repatriates would not necessarily conclude that Siberian detainees made appropriate mates, just as Siberian detainees would not necessarily conclude that what they really needed was a repatriate wife. It was more often than not popular cultural sources, perhaps reflecting the sentiment in society at large, that liked to create marriages of detainees and repatriates.

Yamasaki Toyoko returned to the topic of the ramifications of the end of the colonies in the four-volume novel, *Daichi no ko*. Originally appearing as a serial from April 1988 to April 1989 in the magazine *Bungei shunjū*, it was one of the most sustained treatments of the remaking of a colonial identity. It is the story of Matsumoto Kazuo, who as a seven-year-old is separated from his family in a Manchurian agricultural settlement during the confusion at the end of the war. The leaders in a nearby Chinese village divvy up the farm animals that the Japanese left behind. Kazuo is distributed as a caretaker of some animals to an older, childless Chinese couple who make little distinction between the child and the animals. He escapes to a nearby city where a smuggler attempts to auction him off to the highest bidder. A kindly schoolteacher takes him in. The teacher gives Kazuo, who has forgotten his Japanese name, a new one: Lu Yishin (陸 一 心); literally, "one heart on the continent." The novel then traces his life through the Chinese Civil War, his education as an engineer, and his exposure as Japanese during the Cultural Revolution. During the 1990s, a Sino-Japanese effort released a film based on the novel.

Fictional repatriates have continued to appear in the 1990s. Set in Tokyo in 1984 and 1985, Murakami Haruki's novel *Nejimakidori kuroni-*

---

55. Kunihiro, *Korotō daikenhen.*

kuru (*The Wind-Up Bird Chronicle*), originally published in three volumes in 1994–95, tells the story of the urban and familial adventures of a young man, Okada Tōru. Tōru meets up with a man who served as a military operative in Mongolia and Manchuria during the war, which takes the plot back in time and over to Japan's former colonies in Korea and Manchuria. In one episode, Tōru encounters the fashion designer Akasaka Nutmeg, who tells him her story. She was born in Manchuria and repatriated to Japan as a child. Her father, a veterinarian, remained behind to carry out the grisly task of disposing of all of the animals in a Manchurian zoo and never returned to Japan. Taken in by relatives, Nutmeg and her mother live as charity cases. Nutmeg marries a man repatriated from Korea. In the passage quoted below, she explains that her husband and she were both "like some kind of animal" who had become separated from the herd:

"We were two of a kind," she said. "Both born on the continent. He had also been shipped back after the war, in his case from Korea, stripped of possessions. His father had been a professional soldier, and they experienced serious poverty in the postwar years. His mother had died of typhus when he was very small, and I suppose that's what led to his strong interest in women's clothing. He did have talent, but he had no idea how to deal with people. Here he was, a designer of women's clothing, but when he came into a woman's presence, he would turn red and act crazy. In other words, we were both strays who had become separated from the herd."

They married the following year, 1963.[56]

As in *The Barren Zone*, the appropriate mate for a repatriate appears to be another repatriate, and the two of them become successful designers, in part because they are social mavericks, less constrained by the rules of domestic Japanese society.

Conclusion

In his analysis of the depiction of children in postwar European war films, Pierre Sorlin suggests that films made from 1945 to 1960 rewrote

---

56. Murakami, *The Wind-Up Bird Chronicle*, 477. In Japanese, Murakami uses the phrase "like some kind of animal" (*dōbutsu no yō na mono* 動物のようなもの), translated by Jay Rubin as "strays."

certain aspects of the war in ways that showed that adults wanted to conceal the fact that society had not been able to care for its children: "Films contributed to camouflaging unbearable tensions; they substituted suffering for guilt and contributed, together with other media, to developing the legend of a generation conflict. This fable is one of the most worrying aspects of the postwar cinema. It could have been another subterfuge if we consider that the fear of children served to cover a lack of real care for youth during the hostilities."[57] Japanese cultural sources on repatriation are remarkable for their willingness not to camouflage but rather to explore conflict absent from official sources and the press. Most strikingly, cultural sources explore Japanese-on-Japanese violence.

Repatriates and non-repatriates alike negotiated the episode of repatriation through popular culture. Two women I interviewed both compared their ordeal to Fujiwara Tei's fictionalized memoir, *Nagareru hoshi wa ikiteiru* (Shooting stars live on).[58] One man located his Soviet detention camp by pointing out that his time there overlapped with Yoshida Tadashi, author of the song "Ikoku no oka." [59] Another went out of his way to say that he owned a copy of the film *Ganpeki no haha* (1976).[60] Non-repatriates volunteered songs and films as shorthand for the tragic aspects of the episode.

The processes of repatriation shaped many Japanese writers and artists, which in turn shaped cultural production in Japan. Repatriate characters in literature and film tend to embody both negative and positive associations, contributing to their sustained alterity across the postwar period. They are useful figures—Japanese enough to be found in almost every community but different enough to cause problems. Some repatriate-related works such as the songs "Kaeribune" and "Ikoku no

---

57. Sorlin, "Children as War Victims in Postwar European Cinema," 123–24. Robert Moeller explores the depiction of expellees and POWs in postwar German film, concluding that the films filled a void created by homelessness and were a way that many non-expellees and POWs learned about expulsion. "Heimat, Barbed Wire, and 'Papa's Kino': Expellees and POWs at the Movies," in Moeller, *War Stories*, 123–70.

58. Oral history interview, November 19, 2000; oral history interview, November 20, 2000.

59. Oral history interview, November 19, 2000.

60. Oral history interview, May 31, 2000.

oka" and became hits because of their universal themes of longing for home, but other works used repatriates as internal others, and ran with the tropes of female Manchurian repatriates as contaminated and male Siberian detainees as the source of social problems. Other questions included confusion about identity, the difficulties surrounding delayed repatriation, and the issue of the unrepatriated. One nearly universal theme in popular cultural depictions of repatriation is the cool reception by the people of *naichi*. It is Masuo who delivered the line that most succinctly expresses the overarching sentiment of most popular cultural treatments of repatriates: "We managed to escape from the Russians, the Manchurians, and the Koreans without any problems. In the end, it was the Japanese who got us."[61]

61. Ōshima, *Gishiki*.

FIVE

No Longer Hikiagesha:
"Orphans and Women Left Behind in China"

Japanese nationals who remained in northeast China after the war all had compelling stories of their postwar lives, many of which have come to light through newspaper coverage, memoirs, and academic research.[1] Reporters at the Osaka branch of the *Yomiuri shinbun* followed a few cases in depth, and in 1985, the authors published a short book called *Chūgoku koji* (Chinese orphans), a distillation of their newspaper coverage.[2] The story of Yamamoto Tokuko, her daughter Ōkubo Setsuko (Chinese name Dou Lixin 窦立新; Toku Risshin in Japanese), and the Chinese foster parents who raised her creates a space to imagine the kinds of choices that women with children in postwar Manchuria faced and how those circumstances led to the problem of "orphans and women left behind in China" (*Chūgoku zanryū koji fujin mondai* 中国残留

---

1. In his 1999 dissertation, Gregory Guelcher tells several moving stories of young Japanese women who remained behind in China, often as a means of survival for themselves or their children. Guelcher, "Dreams of Empire." In his 2004 dissertation, Robert Efird profiled several "orphans" and their descendents in Japan. Efird, "Japanese War Orphans and New Overseas Chinese." Ōkubo Maki tells the story of Ikeda Sumie, born just before the end of the war in Manchuria and raised by a loving Chinese foster mother. Ōkubo, *Chūgoku zanryū Nihonjin*.

2. Yomiuri shinbunsha Ōsaka shakaibu, ed., *Chūgoku koji*. The following account is adapted from this book and appears here by permission of Yomiuri shibunsha.

孤児婦人問題). The following account is a condensed version of how Tokuko presented her story to the journalists.[3]

In 1939, the fourteen-year-old Yamamoto Tokuko went to Manchuria with an older sister and worked in a Japanese department store. She was one of twelve children from a poor farming family in Miyagi Prefecture in northeast Japan. Because of a romantic affair deemed inappropriate by the family of the man involved, her sister was sent back to Japan, but Tokuko stayed on by herself, working and living with friends. Toward the end of the war, she fell in love with a recently widowed Japanese man. Japan was in the last throes of the conflict, but Tokuko and her lover remained oblivious, thinking only of when they could marry. When the war ended, Tokuko and her friends were surprised. "Japan lost?" was their response to the emperor's radio broadcast on August 15. Subsequently, communications in Dalian broke down and she could not get in touch with her lover. This was a problem for her because she was six months pregnant.

Dalian became chaotic, with violence on the part of the first wave of undisciplined Russian soldiers, and no way for people to earn a living other than selling their belongings on the street. Tokuko's landlords, friends from whom she rented a room, took care of her, and in December 1945, she gave birth to Setsuko, the name an allusion to the actress Hara Setsuko. She was thrilled to have the baby.

The Russian prisoner troops were withdrawn and returned to Dalian. But then the regular Russian occupation troops came and turned the Japanese out of their homes. Moreover, groups of refugees—Japanese from the settlements—poured into Dalian, with nothing to eat and nowhere to live. Tokuko could not stay and remain a burden to her friends. After all, they had nothing to eat either. With the infant Setsuko, she lodged when possible with acquaintances and begged for food from the local Chiense. Setsuko suffered from hunger because Tokuko did not have enough milk to nurse her. Moreover, Setsuko was dirty: she had not been bathed since she was born. Tokuko had scabies and itched all over. Because of the misery in which Setsuko

---

3. Ibid., 116–61. The book refers to her by her given name "Tokuko" instead of her family name "Yamamoto." I preserve that convention here.

lived, Tokuko wondered whether it would have been kinder to abort her or kill her just after she was born.

A year passed, and Tokuko faced the second winter (1946–47) since defeat. Dalian was frigid in the winter, and Tokuko owned only a summer kimono and slept in unheated rooms. It was under these circumstances that Setsuko had her first birthday, in December 1946. In January 1947, Setsuko's left ear became infected and she cried all the time. When Tokuko put a pin into the boil, a combination of blood and pus oozed out, and left a gaping wound. Tokuko lost strength to care for the baby and began to neglect her, living in a daze of indecision. On January 10, 1947, she went to a Chinese neighborhood to beg for food. A Chinese woman who answered the door responded that the Japanese had brought only woe to China and that she did not care whether Tokuko died, but that as a baby, Setsuko was not guilty and Tokuko should give her the opportunity to live. She knew some people who wanted a child. As instructed, Tokuko went to a particular train station on the following day and handed Setsuko over to a middleman.

A few days later, a friend of Tokuko's stopped by to tell her that work was available at a nearby dance hall. Tokuko took a job dancing with the Chinese and Korean customers for tips. She had not seen white rice for nearly two years, but at the dance hall she was able to eat it again. She saved her money, and in the summer of 1947, she contacted the middleman and went to reclaim, or even buy back, Setsuko.

The middleman took her to Setsuko's new home. Dressed in bright red baby clothes, Setsuko was almost too fat to recognize. Her Chinese foster mother understood Tokuko's intent and regarded her with wariness and loathing. Ignoring the looks of Setsuko's foster mother, Tokuko called to her daughter. The child recoiled, and clung to her Chinese mother. Stunned, Tokuko left.

Rumors circulated that the Japanese would be repatriated, but Tokuko had no intention of leaving Setsuko. One night, in February 1948, the Chinese authorities raided the dance hall and sent the Japanese they found there to an internment camp. Tokuko believed that the reason for the sudden internment was that dance halls went against the spirit, suffusing Dalian at the time, of building a communist society. At the camp, Chinese authorities forced the prisoners to labor as weavers and fed them only corn. Six months later, they were deported to Japan. On

August 19, 1948, on the ship the *Takasago Maru,* Tokuko arrived in Maizuru, Japan.

A telegraph from her father greeted her at the repatriation camp. The names of people arriving on repatriate ships were broadcast on the radio, and Tokuko's parents, who listened faithfully, heard that she would soon reach Japan. The telegraph said, "Bring your child and come home." Before the end of the war, Tokuko had written to her family saying that she planned to marry and was pregnant, but had not written since. She took a train home, where her family greeted her warmly with a special meal of *sekihan* (rice with red beans, served at celebrations). No one asked about the child, and Tokuko never said anything about her. Tokuko went to work, first in an office and then in a number of taverns, but grieved all the while for the daughter she had left behind.

Tokuko married a man who was sympathetic to her history. When Japan and China reestablished diplomatic relations in 1972, Tokuko and her husband went to the Ministry of Health and Welfare and asked them to look for Setsuko. The MHW replied that there was no way to find her with the scanty information Tokuko provided. Tokuko admits that they were probably right, but that it seemed like a cold response. Tokuko and her husband persisted—the MHW had received letters from people in China, asking them to look for their parents, but it did not appear that a letter from Setsuko was among them.

Five years passed. Tokuko then learned of the Te o tsunagu kai (Let's Join Hands Society), an organization devoted to reuniting Japanese left behind in China with their family members in Japan. It was led by Yamamoto Jishō, a former military officer in the Kwantung Army in Manchuria and then a central figure in the civilian attempt to reunite orphans and their families. He had become a priest after the war and devoted his life to searching for his daughter left behind in Manchuria. He then began helping others to search for their lost relatives.[4] In response to Tokuko's inquiry, Yamamoto answered with a long and sympathetic letter, explaining that although he had hundreds of letters from people from China, none of them appeared to be from her daughter. Never-

---

4. Yamamoto's efforts to match possibly Japanese people in China to relatives in Japan was chronicled in the documentary *Saikai,* broadcast on NHK on September 9, 1980. NHK, *Saikai* (video recording); Yamamoto and Hara, *Saikai.*

theless, his organization continued to look for people, and if Tokuko could be patient, he would look for her daughter on their next trip to China. At about this time, in 1981, the MHW sponsored its first group of orphans brought to Japan to look for relatives. Tokuko watched the news coverage intently, hoping in vain to see her daughter.

Yamamoto invited Tokuko to go to Dalian with his organization. At first she refused—she had gone to a fortuneteller who had told her that her daughter was dead—but her husband encouraged her to go. In April 1981, she arrived in Dalian. The place where she had worked as a dancer, the tree-lined streets, and the Dalian train station all remained and were very nostalgic for her. Accompanied by a member of the Chinese Public Security Office and two "orphans" who lived in Dalian, Tokuko drove around looking for the house of Setsuko's foster parents. Her Chinese guides asked elderly people in the neighborhood if they remembered a family in the area taking in a Japanese baby girl just after the end of the war, but with such limited information their search came to naught. Disappointed, Tokuko returned to the hotel. Members of the Te o tsunagu kai tried to comfort her. Yamamoto explained that he had been looking for his daughter for 35 years and Tokuko should be patient and look for one more day—but she lost hope.

Early the next morning, a knock came at the door. One of the Chinese assistants, Mr. Zhang, announced that they had found someone who appeared to be her daughter. That afternoon Tokuko went to the Public Security Office and sat at a table. The officials placed the photograph of a two- or three-year-old girl in front of her. Tokuko said, "That's her!" The translator asked how she could know, from a single photograph of a toddler. "Because that's her!" she replied. The officials displayed a series of photographs of Setsuko, growing older. Tokuko looked at them and wept.

A few minutes later, the officials ushered in a sturdy, dark-skinned woman, wearing the usual people's uniform of China at the time. Tokuko, who was small and light-skinned, remarked, "She's very dark." The translator explained that she was a physical education teacher and spent a lot of time outdoors. The dark-skinned woman rolled back her sleeve, revealing that the skin underneath was pale. Tokuko approached her and looked behind her ear, and there it was: the scar left by her infection as an infant, a wound her Chinese foster mother had worked hard to heal.[5] She knew it was Setsuko. At that point, a child of about eight or nine appeared. Setsuko indicated that she was her daughter, and smiling, the child approached Tokuko. Tokuko had a granddaughter. Setsuko embraced Tokuko, and they both wept, with Setsuko calling her "Mama." Tokuko noticed that all of the officials in the room were weeping as well.

Tokuko learned that Setsuko's foster parents had treasured her and raised her as their own. She met the foster parents again while in Dalian and they treated her courteously. Setsuko harbored no bitterness towards her biological mother and negotiated the reality of her two mothers with grace. Tokuko returned to Japan and through letters the two established a relationship. Eventually Setsuko and her daughter went to Japan.

This vignette captures many of the complexities of the case of women and children left behind in China. Tokuko's story illuminates many of the obstacles and hardships faced by colonial Japanese in postwar Manchuria. It complicates the idea that women abandoned their children in order to save themselves—an unspoken assumption that sometimes contributed to the stigmatization of women from Manchuria. It highlights some of the compelling reasons people did not want to be repatriated. Finally it shows many of the challenges in locating and identifying the orphans, and the sacrifices that their adoptive Chinese parents made, first in raising these children and then in losing them as adults to Japan.

Tokuko and Setsuko's story spans the years from 1945 and 1982, a time during which the procedures and interpretations of repatriation in postwar Japan had evolved. Efforts in the immediate postwar period were devoted to transporting people to Japan, processing them at regional repatriation centers, and sending them home. Then, the government provided other kinds of aid for the resettlement process, including emergency and long-term housing, employment assistance, two kinds of rehabilitation loans, and resettling people onto land as agri-

---

5. Scars, birthmarks, and other features inscribed on orphans' bodies were one of the primary means of identifying them 35 years after the war, and photo albums of these markings circulated among people seeking relatives.

cultural and dairy farmers.[6] By the late 1950s, with the end of organized repatriation from the PRC, the MHW and other bureaucracies turned their attention to bringing the issue of repatriation to an end. Government agencies and repatriate activists devoted their attention to addressing the ramifications of repatriation through compensation, historical narration, and commemoration. This chapter explores how the return of "orphans and women left behind in China" thwarted domestic efforts to bring the issue of repatriation to an end. It shows that ultimately, it was the "orphans" who revealed that the social usefulness of the figure of *hikiagesha* had run its course.

The Movement for Compensation and the Domestication of Repatriation

With the exception of 1,000 yen per person and the baggage they could carry, Japanese people repatriated from overseas were forced to leave all of their other possessions behind. Those assets ranged from personal belongings such as clothing and family photographs to farm equipment, homes, and businesses. From the moment they arrived back in Japan, repatriates joined together to lobby the government to compensate them for their material losses. During the first few years after the war, in a program jointly supported by SCAP and the Japanese government, repatriates were required to register their belongings abroad. The local repatriate papers were filled with notices encouraging people to record their lost property within a month of their return to Japan. In the beginning, the government showed some interest in keeping a record of overseas Japanese assets, but because of the postwar conditions in the former colonies, it became clear that it was not practical to assess or attempt to retrieve them.

Repatriates turned their efforts instead to securing compensation from the Japanese government, and, in 1957, the government passed the "Repatriate benefits allowance law" (Hikiagesha kyūfukin tō shikyū

---

6. According to the history of the Postwar Farming project, 210,000 families were successfully resettled onto farms and dairies in postwar Japan. Sengo kaitaku shi hensan iinkai, *Sengo kaitaku shi*, Kanketsuhen (vol. 3), *jobun*, ii. For a history of other kinds of aid provided to returnees, see Kōseishō engokyoku, *Hikiage to engo 30-nen no ayumi*, 135–36. Writers for *Chūō Kōron* and others argued that these efforts fell short. For example, "Rupo: hikiagete wa kita keredo."

hō). It provided a one-time payment of a "benefit," with the highest amount equal to an urban family's monthly expenditures, to people who met the definition of a repatriate as defined by the law.[7] During the first movement for government recognition of their losses, repatriates had sought "compensation" and the government wanted to offer a "solatium"; ultimately, the law's use of the ambiguous wording of "benefit" served as a compromise.[8] But even the word "benefit" could not conceal the welfare nature of the payments, administered by the MHW and provided only to low-income returnees who had found it difficult to rebuild their postwar lives.[9]

Dissatisfied with the amount and characterization of the first round of payments, activists in the repatriate advocacy group Zenren began to pressure the government for more substantial compensation.[10] In 1967, this movement resulted in a more comprehensive compensation package, administered by the Prime Minister's Office, and cast in language that acknowledged the hardship repatriates faced at the end of the war and the service they had provided to the state.[11] The political scientist John Campbell and the historian James Orr have analyzed the repatriation compensation movement and found in it fertile ground for interpretation. In an exploration of how political interest groups exercise influence, Campbell traces the history of Zenren's efforts in the compensation movement. He explains how repatriate advocates used "advisory councils" (*shingikai*) and other political organizations effectively to advance their cause and wielded their putative voting power to cultivate supporters among rank-and-file politicians in the Liberal Democratic Party (LDP), who then pressured LDP leadership to address the demands of the repatriates. He also shows in fascinating detail how repre-

---

7. Campbell, "Compensation for Repatriates," 107*n*8. According to Campbell, "the maximum grant approximates average monthly expenditures for an urban worker's household in 1957."

8. Campbell, "Compensation for Repatriates," 107.

9. Naikaku sōri daijin kanbō kanrishitsu, *Zaigai zaisan mondai no shori kiroku*, 14–15.

10. The full name of the Zenren is Hikiagesha dantai zenkoku rengōkai (引揚者団体全国連合会; National Federation of Repatriate Groups).

11. "Repatriate Special Subsidy Allowance Law." "Hikiagesha tō ni taisuru tokubetsu kōfukin no shikyū ni kansuru hō" (Repatriate special subsidy allowance law). Campbell translates the title as "Law concerning payments of a special grant-in-aid to repatriates."

sentatives of the opposing sides of the issue—repatriates and the Ministry of Finance—were able to reach a compromise on the amount of the award, ultimately ¥192.5 billion ($535 million at the rate of ¥360 to $1), nearly four times the amount of the original award of ¥50 billion ($140 million).[12] Campbell concludes by showing that Zenren was successful because it was able to project the sense that it controlled votes, although its claims were probably exaggerated.

James Orr analyzes the repatriate compensation movement in the context of compensation efforts by repatriates, atomic bomb victims (*hibakusha*), and landowners whose property was confiscated and redistributed by the Occupation authorities at the end of the war. As Orr explains, one obstacle that these groups faced was the requirement to demonstrate that their claims for state compensation were special and went beyond welfare needs.[13] After all, most people in Japan could claim to have been victimized by state policy during the war—why should the postwar government compensate some people who suffered and not others? Orr shows how they sought and achieved a new kind of recognition from the state, concluding that "these special interest groups manipulated the mythology surrounding war victimhood and the emerging pride in postwar national prosperity in order to construct their experiences as heroic victimhood."[14] He also points out that with the second round of compensation, repatriates' experiences were "incorporated into the national heritage." The liberal media was critical of the government's compensation of repatriates, "but the compensation bill certainly helped validate and legitimize repatriate belief that it indeed was national history."[15] His work shows that the compensation movement brought the issue of the overseas Japanese into the national realm, or at least into the realm of the Prime Minister's Office, by placing repatriates side by side with other "domestic" victims of the war.

Returnees expressed mixed feelings about the compensation efforts. One oral history informant said that he had received the benefit, but dismissed it as "pocket change" (*okozukai*). After a pause, he modified

---

12. Campbell, "Compensation for Repatriates," 103, 112–23.
13. Orr, *The Victim as Hero*, 140.
14. Ibid., 141.
15. Ibid., 168.

his response, saying it did help out with his children's school expenses.[16] A second informant responded to the topic with exasperation. She had filled out the lengthy application for the first round of compensation—repatriates often complained that any repatriate-related process required pages of complicated forms and documentation—only to find that her husband's relative wealth as reported on his income tax returns prevented her from receiving the benefit. After that, she threw her repatriate identification papers away.[17] A third person, nicknamed Gandhi by the surviving members of his Manchurian Youth Corps Brigade, told of going to Manchuria in 1941 as a sixteen-year-old boy, suffering through the winters and preparing the land for the arrival of Japanese agricultural settlers.[18] After three years of service, at the moment when he was eligible to claim his own piece of land, he acknowledged the moral bankruptcy of the project of taking land from the local people. Fortunately, as he put it, he contracted tuberculosis in the winter of 1944–45, and by March 1945 was back in Japan where he was when the war ended. The benefits law acknowledged colonial Japanese like this man who lived abroad but happened to be in Japan when the war ended, so he was eligible for compensation. When asked whether he applied, he said that he felt so guilty about his role in colonialism that he never did. When it was suggested that this was his way of protesting against the state, he insisted that he had no argument with the government—it had paid for his way to Manchuria and brought him back when he was sick. He just did not want to be compensated for his participation in what he came to see as an exploitative venture.

In terms of understanding repatriation in the context of postwar history, the compensation movement is important for several reasons. Responsibility for compensating the repatriates moved from the MHW to the Prime Minister's Office.[19] This moved the issue of recognizing repatriate hardship away from the bureaucracy that ministered to welfare cases and into an office that addressed political issues and answered to

---

16. Oral history interview, May 31, 2000.

17. Oral history interview, February 14, 2000.

18. Oral history interview, May 30, 2000.

19. Campbell pinpoints this transition to the establishment of a small research section (*chōsashitsu* 調査室) in the Prime Minister's Office in March 1963. Campbell, "Compensation for Repatriates," 109.

constituents. In the mid-1960s, and again in the 1980s and beyond, the Prime Minister's Office worked first to compensate and then to commemorate repatriates as a valuable political constituency.

Writing the compensation laws required the government to define a legal category of repatriates eligible for benefits. Before the 1957 law, a *hikiagesha* was a person with a repatriation identification card. Once the law was passed, *hikiagesha* were defined as people repatriated to Japan after August 15, 1945, who maintained their fundamental livelihood overseas (*gaichi*) continuously for more than six months previous to that date (including people who went as settlers on the basis of the 1939 cabinet decision on the colonization of Manchuria who maintained their fundamental livelihood abroad for less than six months), who had no choice except to repatriate because of conditions produced by the end of the war, the orders of foreign authorities, and the loss of the means to earn a livelihood.[20] That definition included or was modified to include a few more categories of people, for example, people from Manchuria who came home after the Soviet attack (August 8) and before the end of the war (August 15), and bona fide overseas residents who happened to be in Japan when the war ended and therefore did not have repatriation identification papers. This legal definition shifted the focus to time spent abroad rather than completion of the repatriation process at home, but it still reflected the social image of a poor person repatriated from overseas who needed welfare support for rehabilitation. People who had established themselves economically in postwar Japan with a yearly income of more than ¥88,200 were excluded.[21]

The 1967 law offered a slightly different definition of repatriates. The income cap was lifted, meaning that to qualify for the payments, repatriates no longer had to be poor. People who had moved to the colonies before Japan's war on China in 1937, that is people who had committed to a life in the colonies before the war, were eligible for a ¥10,000 bonus. Members of the advisory council behind the second compensation package were persuaded by repatriate claims that their suffering was special, and that they had suffered in the service of the state and lost non-material assets, including community ties, social standing, and a

---

20. "Hikiagesha kyūfukin tō shikyū hō," Article II.
21. Orr, *The Victim as Hero*, 161.

sense of security.[22] Liberal critics in the media did not accept these arguments, but in the official realm, the depiction of the repatriate had turned a corner, from people who had been unable to put their lives back together in postwar Japan to people who had demonstrated a long-term commitment to living in the colonies in the service of the state. Arrayed with other victims of the war, repatriates had been domesticated, and, in the official realm at least, repatriates no longer served as foils to "ordinary" Japanese.

The 1967 compensation package did not resolve, once and for all, the repatriation issue, and it was not the last time the government devoted resources to the issue of commemorating repatriation. The government, or more specifically, the Prime Minister's Office, began to put efforts and funds towards commemorating the suffering of constituencies they believed had been overlooked. The trickle of people returning from the former colonies also interfered with efforts to dismantle the systems in place for receiving the overseas Japanese.

Historical Narration, Commemoration, and Bringing Repatriation to an End

Like the efforts to secure recognition from the government in the form of compensation, narration and commemoration of repatriation began a few years after the end of the war. Some of the actors involved were conscious from the beginning of the need to preserve documentation on the return of the overseas Japanese, as evidence for compensation claims and as potentially valuable source material for future scholars. In the afterword to his first volume on the history of repatriation from Korea, Morita Yoshio explains that in November 1945, the president of the Sewakai, Hozumi Shinrokurō, told him to gather for future reference as many materials as possible regarding the repatriation of Japanese from Korea.[23] Morita took this to heart and devoted himself to recording as much as possible about the process.

Documenting repatriation took place on the local, prefectural, and national levels. The regional repatriation centers kept records of their

---

22. Orr, *The Victim as Hero*, 163
23. Morita, *Chōsen shūsen no kiroku*, 1035.

activities and as early as 1947, began to publish them.[24] At least eight pre-
fectures published local histories of the end of the war. Shiga Prefecture's appeared in 1961, but five others appeared in a five-year period
between 1972 and 1976: Ibaragi (1972), Niigata (1972), Gunma (1974), Toyama (1975), and Nagasaki (1976). In 1982, Ishikawa Prefecture published
a slightly different kind of volume, the history of Manchurian settlers
from Ishikawa, with over half the book devoted to memoirs of settlers.
In the following year, Nagano Prefecture published a similar series.[25]
Histories published by Gunma and Toyama represented the trend to
write the history of World War II and aftermath in local terms and show
how extensively the prefectural government aided veterans, repatriates,
war widows, and orphans. They also mirrored a trend of emphasizing
Japan's peaceful and "cultural" present in contrast to its violent past.
The prefaces of both books proffer the following interpretation: the
war was terrible and many Japanese people suffered in the tragedy. Since
the end of the war, however, Japan has been prosperous and become "a
peaceful nation of culture" (*heiwa na bunka kokka*). It was now necessary
to document the history and commemorate the sacrifices of the war
dead in order to educate the nation's children and grandchildren in order
to prevent war from happening again.[26]

The MHW published wide-ranging histories of its efforts in aiding
civilians and soldiers from overseas at the end of the war. The first set
of histories, in three volumes published in 1950, 1955, and 1963, were
accounts of the MHW's role in repatriation and its handling of the men
repatriated from detention in the Soviet Union; over time, the MHW
histories evolved into lavish commemorative volumes including glossy
photographs of national mourning ceremonies.[27] All of the efforts were
meant to document the role of these agencies in the repatriation process,
but they also reveal an impulse to put the story in the past tense.

---

24. See Chapter 2, note 32 for information on the histories of the regional repatriation centers.

25. Takahashi, *"Senki mono" o yomu*, 87, 122.

26. The phrase "peaceful nation of culture" (*heiwa na bunka kokka*) appears on the first
pages of both prefaces in Gunma-ken kenmin seikatsubu sewaka, ed., *Gunma-ken fukuin
engoshi* and Toyama-ken kōseibu shakai fukushika, ed., *Toyama-ken shūsen shori shi.*

27. See Chapter 2, note 32 for information on the MHW histories.

Efforts to commemorate repatriation began on the local level soon after the war and have resulted in a sprinkling throughout the country of monuments, memorials, and museums devoted to repatriation. Maizuru, during the war home to an Imperial Navy base and now the site of a Marine Self-Defense Force base, hosts the most comprehensive repatriate memorial. The longest-lived regional repatriation center, Maizuru received repatriates from all over Asia for thirteen years, from 1945 to 1958. With the closure of the centers in Sasebo and Hakodate in 1950, the Maizuru facility processed almost all of the latecomers: Soviet detainees, people from the PRC who returned between 1953 and 1958, and people from Karafuto and Chishima. For these reasons, Maizuru became the place most closely linked with postwar repatriation.

The process of commemorating repatriation at Maizuru began with the establishment of a monument to repatriation in 1968, ten years after the closure of the Maizuru Regional Repatriation Center. In 1970, Kyoto Prefecture and the City of Maizuru established the Repatriate Memorial Park on a bluff overlooking the remains of the center. More monuments appeared, in 1970, 1978, and 1979, with the 1978 monument consisting of two marble slabs inscribed with the lyrics of the two most popular repatriation-related songs: "Ikoku no oka" and "Ganpeki no haha." On April 24, 1988, the city officials opened the Maizuru Repatriation Museum, the first museum dedicated to repatriation.[28] In 1995, the museum unveiled the carefully restored pier, the spot at which hundreds of thousands of people first set foot in Japan after the war, providing the opportunity for visitors to imagine (and for repatriates to re-experience) the return to Japan.[29] In the museum, visitors are invited to sign their names in the guest book. If relevant, a visitor may also stamp his or her name with a red seal that marks the entry with the words "a repatriate" (*hikiagesha gohonnin*) or "a repatriate's family member" (*hikiagesha gokazoku*), an act of labeling oneself and claiming a link to the history of repatriation. As of 1995, over a million people had visited the museum.[30]

Sasebo's regional repatriation center was second to Maizuru's in longevity, and local residents worked to commemorate the town's role in

---

28. Maizuru-shi, ed., *Hikiagekō Maizuru no kiroku*, 61–62.
29. Maizuru hikiage kinenkan, *Haha naru minato Maizuru*, 61–62.
30. Hashikaku, "Hōmon omoshirokan."

repatriation. In 1983, they organized a group, headed by the mayor of Sasebo, to raise a hundred million yen for the purpose of building their own park and museum. They held benefit events led by famous repatriates and solicited donations from around the country. On May 3, 1986, the Uragashira Repatriate Memorial Peace Museum in Sasebo was completed.[31] Like the Maizuru Repatriation Museum and Park, Sasebo's memorial is dotted with monuments, the most striking of which is the "Repatriate Statue." It features a man in a military uniform, a woman in cotton trousers (*monpei*), and a child carrying a small bundle. One of the man's arms is raised in a quasi-military salute and the other is gently draped around the child, suggesting, perhaps, both the military and civilian aspects of the problem. The woman appears to be searching for something and also pleading for help. Maizuru had laid claim to two of the most popular repatriate-related songs; Sasebo took the third, "Kaeribune," which in 1999 was inscribed in stone.[32] According to an undated flyer displayed at the museum, the facility had offered a repatriation boat tour of the harbor, another opportunity to relive the return to Japan.[33]

Whereas Maizuru remains most closely associated with repatriation, the port of Hakata holds the record for repatriating the largest number of people, estimated at 1,392,429.[34] Hakata also processed the largest number of deportees: 505,496 Koreans and Chinese passed through the Hakata Regional Repatriation Center at the end of the war.[35] In the 1990s, a number of people formed a group to work for the preservation of Hakata's history as the largest repatriation port. Led by former repatriate ship captain Itoyama Masuo and repatriate from Korea Morishita Akiko, the Hikiagekō Hakata o kangaeru tsudoi (引揚港・博多

---

31. "Sasebo-shi Uragashira hikiage kinen heiwa kōen."

32. Tabata and Seshi, "Sore ga tōi rekishi ni naru mae ni"; Ishikawa et al., eds., *Taishū bunka jiten*, 486.

33. The Uragashira Repatriate Memorial Peace Museum is located at the former quarantine station of the Sasebo Regional Repatriation Center because the grounds of the center proper were occupied by Huis ten Bosch, a manicured theme park and living facility based on an imagined seventeenth-century Dutch village. Huis Ten Bosch Resort and Theme Park, http://www.huistenbosch.co.jp [accessed August 15, 2008]; Kaminogō, "Tokushū 2: mō hitotsu no shūsen shori."

34. Kōseishō shakai engokyoku, *Engo 50-nen shi*, 147–58; Kōseishō engokyoku, *Hikiage to engo 30-nen no ayumi*, 32.

35. Hakata hikiage engokyoku (Kōseishō hikiage engoin), *Kyoku shi*, 12.

を考える集い; Think of Hakata as a repatriation harbor association) met for the first time in 1992. Joined by members of alumni associations of colonial schools in Korea and former officials, this citizens' group worked to find ways to commemorate Hakata's role in repatriation.[36] The association held lectures, screened repatriate-related videos, and attended a local high school play about repatriation. It began to gather materials and solicited autobiographical essays, which were published in two volumes, in 1995 and 1998.[37]

The main goal of the association was to establish a monument and a memorial archive for repatriation in Hakata. Although the archive has yet to be established, a striking monument to repatriation was completed in March 1996. Designed by sculptor Toyofuku Tomonori (who had trained with the *tokkōtai*, the special forces, at the end of the war), the monument is a striking abstract metal figure, red in color and eleven meters high, on a four-meter concrete base. It is located on a pier near the international ferry terminal.[38] Whereas the repatriation monuments in Maizuru and Sasebo are confined to the repatriation park, Hakata's monument is a dramatic piece of abstract art, integrated into a larger waterfront revitalization program. The cities of Senzaki in Yamaguchi Prefecture and Hakodate in Hokkaido have also commemorated their histories as repatriation ports.

The Prime Minister's Office joined efforts in commemorating repatriates, or more specifically, their hardship (*kurō* 苦労), with the establishment in 1988 of the Heiwa kinen jigyō tokubetsu kikin (平和祈念

---

36. Hikiagekō Hakata o kangaeru tsudoi, *Sengo 50-nen hikiage o omou: Ajia no yūkō to heiwa o motomete*, 220–27.

37. Hikiagekō Hakata o kangaeru tsudoi, *Sengo 50-nen hikiage o omou: Ajia no yūkō to heiwa o motomete* and Hikiagekō Hakata o kangaeru tsudoi, *Sengo 50-nen hikiage o omou (zoku): shōgen Futsuka'ichi hoyōjo*. The Hakata group became the object of criticism of another group, the Chikuhō yama no kai (筑豊ヤマの会), who argued that the Hakata group's use of historical terms such as Chōsen for Korea amounted to discrimination, indicating that the commemoration efforts and the historical interpretation that accompanied them were contested. "Kyū hyōki wa sabetsu ka: 'Yama no kai' no teisei shazai yōkyū," *Kokura taimusu*, August 7, 1995. Reprinted in Hikiagekō Hakata o kangaeru tsudoi, *Sengo 50-nen hikiage o omou: Ajia no yūkō to heiwa o motomete*, 250.

38. "Stardust: 'Hikiage' kara hanseki Hakatakō ni tōjō shita Toyofuku Tomonori no kinenhi," 123–24.

事業特別基金; Public Foundation for Peace and Consolation).[39] The generously funded foundation is devoted to recognizing three groups: repatriates, Siberian detainees, and veterans who had not served long enough to qualify for a military pension (*onkyū kekkaku sha* 恩給欠格者). The fund devoted resources to preserving oral testimony and publishing relevant materials on the experiences of these people. It established a program to recognize their hardship by offering a small payment, watches, and chalices to the Siberian detainees, and a certificate of recognition to qualified repatriates. The work of the Fund culminated in November 2000, with the opening of the Heiwa kinen tenji shiryōkan (平和祈念展示資料館; Commemorative Peace Museum) on the 48th floor of the Shinjuku Sumitomo Building in Tokyo. A portion of the floor was devoted to the administration of the foundation and the rest to a museum designed to commemorate the experiences, in three discrete sections, of the three groups. Opened just a year after Shōwakan, the Heiwa kinen tenji shiryōkan is the second national museum devoted to commemorating the suffering during the war. From the 1970s, people on the local level had worked to commemorate repatriation. With the establishment of the foundation in 1988, the work of repatriate commemoration reached the national stage.

Bureaucratic Efforts in Ending Repatriation

Bureaucrats at the MHW participated in these postwar efforts to compensate, narrate, and commemorate repatriates and their history. They administered the first compensation program and published administrative overviews. As the agency responsible for the processes of repatriation, they also worked in more empirical ways to bring the issue of repatriation to a close. With the end of organized repatriation from the PRC in 1958, they shut down the last regional repatriate center at Maizuru.

---

39. The fund began as an "authorized corporation" (*ninka hōjin* 認可法人) linked to the Prime Minister's Office, but because of government restructuring in 2003, the fund became an "incorporated administrative agency" (*dokuritsu gyōsei hōjin* 独立行政法人) with the prime minister remaining as its head. The museum opened in November 2000 and received its 300,000th visitor in December 2007 (Heiwa kinen jigyō tokubetsu kikin, 2008).

Another way the MHW tried to bring repatriation to an end was to pare down the lists of people still missing by changing their categorization from "unrepatriated" to "dead."[40] Declaring people dead was a structured process whereby bureaucrats solicited potentially interested family members and offered them an opportunity to go through the process of having their missing family member declared dead. Some families probably welcomed the chance to resolve, at least bureaucratically, the issue of missing family members, thirteen years after the war. Moreover, the government recognized the deaths of both missing military and civilians overseas as "state" deaths and offered a small solatium. The process was useful to the MHW, which, being a bureaucracy, was trying to manage, administratively, the issues of missing persons and death. In one of its reports, it noted that as of 1959, the list of "unrepatriated" contained 31,132 names, but by the end of 1963, the list of "unrepatriated" had been "rapidly reduced" to 6,145 names,[41] mainly through the process of the death declarations. When examined in the context of the bureaucracy's attempt to resolve the issue, and the possible benefits for families, the impulse to declare unrepatriated people dead does not seem farfetched. But some of the people who had been declared dead were still alive in China. As Robert Efird has shown, some later returnees were prevented from reclaiming their Japanese citizenship because they had been declared dead and purged from family registers.[42] Through various administrative and symbolic gestures, the MHW tried to bring the issue of repatriation to an end, but the presence of Japanese in China made it difficult to declare the repatriation process complete.

Orphaned by Empire

Government-sanctioned repatriation from China ended in 1958, but the establishment of diplomatic ties between Japan and the PRC in 1972 made it possible for Japanese nationals still in China to return to Japan.

---

40. The process of the death declarations was initiated in the late 1950s and expressed in a 1958 "Special Measures" law. Kōseishō engokyoku, *Hikiage to engo 30-nen no ayumi*, 232.

41. Ibid., 233.

42. Efird, "Japan's 'War Orphans,'" 374.

The first returnees in the early 1970s were people who were adults at the end of the war but for any number of reasons did not return to Japan by 1958. Most were women, but one oral history informant was a former military man who had been demobilized in China just before surrender and had made his life there.[43] He had wanted to return to Japan and did so when it became possible in 1972. By that time, he was 55 years old. He worked when possible, but in part because it was too late to qualify for a national pension, he ended up in public housing on welfare. Others who returned in the early 1970s were women and children whose Japanese families had never stopped looking for them and with the opening of official channels were able to bring them back. Returnees continued to be slotted into the previously constituted categories of "repatriate," in terms of receiving "repatriate allowances" upon return.[44] Because their families and communities took care of them, the returnees of the early 1970s presented relatively few problems to the government in caring for them.

From the early 1980s, the nature of the issue of returnees to Japan changed. The later returnees had been infants and children at the end of the war and had been raised in a Chinese environment. As noted by the MHW, they differed from Japanese people in terms of language, lifestyle, habit, and way of thinking. In all of those realms, the returnees had become Chinese.[45] Moreover, the orphans had married Chinese people and had children and grandchildren of their own. When they came to Japan, they wanted to bring their families with them. As the MHW explained, for the family members who accompanied the Japanese person to Japan, the word "return to one's country" (*kikoku* 帰国) was not accurate; in reality, they were attempting to move their families to a foreign country. The legal language finally caught up with reality with the 1994 passage of the "Kikokusha shien hō" (Support for returnees law), which removed the word "orphan" from the official designation of these peo-

---

43. Oral history interview, February 18, 2000. According to our conversation, because he had an ear for the Chinese language, he served the Japanese military as a spy. Leaving the military and living anonymously were ways to avoid Allied and Communist Chinese prosecution for war crimes.

44. Kōseishō engokyoku, *Hikiage to engo 30-nen no ayumi*, 118–19.

45. The phrasing is "Chūgokujin to natteiru" (中国人となっている). Kōseishō shakai engokyoku, *Engo 50-nen shi*, 426.

ple and called them instead "Japanese nationals left behind in China" (*Chūgoku zanryū hōjin* 中国残留邦人), and discussed their arrival in terms of a "permanent return" instead of repatriation.[46]

From 1981, the MHW began to work more actively for the people left behind in China. They coordinated at least 23 "relative-seeking" trips (*nikushin sagashi* 肉親探し; literally, "seeking the flesh of relatives"), in which they brought, at government expense, possibly Japanese people from China to look for relatives in Japan. They participated in the political processes with the Diet through advisory councils to try to solve the problems associated with the orphans. They held information sessions throughout China for people who were considering pursuing the process of being identified as an orphan and moving to Japan permanently. And they facilitated the establishment and operation of resettlement centers throughout Japan.[47] From 1972 until March 2000, 6,021 of the Japanese nationals left behind in China had returned to Japan. Counting the accompanying family members, the total number of people was 19,163. An estimated 700 Japanese nationals remained in China at that point.[48] Government accounts of the process describe the MHW playing an active role in bringing Japanese nationals and their families back to Japan to settle, and there were undoubtedly bureaucrats at the MHW who worked with devotion towards that end.

Nevertheless, critics were quick to point out a number of flaws in the MHW's response to the issue of the remaining colonial Japanese in China. Until 1994, returnees had to have a personal guarantor in order to resettle permanently in Japan. This had the impact of foisting the economic and social responsibility for the recent arrivals onto private citizens or organizations who served as guarantors. The government also developed a system of "identifying" the orphans. People in China who believed that they were Japanese were categorized as "identified" or "not identified." It was possible for a person to be recognized as Japanese but

---

46. The full name of the legislation is "Chūgoku zanryū hōjin tō no enkatsu na kikoku no sokushin oyobi eijū kikokugo no jiritsu no shien ni kansuru hōritsu" 中国残留邦人 等の円滑な帰国の促進及び永住帰国後の自立の支援に関する法律 (The law concerning promoting the smooth return of Japanese nationals left behind in China and supporting their independence after their permanent return).

47. Kōseishō shakai engokyoku, *Engo 50-nen shi*, 420–30.

48. "Chūgoku kikokusha shien ni kansuru kentōkai hōkokusho," 2–3.

still remain as "not identified." As Robert Efird has explained, the orphans were created by the practices of state memory, and being recognized by the government as Japanese was not enough to claim automatic Japanese citizenship:

> It is important to emphasize that official designation as a "war orphan" did not and still does not automatically include or confer Japanese citizenship. This has been true no matter how compelling the evidence of a person's Japanese background or birth. Without proof of parentage in the form of a blood test that unambiguously anchors an individual to a living Japanese relative and his or her family registration (*koseki-sho*), a central constituent of Japanese state memory, government officials will not "recognize" that individual as a Japanese citizen.[49]

Ultimately, the government processing of the later returnees revealed the reality that being born of Japanese citizens who were in Japanese colonies, often on government sponsored programs, was not enough to give a person an automatic claim on the right to Japanese citizenship. Ironically, perhaps, it also removed retroactively any doubt about the Japaneseness of earlier returnees: compared to the orphans, *hikiagesha* were clearly Japanese.

Conclusion

From the 1950s, public discussions on repatriation moved in the directions of compensation, historical narration, and commemoration. Through these acts, the agencies involved with repatriation attempted to put the episode in the past. Such attempts to declare the end of repatriation were thwarted, however, by the fact that thousands of Japanese nationals remained abroad in former colonial spaces. With the resumption of diplomatic ties with the PRC in 1972, some of the remaining Japanese were able to return home. By the 1980s, Japanese society saw the return of dramatically different overseas Japanese—people who had been raised in China and were culturally Chinese. This required changes in the language and system for receiving them. The historical context that had produced the *hikiagesha* and the orphans were the same, but the context to which they returned differed dramatically, and for that reason, they played different roles. Immediate postwar returnees arrived

---

49. Efird, "Japan's 'War Orphans,'" 374–75.

in a destitute Japan and served as a buffer between the metropolitan Japanese and the failed colonial project. Returnees in the 1980s found a country of extraordinary prosperity, which often informed their decision to move their families to Japan. The later returnees were slotted not into the past discourse of *hikiagesha* but into a new framework of foreign migrants. This was due, in part because of their apparent foreignness, but also because there was no longer a need to distinguish between postwar Japan and the colonies. The *hikiagesha* and the "orphans" were the products of the same history and even, in some cases, such as Toku-ko and Setsuko, of the same families. It was the new categorization of the orphans that showed that the usefulness of the *hikiagesha* had run its course.

Epilogue:
The Postwar History of Tsukada Asae

The schoolteacher Tsukada Asae survived her violent postwar year in Manchuria, motivated mainly by a sense of duty to shepherd her pupils back to Japan. She arrived, near death, in Japan in the fall of 1946. In her hospital bed, convinced that she was going to die, she wrote a report of the last days of the Senzan farming community because she was afraid that the men who had been drafted would return to Japan and never know what had happened to their families.[50] She was correct in her prediction that some of the men from Senzan would make it back to Japan: of the draftees, 64 ended up in Soviet detention, where 21 of them died. The remaining 43 were released from Soviet captivity and repatriated to Japan between 1946 and 1949 only to find that their families and community had been decimated.[51] Although these men perhaps felt a sense of loss and betrayal upon their return, thanks to Tsukada's records they at least had the option of knowing what had happened—unlike many other Soviet detainees whose families perished in Manchuria.

Tsukada survived and went back to her job as an elementary school teacher in her hometown in Nagano. For twenty years she devoted her-self to teaching, but upon retirement in 1965, at age 55, she poured her

---

50. Tsukada, "Haisen zengo no Senzan Sarashina gō kaitakudan hinan jōkyō kiroku."
51. Nagano-ken kaitaku jikōkai Manshū kaitaku shi kankōkai, ed., *Nagano-ken Manshū kaitaku shi*, vol. 3, 556.

energy into commemorating the Japanese agricultural settlers who had died in Manchuria. She wrote a letter to the local newspaper arguing for the need to mourn the settlers; a year later, Tsukada and approximately twenty members from Nagano visited the PRC, in the midst of the Cultural Revolution, to commemorate the Japanese dead and seek the living. Tsukada worked for the return of Japanese orphans left behind and arranged for at least one of the boys to return to Japan as an adult with his family.

Tsukada also came to think about her role in Japanese aggression abroad, and sought out the Chinese woman, known to her as Mrs. Zhang, who sheltered her during the winter of 1946. Tsukada sent modest compensation and gifts, and the two remained in contact. Although the people of Japan have been criticized for not addressing their history of war and empire, Tsukada, at the end of her life, acknowledged that she had been a perpetrator as well as a victim of the Japanese empire in Asia.

But mainly she mourned for the children who died. Twenty of her second-grade students were alive with her in the fall of 1945, but only two survived to make it back to Japan in the first years after the war. Tsukada's grief over the deaths of these children was pinned on one child, Hayashibe Rie, who died on the ship while waiting to land at the port city of Hakata.[52] Tsukada mourned this death by making an annual pilgrimage to Hakata from her home in Nagano. In the early twenty-first century, the journal is quite comfortable, with most of the trip on the Shinkansen. During the first decades after the war, it would have been arduous and expensive. In the postwar period, Tsukada was able to live out her childhood fantasy of travel, and went to remote places in the world, including Afghanistan. When I spoke to her in the fall of 2000, she admitted that five years previously she had stopped her annual trips to Hakata to mourn the child. When she turned 85, still blind in one eye and deaf in one ear, the trip became too taxing. But she kept a small doll on her mantle, one that she claimed resembled the child who had died, as a memorial to the girl. A few months after I spoke with her, at the age of 90, she died at her home in Nagano.

---

52. Shinonoi heiwa katsudō iinkai, "Kodomotachi ni ikasareta 85-nen."

CONCLUSION

Third Party Decolonization
and Post-Imperial Japan

One of the most compelling narratives in modern Japanese history is the story of late nineteenth-century leaders, sensing the need to secure Japan's diplomatic, economic, and social place in the Euro-American world order, who transformed Japan into a recognizable and powerful nation-state. These efforts were complicated by the need to embrace industrialization and negotiate the ideas of modernity. As Peter Duus and Robert Eskildsen have shown, one distinctive feature of this period is that ideas about imperial expansion were deeply intertwined with the process of building the nation-state.[1] This is not to argue for the uniqueness of the Japanese empire—it did have particularities, but in terms of how it functioned it was more similar than different when compared to contemporary national empires;[2] rather, it is to argue as

---

1. Duus, *The Abacus and the Sword*; Eskildsen, "Of Civilization and Savages." In his challenge to the idea of the so-called Taishō Democracy, Andrew Gordon also argues for recognizing imperialism as central, especially in the realm of labor history. He proposes "the notion of a trajectory from imperial bureaucracy to imperial democracy to fascism." Gordon, *Labor and Imperial Democracy in Prewar Japan*, 9. Louise Young illuminates the links between modernity and imperialism in *Japan's Total Empire*.

2. The first wave of English-language scholarship on the Japanese empire tended to emphasize its particularities compared to European empires: the perception that Japan colonized people of a similar race; that Japan colonized its geographical neighbors; and that it had a different economic constellation from other empires. Beasley, *Japanese Im-*

Eskildsen does that "mimetic imperialism helped shape national identity and the new political order in the Meiji period."[3]

The colonial project was terminated, not after domestic discussions, but by defeat in war followed by the arrival of a powerful third party in the form of the Allied militaries. That third party then provided the means, and sometimes the rationale, for undoing the ethnic mixing that had accompanied colonialism in East Asia. A look at how this third party decolonization played out, in Okinawa and compared to other post-imperial migrations, reveals some of the particularities of the end of Japan's empire.

Repatriation and Deportation in Okinawa

Okinawa's incorporation into the Meiji imperial order had an ambiguously colonial beginning, and, because the Americans cycled Okinawa through the processes of repatriation and deportation, its removal from that order was entangled with decolonization. The Meiji state had worked hard to incorporate, discursively at least, the Ryukyu archipelago and its people as part of the nation-state of Japan, "disposing" of Okinawa as a prefecture in 1879.[4] The people from the Ryukyus, however, suffered economic deprivation and social discrimination and came to occupy an ambiguous position between people of the Japanese home islands and the colonial subjects of Korea, Taiwan, and China. As Alan Christy has shown, intellectuals of the Meiji period argued that the Ryukyuans and Japanese had the same archaic origins and were therefore of the same racial group. In order to make sense of the riddle of the obvious differences between the lifestyles in Japan and those of the Ryukyus,

---

perialism 1894–1945; Myers and Peattie, eds., *The Japanese Colonial Empire, 1895–1945*. In terms of the processes of colonization—the cooptation of elites, intellectual and social struggles with subjugation or assimilation, and exploitation of others in defining the self—Japan's colonial practices have more in common with other empires of the same time. I agree with Leo Ching that, "at some level, we must acknowledge that most forms of modern colonialism share a certain generality—that is, the rule of force of a people by an external power. There might be historical and philosophical differences in the methods of colonization, but the fundamental structure of the relation between colonizer and colonized remains quite similar." Ching, *Becoming "Japanese,"* 19.

3. Eskildsen, "Of Civilization and Savages," 403.
4. Taira, "Troubled National Identity."

the Okinawans were cast as Japanese, but as backward ones, people who had fallen behind on the march to progress.[5]

During the war, Americans began to promote new ideas about the Ryukyus, its people, and their appropriate place in the world. As early as July 1943, American planners discussed a number of postwar possibilities, including transferring the Ryukyus to China, placing them under international administration, and giving conditional retention to Japan.[6] These possibilities surfaced several months later at the Allied Cairo Conference in November 1943. According to the historian Ōta Masahide, it is possible that the Allies considered the Ryukyus as part of the "territories which she has taken by violence and greed," which meant that Japan was to be expelled. Japan surrendered in 1945 by accepting the Potsdam Declaration, which read, in part, "the terms of the Cairo Declaration shall be carried out and Japanese sovereignty shall be limited to the islands of Honshu, Hokkaido, Kyushu, Shikoku and such minor islands as we determine." Here again, it was not clear where Okinawa stood in terms of the Cairo Declaration or whether it counted as "minor islands" that the Allies would determine, an ambiguity that was useful to the

---

5. Christy, "The Making of Imperial Subjects in Okinawa." Tessa Morris-Suzuki argues this point in terms of Ryukyuans being transformed from geographical others (barbarians) in the early modern period into temporal others (people "stranded in an earlier phase of historical evolution") in the modern period (Morris-Suzuki, "A Descent into the Past," 91). Michael Molasky's discussion of his uses of the terms "Ryukyu" and "Okinawa" is useful. "Ryukyu" refers to the geographical entity of the Ryukyu archipelago as a separate political and cultural entity before it was annexed by the Meiji government in 1879—as such, the term is preferred by Okinawan nationalists, anthropologists, and historical linguists. "Okinawa" is the name of the prefecture and its main island. Molasky makes a further distinction between Okinawa and Japan in 1945–52 and since 1972. In the earlier period, Okinawa and Japan were occupied by different administrative entities, and "Okinawa" referred to the Okinawan occupation; since 1972, with the reversion of Okinawa to Japan, "Okinawa" is paired with "mainland Japan" or "Japan's main islands." Molasky, *The American Occupation of Japan and Okinawa*, 3–4. Contemporary American sources, in line with their agenda to see the Okinawans as distinct from the Japanese, emphasize "the Ryukyus" and "the Ryukuans." I use "the Ryukyus" or "the Ryukyu archipelago" to refer to the geographical entity, and "Okinawans" to refer to the people, except when highlighting the "Ryukyuans" as depicted as a distinct ethnicity.

6. Ōta, "The U.S. Occupation of Okinawa and Postwar Reforms in Japan Proper," 297, 305, especially note 40.

United States in placing Okinawa under American jurisdiction and in bargaining with Japan.[7]

In the early 1940s, American anthropologists began to promote the view that the Ryukyuans were "ethnologically" different from the Japanese.[8] This idea appealed to U.S. military strategists, who believed that Okinawan resentment towards the people of mainland Japan might be useful in waging the war against Japan. By the time the U.S. military had defeated the Japanese forces on Okinawa on June 21, 1945 and then moved into its military occupation of the islands, they had re-narrated the Okinawans into a distinct ethnic group in a land that was not necessarily an inherent part of Japan. What this meant for Okinawans in terms of repatriation and deportation is best presented in the language of the Occupation authorities, in the spring of 1946: "The following plan governs the repatriation of Ryukyuans from Japan to their home islands, and of Japanese from the Ryukyus to Japan."[9] This reveals the American thinking on the matter: that the Ryukuans and the Japanese were different peoples who belonged in different homelands. In transfers fraught with challenges, American and Japanese officials moved the Okinawans—by February 1946, 13,000 Okinawans had been deported, and by December 31, 1950, 180,016 had been moved.[10]. The United States tended to see the deportation of Okinawans in Japan in the same light as the deportation of other colonials, ordering the registration of "Koreans, Chinese, Ryukyuans and Formosans" within Japan for the purpose of surveying their wishes for repatriation.[11] Japanese officials did not group the Okinawans with other colonials, but did not claim them as "compatriots" (*dōhō*) either.[12] The United States ordered repatriation, but then closed the main island of Okinawa to all returnees because of the logistical challenges they faced in administering the for-

---

7. Ibid., 297.

8. Ibid., 285–86.

9. "Repatriation to and from the Ryukyus," Annex III Section IV of "Repatriation," SCAPIN 822, March 16, 1946, in Takemae, ed., *GHQ shirei sōshūsei*, vol. 4, 1303–5.

10. Kōseishō engokyoku, *Hikiage to engo 30-nen no ayumi*, 149, 152, 154–55.

11. "Registration of Koreans, Chinese, Ryukyuans and Formosans," SCAPIN 746, February 17, 1946, in Takemae, ed., *GHQ shirei sōshūsei*, vol. 3, 1122–23.

12. The wording is "people from Okinawa Prefecture to be deported" (*sōkan Okinawa kenmin* 送還沖縄県民). Kōseishō shakai engokyoku, *Engo 50-nen shi*, 156.

mer battlefield. Okinawans languished in deportation camps in Nagoya, Kagoshima, and elsewhere, with little food, clothing, or medical care, while the American and Japanese authorities pointed fingers at each other for neglecting them. The MHW blamed the poor treatment of Okinawans, who were Japanese citizens, on the Americans, arguing that stripping Japan of its diplomatic sovereignty and wresting Okinawa away from Japan made foreigners out of Okinawans.[13]

The removal of Okinawa and its people from the disintegrating Meiji imperial order tells us more about American ideas on the Ryukyu people, and their ability to deploy those ideas, than it does about how people on the home islands of Japan viewed them. Nevertheless, the removal of Okinawa, in part by trying to separate the populations of the home islands and the Ryukyus through repatriation and deportation, contributed to having Okinawa frozen in time and space, just out of geographical and political reach of the home islands, and that made it easier for people in Japan to move forward with a new rendering: self-evident borders around a homogeneous people.

Okinawa returned to Japanese rule in 1972, and the people of Okinawa, like the *hikiagesha*, were eventually incorporated into the nation. The "third country nationals," or *sangokujin* (abbreviated from *daisangoku-jin*), were not. In April 2000, Tokyo Mayor Ishihara Shintarō used the word *sangokujin* in a speech to refer to non-Japanese Asians who, in his view, presented a threat to Japanese domestic security in the event of an earthquake or other catastrophe. His inflammatory statement, delivered to members of the police force, harkened back to the Great Kantō Earthquake of 1923, in which Koreans, rumored to be starting the fires that destroyed much of Tokyo, were massacred. Although Ishihara is an award-winning novelist with a strong command of the language, he claimed that *sangokujin* was a neutral term that was invented by the Allies to distinguish Koreans and other Asians from other foreigners.[14] Although that is technically true, the history of imperialism

---

13. Kōseishō engokyoku, *Hikiage to engo 30-nen no ayumi*, 154–55. Problems surrounding the dismantling of the Japanese settler colony in Karafuto also showed the complications that ensued in places on the cusp between empire and home. Morris-Suzuki, "Northern Lights."

14. Ishihara defended himself by citing his dictionary, which defined the term "as nothing more than a foreigner" and added that "people should stop reading so much into

in Japan and the treatment of foreigners in postwar Japan created a situation in which "third country national" meant "non-White foreigner"—former colonial subjects whose presence no longer made sense because there was no empire to define them.

The "Unmixing of Peoples" in Postwar East Asia in a Comparative Context

It is instructive to think through the history of Japanese repatriation in the context of other cases of the "unmixing of people," many instances of which occurred in twentieth century Europe after geopolitical space was rearranged at the end of empires and wars.[15] In seeking to understand past migrations and anticipate possible future migrations of ethnic Russians to the Russian Federation from other parts of the former Soviet Union after its collapse in 1991, Rogers Brubaker first evaluates several post-imperial migrations "that ensued when a ruling ethnic or national group in a multinational empire was abruptly transformed, by the shrinkage of political space and the reconfiguration of political authority along national lines."[16] After evaluating the flows of three groups of people—Balkan Muslims in the Ottoman Empire, Hungarians in the Habsburg Empire, and Germans in Imperial Germany—Brubaker generates a set of analytical points to apply productively to the Russian case. Brubaker focuses on the end of the traditional land-based empires of Central and Eastern Europe, the Ottoman, Hapsburg, and Russian empires, and not on modern colonial empires like Japan's. Nevertheless, the shrinkage of political space under Japanese rule after defeat in 1945 and the reconfiguration of political authority along national lines abruptly transformed the status of the ruling Japanese colonists in what had been a multinational empire, at which point a post-imperial migration ensued. For this reason, it is illuminating to process this case through this framework.

---

the term." Magnier, "Tokyo Governor Assails Critics, Says Remarks Were Misunderstood."

15. Michael Marrus attributes the phrase "the unmixing of peoples" to Lord Curzon (*The Unwanted*, 41). Rogers Brubaker uses this term as well in "Aftermaths of Empire and the Unmixing of Peoples," 157.

16. Brubaker, "Aftermaths of Empire and the Unmixing of Peoples," 156.

Brubaker's first insight is that ethnic unmixing in the aftermath of empire varies in the degree, timing, and modalities of the migrations, and that this variation changes over time, in different regions, and across social classes.[17] As we have seen, these variations occurred in the Japanese case. In terms of *degree*, Japanese repatriation was meant to be total, with all Japanese nationals removed from the colonies and all colonial subjects removed from Japan. Nearly all Japanese nationals *were* removed from most of the former colonies, but the exceptions were significant, especially the approximately 10,000 people who remained behind in northeast China, testifying to the impossibility of moving everyone who was supposed to be moved. Also, approximately 600,000 Koreans refused deportation, forming the core of "resident Koreans" who remain in Japan. As for the *timing*, post-imperial Japanese migration is distinctive in the abrupt and disjointed way in which it was triggered. It was abrupt in that the colonial Japanese did not anticipate defeat or status transformation. With the exception of settlers and soldiers in Manchuria, Japanese colonists did not flee an invading army in the same way that Germans in East Prussia fled the Soviet Army in early 1945. Instead, most heard about defeat on the radio. The end of the empire was disjointed in that military battles fought in regions outside of the colonies—for example, in the Pacific, Southeast Asia, and Okinawa—led to the end of colonial rule in Taiwan, Korea, and parts of China, making it hard for some colonists to understand that they could no longer remain in their colonial homes. Military defeat brought status transformation to colonial Japanese but it did so from afar. The timing of the repatriates' return, the region from which they returned, and their class were critical elements, not in the decision to return, which was mandated by the Allies, but rather in their reception at home, as described in Chapters 2 and 3 in this book.

In a corollary to his first point on the variety of the degree, timing, and modalities of ethnic unmixing, Brubaker argues that there was nothing foreordained about the migrations. In the cases he examined, the reconfiguration of political space along national lines did not automatically entail a corresponding redistribution of the population, and instead depended on several variables, including how the potential mi-

17. Ibid., 166–67.

grants were transformed from their dominant position into one of a national minority, how rooted they were, the availability and suitability of a national homeland to which to return, and the potential migrants' sense of their prospects if they remained in the successor state. Setting aside for a moment the mandatory nature of the Allied-sponsored transfer, it is instructive to assess these variables in the Japanese case. Defeat in war transformed decisively and publicly the status of colonial Japanese. Everyone throughout the colonies knew that the Japanese had lost the war, and with that, the privileges protected by their state. As for rootedness, colonial entrepreneurs in Korea and Taiwan, long-term residents of treaty ports in China, and agricultural settlers in Manchuria may have felt closely tied to their colonial homes, but the colonial Japanese were third-generation colonists at most and had not had time to develop deep ties with the land or inclination to integrate themselves into local communities.[18]

At first glance, the country of Japan presents an obvious national homeland for the overseas Japanese. No other territory called out as a place for Japanese nationals to go.[19] Within Japan, strong notions of ties between each Japanese person and his or her *furusato*, or native home, made the return of a Japanese person to Japan appear to be a natural move. The metropolitan government at the time, though, was trying to manage a devastated nation of 72 million people on the brink of starvation and expressed concerns about how to handle the additional burden of nearly 9 percent of its population. In the aftermath of the war, some Japanese officials believed that colonists in relatively peaceful areas would be better off if they "stayed put" for the time being. As we have seen, some metropolitan Japanese harbored suspicions as to whether the returnees would be able to reintegrate harmoniously into Japanese society. The U.S. military authorities did not share these nuanced views of who counted as a Japanese person and where they belonged. After

---

18. On the "extreme domestic insularity" of the Japanese concession in Tianjin, see Rogaski, *Hygienic Modernity*, 262. On insularity in Shanghai, see Henriot, "'Little Japan' in Shanghai."

19. In a 1945 report on the problem of overseas Japanese nationals, an American analyst for the Office of Strategic Services concluded that no place other than Japan could serve as a destination for those abroad. United States, Office of Strategic Services. "Japanese Civilians Overseas," 38.

four years of extensive study of "the Japanese" in order to "know their enemy," the authorities apparently knew a Japanese when they saw one and arranged the transfer of unambiguously Japanese people back to an unambiguous Japan.[20]

Most of the colonial Japanese had already left other parts of Asia by the time the establishment of the East Asian "successor states" of the Republic of Korea (1948), the Democratic People's Republic of Korea (1948), the People's Republic of China (1949), and the Republic of China (1949). For that reason, colonial Japanese did not have the opportunity to ascertain prospects for life there, even if the Allies had permitted it. Moreover, because of the form of the Japanese colonies, with Japanese authorities positioning themselves as tutors to the colonial population and living separately in Japanese enclaves, it is difficult to imagine Japanese settlers adjusting to a new status of citizen or permanent resident on equal footing with Koreans, Chinese, or Taiwanese citizens and integrating into their communities, especially since their states were built on Korean and Chinese ethnic nationalism fused with communist or anti-communist ideologies.

It is striking that in the Japanese case, all of the variables that determine whether a new national minority stays or moves—the decisiveness of their transformation, their lack of rootedness, the sense of an appropriate homeland, and the lack of an opportunity to evaluate prospects in a successor state—were weighted on the side of pushing them to go. Into that context, the Allies appeared, providing the means for people to move, including crossing an ocean to reach Japan. This leads to a possible modification of Brubaker's claim that post-imperial migrations are not foreordained. If the end of empire is combined with the military defeat of the dominant, state-bearing nationality, even if they are defeated by someone other than the indigenous residents of the colonies, the push factors increase dramatically. One exception to this modification presents itself immediately: military defeat led to the collapse of Imperial Germany in 1918, and yet, as Brubaker tells us, not all ethnic Germans in

---

20. Capra, *Know Your Enemy—Japan*. One American official considered the possibility that overseas Japanese might be able to stay in Taiwan or Korea, but he or she appeared to be in a minority. United States, Office of Strategic Services. "Japanese Civilians Overseas," 40–42.

the East returned to Germany at that time.[21] Nevertheless, compared to cases such as the breakup of the Soviet Union, where the empire ended without the state-bearing nationality being defeated in war, cases such as Japan and Germany after World War II, and France in the Algerian War, in which military defeat accompanies the end of empire, point to the likelihood of migration or expulsion.

A comparison of Japanese repatriation and European Algerian flight at the end of French rule highlights the specifically post-imperial aspects of the Japanese case. After France established colonial rule in Algeria in 1830, an assortment of Europeans—French, but also other nationalities from around the Mediterranean—settled in Algeria, and over time formed a community. They produced children, and by 1896, Algerian-born Europeans outnumbered European immigrants.[22] By the time of the beginning of the Algerian War for Independence in 1954, 79 percent of the European population of 984,000 had been born in Algeria.[23] Over time, these "French Algerians" produced a distinctive identity.

In 1954, the Algerians, seeking to change or end French colonial rule, waged a war against the European rulers. The conflict ended in 1962, with Algeria gaining independence. Because of the brutality of the war and the end of the colonial formation, European colonists were not able to remain. From April 1962, the European Algerians fled and nearly a million people arrived on the shores of France over the next three months.[24] Although some of the returnees were able to integrate smoothly back into French society, others struggled because their communities were dispersed throughout France, and because they were viewed by metropolitan French as the purveyors of empire. Still others ended up on the edges of France, in Corsica and elsewhere.

Hikiagesha and *pied noir* faced similar kinds of problems upon their return to the metropolitan society, including having to negotiate the labels applied to them. The historian Benjamin Stora has mused on the origins of the phrase *pied noir* and when the European Algerians became

---

21. Brubaker, "Aftermaths of Empire and the Unmixing of Peoples," 162–66.

22. Stora, *Algeria*, 9.

23. Ibid., 8. Matthew Connelly also cites 984,000 as the figure of the European settler population in Algeria in 1954. Connelly, *A Diplomatic Revolution*, 18.

24. Stora, *Algeria*, 99.

aware of it: "*Pieds noirs* . . . how are we to determine the exact origin of this term? Some say it may have been invented by the Arabs, surprised to see soldiers landing in 1830 with black boots on their feet. Others suggest it was the color of the feet of the wine growers in Algeria, tramping grapes to make wine. Whatever the explanation, the French of Algeria did not encounter that characterization until they arrived in the metropolis—in 1962."[25] Matthew Connelly proposes a different etymology and timetable of awareness: "French people of the metropole called Muslim immigrants stoking coal on cargo-boats *pieds noirs* because of their black feet. The term became a way to insult settlers, but by the 1950s Algeria's nearly one million citizens of European descent had made this epithet their own."[26] Regardless of its origin, or precisely when European Algerians encountered the label *pied noir*, the category took on new importance and meaning as it came to describe the dislocated population in France, and as the *pieds noirs* came to serve as scapegoats for the French colonial project.[27] It is clear that the stigmatization of former colonial participants is one of the ways that metropolitan societies move away from their histories of colonization.[28]

The Japanese and French cases differ in significant ways. In the Japanese case, the Allies triangulated the process by placing themselves between the colonial Japanese and the native residents, and played an important—if unanticipated—role in the transition of the colonial spaces in East Asia into national ones. This third party decolonization had important ramifications for the end of empire in East Asia and the subsequent post-imperial migrations. A second difference is the matter of the year, 1945, a time marked by civilian transfers, migrations, expulsions, and genocide.

Comparing the Japanese case to the 1945 expulsions of ethnic Germans provides the means to explore these two distinctive aspects of the case: the Allied role and the year 1945. The experiences of German-speaking people in Europe east of Germany and Japanese nationals in

---

25. Ibid., 8. Stora refers to colonial Algerians as "those who would later be called *pieds noirs*" (*Algeria*, 100) and "those who were henceforth to be called *pieds noirs*" (*Algeria*, 108).

26. Connelly, *A Diplomatic Revolution*, 11.

27. Stora, *Algeria*, 114.

28. Smith, ed., *Europe's Invisible Migrants*; Elkins and Pedersen, *Settler Colonialism in the Twentieth Century*.

East Asia differ significantly in their historical circumstances. As part of early modern migrations and colonizations, German-speaking peoples had settled throughout Central and Eastern Europe as far east as Russia.[29] Some ethnic Germans had lived in Eastern Europe and Russia for centuries, and not always as aggressors. Invited by Catherine the Great, German-speaking Mennonites settled in what is now Ukraine in the late eighteenth century to escape military service. German speakers had been in what is now the Czech Republic since the 1600s.[30] Some people later deemed "ethnic Germans" had never been citizens of the German state and had only the remotest of ties to Germany. No analogue to Japanese versions of these people exists.

After the end of World War I, with the defeat of Imperial Germany and the end of the Habsburg Empire, and the subsequent reduction of German territory, about 6.5 million Germans in Europe became national minorities. Approximately 600,000 to 800,000 in regions awarded to Poland moved to Germany, but most of the others remained in the successor states of Czechoslovakia, Yugoslavia, Romania, and Hungary.[31] With the establishment of National Socialist rule in 1933, and especially the military expansions of 1939, "Germans of the Reich" spread eastward to rule areas that fell under German conquest, including Czechoslovakia and Poland. The regime sought closer ties with ethnic Germans (*Volksdeutsche*) outside of Germany's borders and elevated them in ethnic reclassification schemes. In other cases, as part of Heinrich Himmler's "ethnic redistribution" plans, the government resettled ethnic Germans from the Baltics into newly emptied Jewish and Polish homes in Poland, in an effort to bring German speakers back to an expanded Germany.[32]

When the Third Reich began to lose the war, all categories of Germans—"Germans of the Reich," ethnic Germans, and autochthons (people with remotely German ancestry such as Kashubians, Silesians, and others)—were exposed to military and civilian attack. In January 1945, Germans in East Prussia began to flee as Soviet troops advanced

---

29. Wolff, *The German Question since 1919*.

30. Glassheim, "National Mythologies and Ethnic Cleansing," 467–68.

31. Brubaker, "Aftermaths of Empire and the Unmixing of Peoples," 166–67.

32. Aly, *'Final Solution,'* 5. As Aly's title suggests, the "ethnic redistribution" of ethnic Germans from the east was part of the National Socialist plan to reshape the demographic landscape in Europe through the murder of all European Jews.

towards Berlin. Soon after, people in Poland, Czechoslovakia, Yugo-slavia, Romania, and Hungary began to expel their local German pop-ulations. The spontaneous expulsions, marked by extraordinary violence, lasted from the spring of 1945 until about the time of the Potsdam meet-ings at the end of July 1945.[33] They were followed by more organized transfers, which lasted until the end of 1946.[34] Ultimately, an estimated 12 million ethnic Germans from Central and Eastern Europe—7 million from Poland (including parts of Poland taken by Russia, and parts of Germany awarded to Poland after the war), 3 million from Czecho-slovakia, and the rest from Yugoslavia, Romania, and Hungary—were expelled, and 2 million people are estimated to have died during the process.[35]

Whereas the historical background of German expulsion and Japa-nese repatriation differed, the history of the two migrations intersected temporally in 1945. Defeat at the hands of the Allies triggered the status transformation of Germans and Japanese in territory their militaries no longer controlled. Other parallels are apparent. Germans and Japanese who ended up in Soviet hands in the immediate postwar period suf-fered similarly grim fates. The rapes of German and Japanese women forced the home governments to address the postwar ramifications of the violence. Japanese soldiers who surrendered to the Soviet military joined as many as 3 million German POWs in Soviet detention camps, often in Siberia. Japanese and Germans were sometimes held in nearby camps and there is evidence that they had some contact. One Soviet detainee explained that Russian officials issued orders only in Russian. Multilingual Germans then translated the orders into English for bi-lingual Japanese, who would then translate for their fellow detainees.[36] Descriptions of German and Hungarian POWs appeared in Japanese

---

33. Naimark, *Fires of Hatred*, 111, 117.

34. Eagle Glassheim discusses the "wild transfers" in the summer of 1945, followed by "organized transfers" in 1946 of ethnic Germans from Czechoslovakia. Glassheim, "National Mythologies and Ethnic Cleansing," 463–64.

35. Nearly 3 million were expelled from Czechoslovakia (Naimark, *Fires of Hatred*, 120). Seven million Germans found themselves within the new postwar borders of Poland (Judt, *Postwar*, 26).

36. Oral history interview, October 27, 1999.

POW debriefing reports.[37] Japanese POWs appear as characters in German movies that depict life in the camps.[38] There were connective, as well as comparative, aspects in this case.

The episodes diverge again in how each home society dealt with the returnees and the problems that accompanied them. Both Germany and Japan had pro-natalist policies and anti-abortion laws on the books at the end of the war. Concerns about mixed-race children, especially those who were the product of rape, outweighed concerns about breaking the abortion laws. Officials looked the other way when the abortions were performed on the women. Sexually assaulted German women in postwar society were almost certainly stigmatized, and like Japanese women, they probably had nothing to gain by disclosing their experiences. Compared to Japan, however, women there seemed more willing to discuss it. Atina Grossmann explains that although women tended not to speak of it in public, they could talk about it with their daughters and other female relatives.[39] It is difficult to imagine Japanese women speaking frankly on this topic in public or even in private. Grossmann argues that German women managed to avoid feelings of shame, and in fact, were able to use their rape experience to mitigate other negative feelings. Grossmann concludes that German women "felt victimized, violated, humiliated, but finally not guilty or responsible."[40] We do not yet know how, or even if, Japanese women used this experience as a means of negotiating guilt or responsibility.

Men returning to Germany from Soviet detention were sometimes depicted as malingerers or sexually dysfunctional. This was complicated by whether they returned to East or West Germany.[41] In other cases, ex-pellees appeared to integrate well into their new homes in postwar Germany. Mark Roseman states that he expected to find evidence of conflict in the resettlement of ethnic German miners expelled from Poland who sought work in the Ruhr Valley. They chose the region because they had

---

37. "Doitsujin, Hangarījin nado."

38. For example, the film *Der Teufel spielte Balalaika* (1961) depicts German and Japanese POWs forced to break rocks in a Soviet quarry. Discussed in Moeller, *War Stories*, 127.

39. "Gendered Defeat: Rape, Motherhood, and Fraternization," in Grossmann, *Jews, Germans, and Allies*.

40. Grossmann, "A Question of Silence," 62.

41. Biess, "Men of Reconstruction—The Reconstruction of Men."

family ties or the promise of mining jobs—difficult, but relatively lucrative and stable. With the exception of local resentment over government compensation paid to expellees, Roseman concludes that the newcomers faced few long-term problems reintegrating into the community.[42] And by the mid-1950s, German POWs from the Soviet Union sometimes stood as symbols for traditional, masculine values, in contrast to the consumerism and fussiness of postwar West German society.[43] With the possible exception of Iki, the protagonist of Yamasaki's 1975 novel *The Barren Zone*, Japanese detainees depicted in artistic or media sources rarely served as symbols of masculinity or traditional values.

Perhaps the most distinctive difference in the expulsions of ethnic Germans and postwar repatriation in Japan is how each home society made use of that history across the postwar period. Robert Moeller analyzes how, in West Germany, the stories of expulsion were folded into the realms of official history writing, politics, and popular culture, and concludes that in the 1950s the stories of the expulsion and the Soviet detention of thousands of German POWs came to stand for German suffering during World War II, providing the means for people in West Germany to share in a story of national victimization in war, in a narrative of suffering parallel to the better-known victims of National Socialism.[44]

The story of repatriation, however, never became Japan's national story of World War II, and therefore, the images of repatriates did not function in the same way. In the first place, Japan did not need the repatriation story because there were more compelling stories of victimization available. Hiroshima and Nagasaki became powerful national and international symbols of the fact that Japan was the only nation to have been bombed by atomic weapons. The story of the peace-loving Japanese people led astray by renegade military leaders, one that was supported by the Occupation authorities, was another powerful narrative.[45] Japanese civilians as the victims of urban firebombing campaigns

---

42. Roseman, "Refugees and Ruhr Miners."

43. "Heimat, Barbed Wire, and 'Papa's Kino': Expellees and POWs at the Movies," in Moeller, *War Stories*, 123–70.

44. Moeller, *War Stories*.

45. "What Do You Tell the Dead When You Lose?" in Dower, *Embracing Defeat*.

are a third. All of these storylines stress the suffering of the people in *naichi*. Because most repatriates were abroad during the atomic and conventional bombings, they were excluded from the victim's circle. Because repatriation was never Japan's national story of World War II, it was not necessary to put a noble face on the repatriates. It was the colonial element, as well as being outside the borders of the home islands of Japan at defeat, that disqualified their stories from the national stories of suffering. Looking at the Japanese, the French, and the German cases together suggests that stories of suffering in war are eligible as national stories, but that stories of suffering at the end of a colonial project, even if the stories are compelling in terms of "our" men and women suffering at the hands of other peoples, are disqualified from serving as national stories of suffering.

Finally, comparing Japanese repatriation and German expulsion invites us to consider the question of ethnic cleansing. The motivation on the part of local populations to expel the ethnic Germans, even if they had been neighbors for decades or centuries, is not hard to imagine: revenge and retribution for years of abuse. But that was not the only factor. The government and people of Poland expelled Ukrainians and surviving Jews as well as Germans; the government and people of Czechoslovakia expelled Hungarians as well as Germans.[46] The expulsions were part of a larger impulse to create more ethnically homogeneous national spaces, an impulse that found its opportunity in the chaos of the immediate postwar moment. After all of the killings, wartime population transfers, expulsions, and migrations, the people of Eastern Europe had been sorted into comparatively homogeneous spaces.[47]

The sorting of Europe took place in two steps, a geographic one after World War I and a human one after World War II. As Tony Judt explains, "At the conclusion of the First World War it was borders that were invented and adjusted, while people were on the whole left in place. After 1945 what happened was rather the opposite: with one major exception [Poland] boundaries stayed broadly intact and people were moved instead."[48] In the case of postwar East Asia, those two steps were

---

46. Naimark, *Fires of Hatred*, 136–37.
47. Judt, *Postwar*, 27–28.
48. Ibid., 27.

collapsed into one: the borders were adjusted *and* people were moved. As a result, by 1946, both Europe and East Asia were regions in which ethnic mixing had been largely undone.

How can the postwar migrations in East Asia be characterized best? Because the Allied militaries and local Japanese authorities cooperated quickly after defeat to begin moving Japanese civilians back to Japan, it is impossible to know what would have happened between Japanese colonists and local populations had they been left on their own. As it stands, Japanese repatriation does not qualify as an expulsion or ethnic cleansing.[49] The discourse of the need to create ethnically homogeneous spaces in China, Korea, and Taiwan did not accompany the departure of the Japanese in 1945. Rather, it was a mandatory repatriation that had the effect of removing colonizers from formerly colonial spaces in addition to the more pressing goal, in the eyes of the Allies, of removing Japanese soldiers from the battlefield.

My goal in this book has been to tell the story of repatriation as Japanese people lived it, and the opportunity remains to explore 1940s American attitudes towards population transfers in East Asia. Language extolling the benefits of spaces rid of their Japanese military and colonial populations appears in American overviews of the motivation to repatriate them. The repeated use of the word "cleared" to describe regions that had been rid of the Japanese resonates with one strand of Allied thinking in Europe that did not oppose population transfers or even expulsions.[50] One iteration of those views, quoted by Norman

---

49. For a concise discussion of "ethnic cleansing," see Naimark, *Fires of Hatred*, 2–4.

50. Discussions of regions "cleared" of Japanese appear in Supreme Commander for the Allied Powers, *Reports of General MacArthur*. It is possible that the authors of the reports were using the word in a military sense. Some examples: "By this time [July 1946] South Korea had been cleared" (158); "The clearance of the Japanese from South Korea was accomplished more expeditiously and completely than from any other area" (162–64); "When General MacArthur decided that all United States controlled areas were to be cleared by the end of 1946, a plan was set up to clear the remaining Japanese from the Philippine Islands" (168); "Except for stragglers, Central China was cleared in July 1946" (173); "Formosa was cleared by 15 April 1946" (173). Occupation forces within Japan also used the word "clear" when referring to the deportation of Koreans from Japan, as in "Koreans will be cleared from areas in the following order" ("Repatriation of Non-Japanese from Japan," SCAPIN 224, November 1, 1945, in Takemae, ed., *GHQ shirei sō-shūsei*, vol. 2, 340–43; here, 341).

Naimark, includes Winston Churchill's 1944 remarks on the likelihood of postwar German expulsions:

For expulsion is the method which, so far as we have been able to see, will be the most satisfactory and lasting. There will be no mixture of populations to cause endless trouble as in Alsace-Lorraine. A clean sweep will be made. I am not alarmed at the prospect of the disentanglement of the population, nor am I alarmed by these large transferences, which are more possible than they were before through modern conditions.[51]

American officials debated some aspects of repatriation, with at least one military officer arguing against devoting any resources to aiding their recent enemies. Statements justifying different standards of treatment for "Orientals" and "Occidentals" in the transfer remind us that the Allies objectified those they moved.[52] But there appears to have been little debate on whether the Allied "disentanglement of the population" in East Asia was at all problematic.

In some instances in the former colonial spaces, locals ousted Japanese residents from their homes and looted them. Theft, beatings, rapes, and occasional murders of Japanese civilians at the hands of former colonial subjects appear in official sources and memoirs. Stories of Korean and Chinese violence toward the Japanese in northern Korea during the Soviet invasion continue to seep out. Mass graves of overseas Japanese civilians in Asia, like recently discovered graves containing what are believed to be the remains German civilians who died in 1945 in Poland, may still be uncovered. Japanese abroad in post-colonial East Asia suffered terribly, from cold, hunger, disease, and humiliations, and, as families and communities, faced terrible choices in how to survive. Nevertheless, given the loss of state protection and the subsequent vulnerability of Japanese soldiers and colonial participants, the violence toward them could have been much worse. This assessment will provide no comfort to the family members of people who were killed after the war, or to women exposed to sexual violence, or to the three million people who lost nearly all of their possessions and their colonial homes,

---

51. Winston Churchill, in a 1944 speech to the British House of Commons, accepting the idea of the postwar transfers of Germans, quoted in Naimark, *Fires of Hatred*, 110.

52. Supreme Commander for the Allied Powers, *Reports of General MacArthur*, 150, 155.

but the fact that over 95 percent of this population made it back to Japan within four years after the end of hostilities is remarkable given the context of the violent war.

My conclusions in this historical case abrade two of my own political beliefs in the first decade of the twenty-first century: that American military and civil authorities should not act unilaterally to make and enforce decisions about the fate of millions of people in other parts of the world, and that moving people to create homogeneous spaces is not justifiable or desirable. Compared to other cases, however, it does seem likely that the American decision to move Japanese people immediately back to Japan, a decision that was conveyed and enforced publicly throughout the former empire, saved Japanese lives.

In the final assessment, Japanese repatriation was a part of the process of decolonization and coincided with Japan's catastrophic defeat at the hands of the Allies. Because the Allies believed that the former Japanese colonies would be more stable if rid of the colonists, and because the U.S. military was willing to devote resources to moving civilians as well as soldiers back to Japan, the human dismantling of Japan's empire happened rapidly and with little discussion. It stands as a compelling example of the unmixing of a population, in the transition from imperial formations, which mixed people, into post-colonial and post-imperial national ones, which sorted them.

Reference Matter

Works Cited

Primary and Secondary Sources

Abe Kōbō 安部公房. *Abe Kōbō zenshū* 安部公房全集 (Complete works of Abe Kōbō). Vol. 12. Tokyo: Shinchōsha, 1998.

———. *Kemonotachi wa kokyō o mezasu* けものたちは故郷をめざす (Wild beasts seek home). Tokyo: Kōdansha, 1970. Originally published in *Gunzō* 群像 (January–April 1957).

———. "Sakuhin nōto" 作品ノート (Notes on writing). In *Abe Kōbō zenshū* 安部公房全集 (Complete works of Abe Kōbō). Vol. 1. Tokyo: Shinchōsha, 1997.

Aida Yūji. *Prisoner of the British: A Japanese Soldier's Experiences in Burma*. Trans. Louis Allen and Hide Ishiguro. London: The Cresset Press, 1966.

Akiyoshi Toshiko 穐吉敏子. *Jazu to ikiru* ジャズと生きる (Living through jazz). Tokyo: Iwanami shoten, 1996.

Aly, Götz. *'Final Solution': Nazi Population Policy and the Murder of the European Jews*. London: Arnold, 1999 [1995].

Amemiya, Kozy Kazuko. "The Road to Pro-Choice Ideology in Japan: A Social History of the Contest between the State and Individuals over Abortion." Ph.D. diss., University of California at San Diego, 1993.

Ara Takashi 荒敬, ed. *Nihon senryō, gaikō kankei shiryōshū* 日本占領・外交関係資料集 (Documents on the occupation and foreign relations of Japan). Vol. 3. Tokyo: Kashiwa shobō, 1991.

Asahi shinbun 朝日新聞, 1945–2008.

Asahi shinbunsha 朝日新聞社, ed. *Koe* 声. Vol. 1. Tokyo: Asahi bunko, 1984.

Asahi shinbunsha 朝日新聞社. *Nihon shinbun fukkokuban* 日本新聞復刻版 (Reproduction of *Nihon shinbun*). 3 vols. Tokyo: Asashi shinbunsha, 1991.

Asano Toyomi 浅野豊美. *Datsu shokuminchika purosesu toshite no sengo Nihon no tai Ajia gaikō no tenkai to kokunai seiyaku yōin* 脱植民地化プロセスとしての戦後日本の対アジア外交の展開と国内制約要因 (The development of postwar Japan's relations with the rest of Asia and the cause of domestic restrictions as a process of decolonization). Nihon gakujutsu shinkōkai kagaku kenkyūhi hojokin kiban kenkyū (B) kenkyū seika hōkokusho, 2007.

Banba Tsuneo 番場恒夫. "Marai hantō hikiage hōkokusho" 馬来半島引き揚報告書 (Report on repatriation from the Malaysian peninsula). Nihon kōkan kabushiki kaisha gaichika, 1945. Available in Katō Kiyofumi 加藤聖文, ed. *Kaigai hikiage kankei shiryō shūsei* 海外引揚関係史料集成 (Collection of historical documents on repatriation from overseas). Vol. 33. Tokyo: Yumani shobō, 2002.

Barnhart, Michael A. *Japan Prepares for Total War: The Search for Economic Security, 1919–1941*. Ithaca, NY: Cornell University Press, 1987.

Bayly, C. A. and Tim Harper. *Forgotten Wars: The End of Britain's Asian Empire*. London and New York: Allen Lane, 2007.

Beasley, W. G. *Japanese Imperialism 1894–1945*. Oxford, UK: Clarendon Press, 1987.

Biess, Frank. "Men of Reconstruction—The Reconstruction of Men: Returning POWs in East and West Germany, 1945–1955." In *Home/Front: The Military, War, and Gender in Twentieth Century Germany*, ed. Karen Hagemann and Stefanie Schüler-Springorum, 335–58. Oxford, UK: Berg, 2002.

Borton, Hugh. *American Presurrender Planning for Postwar Japan*. New York: East Asian Institute, Columbia University, 1967.

Boyle, John Hunter. *China and Japan at War, 1937–1945: The Politics of Collaboration*. Stanford, CA: Stanford University Press, 1972.

Bramwell, Anna, ed. *Refugees in the Age of Total War*. London: Unwin Hyman, 1988.

Brooks, Barbara. "Japanese Colonial Citizenship in Treaty-Port China: The Location of Koreans and Taiwanese in the Imperial Order." In *New Frontiers: Imperialism's New Communities in East Asia, 1843–1953*, ed. Robert Bickers and Christian Henriot, 109–24. Manchester, UK and New York: Manchester University Press, 2000.

———. *Japan's Imperial Diplomacy: Consuls, Treaty Ports, and War in China, 1895–1938*. Honolulu, HI: University of Hawai'i Press, 2000.

———. "Peopling the Japanese Empire: The Koreans in Manchuria and the Rhetoric of Inclusion." In *Japan's Competing Modernities*, ed. Sharon Minichiello, 24–44. Honolulu, HI: University of Hawai'i Press, 1998.

Brubaker, Rogers. "Aftermaths of Empire and the Unmixing of Peoples." In *After Empire: Multiethnic Societies and Nation-Building*, ed. Karen Barkey and Mark von Hagen, 155–80. Boulder, CO: Westview Press, 1997.

Buckley, Roger. *Occupation Diplomacy: Britain, the United States, and Japan 1945–1952*. Cambridge, UK: Cambridge University Press, 1982.

Campbell, John Creighton. "Compensation for Repatriates: A Case Study of Interest-Group Politics and Party-Government Negotiations in Japan." In *Policymaking in Contemporary Japan*, ed. T. J. Pempel, 103–42. Ithaca, NY: Cornell University Press, 1977.

Capra, Frank, dir. *Know Your Enemy—Japan*. *Why We Fight* series. Washington, DC: U.S. War Department, 1945.

Chen Yingzhen. "Imperial Army Betrayed." In *Perilous Memories: The Asia-Pacific War(s)*, ed. T. Fujitani, Geoffrey M. White, and Lisa Yoneyama, 181–98. Durham, NC: Duke University Press, 2001.

Ching, Leo T. S. *Becoming "Japanese": Colonial Taiwan and the Politics of Identity Formation*. Berkeley, CA: University of California Press, 2001.

Choi, Chungmoo. "The Discourse of Decolonization and Popular Memory: South Korea." *positions* 1, no. 1 (Spring 1993): 77–102.

———. "The Politics of War Memories toward Healing." In *Perilous Memories: The Asia-Pacific War(s)*, ed. T. Fujitani, Geoffrey M. White, and Lisa Yoneyama, 394–409. Durham, NC: Duke University Press, 2001.

Christy, Alan S. "The Making of Imperial Subjects in Okinawa." *positions* 1, no. 3 (Winter 1993): 607–39.

Chūgoku hikiage mangaka no kai 中国引揚げ漫画家の会, ed., *Boku no Manshū: mangaka tachi no haisen taiken* ボクの満州: 漫画家たちの敗戦体験 (My Manchuria: the experience of defeat of *manga* artists). Tokyo: Aki shobō, 1995.

"Chūgoku kikokusha shien ni kansuru kentōkai hōkokusho" 中国帰国者支援に関する検討会報告書 (Report of the investigative committee on supporting returnees from China). Web. December 4, 2000. http://www1.mhlw.go.jp/shingi/s0012/s1204-1_16.html. Accessed May 9, 2008.

"Chūgoku zanryū hōjin tō no enkatsu na kikoku no sokushin oyobi eijū kikokugo no jiritsu no shien ni kansuru hōritsu" 中国残留邦人等の円滑な帰国の促進及び永住帰国後の自立の支援に関する法律 (The law concerning promoting the smooth return of Japanese nationals left behind in China and supporting their independence after their permanent return). Law no. 30, April 6, 1994.

Chung, Young-Soo and Elise K. Tipton. "Problems of Assimilation: The Koreans." In *Society and the State in Interwar Japan*, ed. Elise K. Tipton, 169–92. London and New York: Routledge, 1997.

CNN Presents. *The Cold War.* 24 Episodes. Vol. 1, episode 2, 1998.

Connelly, Matthew. *A Diplomatic Revolution: Algeria's Fight for Independence and the Origins of the Post-Cold War Era.* Oxford, UK: Oxford University Press, 2002.

Coox, Alvin D. *Nomonhan: Japan against Russia, 1939.* Stanford, CA: Stanford University Press, 1986.

———. "The Pacific War." In *The Cambridge History of Japan: Volume 6: The Twentieth Century*, ed. Peter Duus, 315–82. Cambridge, UK: Cambridge University Press, 1988.

Coughlin, William J. *Conquered Press: The MacArthur Era in Japanese Journalism.* Palo Alto, CA: Pacific Books, 1952.

Cumings, Bruce. *The Origins of the Korean War: Liberation and the Emergence of Separate Regimes, 1945–1947.* Princeton, NJ: Princeton University Press, 1981.

Currie, William Joseph. "Metaphors of Alienation: The Fiction of Abe, Beckett and Kafka." Ph.D. diss., University of Michigan, 1973.

Dazai Osamu 太宰治. *Shayō, Ningen shikkaku* 斜陽・人間失格 (*The Setting Sun* and *No Longer Human*). Tokyo: Shinchō gendai bungaku, 1979.

Dennis, Peter. *Troubled Days of Peace: Mountbatten and South East Asia Command, 1945–1946.* New York: St. Martin's, 1987.

Department of State. *Foreign Relations of the United States [FRUS]: The Conference of Berlin (The Potsdam Conference), 1945.* Vol 2. Washington, DC: Government Printing Office, 1960.

Department of State. *Foreign Relations of the United States [FRUS]: The Conferences at Malta and Yalta, 1945.* Washington, DC: Government Printing Office, 1955.

Dōhō kōsei shinbun 同胞更生新聞, 1946.

"Doitsujin, Hangarījin tō to Nihonjin ni taisuru minshu keimō undō no sa'i ni tsuite" ドイツ人ハンガリー人等と日本人にたいする民主啓蒙運動の差異について (Differences in the reeducation campaigns aimed at Germans and Hungarians and the Japanese). Report. *Shiberia minshu undō no jōkyō ni kansuru kikansha no kikanji ni okeru ippan hōkoku*, July 14, 1948. Boeichō: Box 73, bunko, yuzu 109.

Dower, John. *Embracing Defeat: Japan in the Wake of World War II.* New York: W.W. Norton, 1999.

Duus, Peter. *The Abacus and the Sword: The Japanese Penetration of Korea, 1895–1910.* Berkeley, CA: University of California Press, 1998.

Duus, Peter, Ramon H. Myers, and Mark R. Peattie, eds. *The Japanese Informal Empire in China, 1895–1937.* Princeton, NJ: Princeton University Press, 1989.

———, eds. *The Japanese Wartime Empire, 1931–1945.* Princeton, NJ: Princeton University Press, 1996.

Efird, Robert. "Japanese War Orphans and New Overseas Chinese: History, Identification and (Multi)ethnicity." Ph.D. diss., University of Washington, 2004.

―――. "Japan's 'War Orphans': Identification and State Responsibility." *Journal of Japanese Studies* 34, no. 2 (Summer 2008): 363–88.

Elkins, Caroline and Susan Pedersen, eds. *Settler Colonialism in the Twentieth Century: Projects, Practices, Legacies.* New York and London: Routledge, 2005.

Endō Yumi 遠藤由美. "J. M. Neruson hikiagesha kyōiku jigyō no tenkai to tokushitsu" J. M.ネルソン引揚者教育事業の展開と特質 (J. M. Nelson and the development and particularities of repatriate education). *Gekkan shakai kyōiku* 月刊社会教育 31, no. 1 (1987): 68–77.

Eskildsen, Robert. "Of Civilization and Savages: The Mimetic Imperialism of Japan's 1874 Expedition to Taiwan." *American Historical Review* 107, no. 2 (April 2002): 388–418.

Etō Jun 江藤淳, ed. *Senryō shiroku* 占領史録 (Historical records of the Occupation). Vol. 2. Tokyo: Kōdansha, 1982.

Fogel, Joshua A. "Integrating into Chinese Society: A Comparison of the Japanese Communities of Shanghai and Harbin." In *Japan's Competing Modernities: Issues in Culture and Democracy, 1900–1930,* ed. Sharon Minichiello, 45–69. Honolulu, HI: University of Hawai'i Press, 1998.

Fujitani, T. "The Reischauer Memo: Mr. Moto, Hirohito, and Japanese American Soldiers." *Critical Asian Studies* 33, no. 3 (2001): 379–402.

Fujiwara Tei 藤原てい. *Nagareru hoshi wa ikiteiru* 流れる星は生きている (Shooting stars live on). Tokyo: Hibiya shuppansha, 1949.

Fukuoka Yasunori. *The Lives of Young Koreans in Japan.* Trans. Tom Gill. Melbourne: Trans Pacific Press, 2000.

Furukawa Atsushi 古川純. "Zasshi *Kaizō* ni miru senryōka ken'etsu no jittai" 雑誌「改造」にみる占領下検閲の実態 (Censorship under the Occupation as seen in the magazine *Kaizō*). *Tōkyō keidai gakkaishi* 東京経大学会誌, nos. 116–17 (1980): 133–83.

Gallicchio, Marc S. *The Cold War Begins in Asia: American East Asian Policy and the Fall of the Japanese Empire.* New York: Columbia University Press, 1988.

Gane, William J. "Foreign Affairs of South Korea, August 1945 to August 1950." Ph.D. diss., Northwestern University, 1951.

Garon, Sheldon. *Molding Japanese Minds: The State in Everyday Life.* Princeton, NJ: Princeton University Press, 1997.

―――. "The World's Oldest Debate? Prostitution and the State in Imperial Japan, 1900–1945." *American Historical Review* 98, no. 3 (1993): 710–33.

Gillin, David and Charles Etter. "Staying On: Japanese Soldiers and Civilians in China, 1945–1949." *Journal of Asian Studies* 52, no. 3 (May 1983): 497–518.

Glassheim, Eagle. "National Mythologies and Ethnic Cleansing: The Expulsion of Czechoslovak Germans in 1945." *Central European History* 33, no. 4 (November 2000): 463–86.

Gluck, Carol. "The Human Condition." In *Past Imperfect: History According to the Movies*, ed. Mark C. Carnes, 250–53. New York: Henry Holt and Company, 1995.

———. "The Past in the Present." In *Postwar Japan as History*, ed. Andrew Gordon, 64–98. Berkeley, CA: University of California Press, 1993.

Gojo kaihō 互助会報 (subsequently, *Hikiage minpō* 引揚民報), 1946.

Gomikawa Junpei 五味川純平. "Genten toshite no waga *Sensō to ningen*" 原点 としてのわが『戦争と人間』 (My *War and People* as the point of origin). *Ushio* 潮 (Aug. 1971): 191–95.

———. *Ningen no jōken* 人間の条件 (The human condition). 6 vols. Kyoto: San'ichi shobō, 1956–58.

Gordon, Andrew. *Labor and Imperial Democracy in Prewar Japan*. Berkeley, CA: University of California Press, 1991.

———. *A Modern History of Japan, from Tokugawa Times to the Present*. Oxford, UK: Oxford University Press, 2003.

———. *The Wages of Affluence: Labor and Management in Postwar Japan*. Cambridge, MA: Harvard University Press, 1998.

Gosho Heinosuke 五所平之助, dir. *Kiiroi karasu* 黄色いからす (The yellow crow). Tokyo: Shōchiku, 1957.

Government Section, Supreme Commander for the Allied Powers. *Political Reorientation of Japan*. Washington, DC: Supreme Commander for the Allied Powers, 1968 [1948].

Grossmann, Atina. *Jews, Germans, and Allies: Close Encounters in Occupied Germany*. Princeton, NJ: Princeton University Press, 2007.

———. "A Question of Silence: The Rape of German Women by Occupation Soldiers." *October* 72 (Spring 1995): 43–63.

Guelcher, Gregory. "Dreams of Empire: The Japanese Agricultural Colonization of Manchuria (1931–1945) in History and Memory." Ph.D. diss., University of Illinois at Urbana-Champaign, 1999.

Gunma-ken kenmin seikatsubu sewaka 群馬県県民生活部世話課, ed. *Gunma-ken fukuin engo shi* 群馬県復員援護史 (The record of demobilization and welfare in Gunma Prefecture). Gunma: Gunma-ken, 1974.

Hakata hikiage engo kyoku (Kōseishō hikiage engoin) 博多引揚援護局(厚生省引揚援護院), ed. *Kyoku shi* 局史 (The history of the regional repatriation center). Fukuoka: Hakata hikiage engo kyoku, 1947.

Hani Susumu 羽仁進, dir. *Kanojo to kare* 彼女と彼 (She and he). Tokyo: Iwanami Eiga, 1963.

Hasegawa Machiko 長谷川町子. *Sazaesan* サザエさん. Vol. 1. Tokyo: Shimai-sha, 1959.

Hashikaku Tadao 橋角忠雄. "Hōmon omoshirokan: Kyōto-fu Maizuru hikiage kinenkan—hitomi o tojireba 'Ganpeki no haha' no uta ga. . . ." 訪問おもしろ館：京都府舞鶴引揚記念館 ——瞳を閉じれ ば「岸壁の母」の唄が. . . . (Interesting museums to visit: Kyoto's Maizuru Repatriation Museum—if you close your eyes, the song "Ganpeki no haha. . . ."). Gekkan shakaitō 月刊社会党 480 (June 1995): 73–82.

Hein, Laura and Mark Selden, eds. *Censoring History: Citizenship and Memory in Japan, Germany, and the United States.* Armonk, NY: M.E. Sharpe, 2000.

Heiwa kinen jigyō tokubestu kikin 平和祈念事業特別基金 (The Public Foundation for Peace and Consolation). Web. http://www.heiwa.go.jp/. Accessed August 15, 2008.

———, ed. *Keijō Nihonjin sewakai kaihō* 京城日本人世話会々報 (The newsletter of the Keijō Nihonjin sewakai). Tokyo: Heiwa kinen jigyō tokubetsu kikin, 1999 [1945–46].

Henriot, Christian. "'Little Japan' in Shanghai: An Insulated Community, 1875–1945." In *New Frontiers: Imperialism's New Communities in East Asia, 1843–1953,* ed. Robert Bickers and Christian Henriot, 146–69. Manchester and New York: Manchester University Press, 2000.

Hikiage dōhō 引揚同胞, 1946.

Hikiage dōhō shinbun 引揚同胞新聞, 1948–1949.

Hikiage engo chō 引揚援護庁. *Hikiage engo no kiroku* 引揚援護の記録 (A record of repatriation and aid). Tokyo: Kōseishō, 1950.

"Hikiage kaitakumin no nyūshoku ni tsuite no shitsumon chūisho ni taisuru tōben no ken" 引揚開拓民の入植についての質問注意書に対する答弁の件 (Questions regarding the agricultural resettlement of repatriated agricultural settlers). April 27, 1948. Kokuritsu kōbunshokan, 2A 28-3 rui 3321.

Hikiage minpō 引揚民報 (previously, *Gojo kaihō* 互助会報), 1946.

"Hikiage o motomete: kaetta hitobito 300-mannin no hikiagesha o matteita mono" 引揚げを求めて：帰った人々三百万人の引揚者を待っていた者 (Calling for repatriation: those who waited for the return of 3 million repatriates). *Shūkan shinchō* 週刊新潮 (February 11, 1957): 86–91.

Hikiagekō Hakata o kangaeru tsudoi 引揚港・博多を考える集い. *Sengo 50-nen hikiage o omou: Ajia no yūkō to heiwa o motomete* 戦後 50 年引揚げを思う：アジアの友好と平和をもとめて (Thinking about repatriation 50 years after the war: seeking friendship and peace in Asia). Fukuoka: Hikiagekō Hakata o kangaeru tsudoi henshū iinkai, 1995.

———. *Sengo 50-nen hikiage o omou (zoku): shōgen Futsuka'ichi hoyōjo* 戦後 50 年引揚げを思う(続)：証言二日市保養所 (Thinking about repatriation 50 years after the war, continued: testimony on the Futsuka'ichi Sanatorium). Fukuoka: Hikiagekō Hakata o kangaeru tsudoi henshū iinkai, 1998.

Hikiagekō Hakata wan: gaichi kara no hikiageshatachi no sonogo 引揚港・博多湾: 外地からの引き揚げ者たちのその後 (Repatriation harbor, Hakata Bay: the afterlives of repatriates from the colonies). RKB Mainichi Hōsō, 1978. Documentary, broadcast in Kyushu on June 28, 1978.

"Hikiagesha kyūfukin tō shikyū hō" 引揚者給付金等支給法 (Repatriate benefits allowance law). Law no. 109, May 17, 1957.

"Hikiagesha tō ni taisuru tokubetsu kōfukin no shikyū ni kansuru hōritsu" 引揚者等に対する特別交付金の支給に関する法律 (Repatriate special subsidy allowance law). Law no. 104. 55th Diet Session (Special), August 1, 1967.

"Hikiagesha no chitsujo hoji ni kansuru seirei" 引揚者の秩序保持に関する政令 (Cabinet order for preserving order among repatriates). Ordinance no. 300, August 11, 1949.

Hikiagesha no koe 引揚者の声, 1946.

"Hikiagete wa mita keredo" 引揚げてはみたけれど (I was repatriated but...). *Shinsō* 真相 (January 1950): 53–56.

Hikiage zenren tsūshin 引揚全連通信, 1956–.

Hirashima Toshio 平島敏夫. *Rakudo kara naraku e: Manshūkoku no shūen to 100-man dōhō hikiage jitsuroku* 楽土から奈落へ: 満洲国の終焉と百万同胞引揚げ実録 (From heaven to hell: the record of the end of Manchukuo and the repatriation of a million compatriots). Tokyo: Kōdansha, 1972.

"Hokuman hikiage fujin no shūdan ninpu chūzetsu shimatsuki: akai heitai no ko ga umarenu wake" 北満引揚婦人の集団妊娠中絶始末記: 赤い兵隊の子が生まれぬ訳 (The record of dealing with the mass abortions of pregnancies of women repatriated from North Manchuria: the reason that no children of Red soldiers were born). *Sandē mainichi* サンデー毎日 (March 29, 1953): 4–10.

Honda Yasuharu 本田靖春. "Nihon no 'Kamyu' tachi: 'hikiage taiken' kara sakkatachi wa umareta" 日本の「カミュ」たち:「引揚げ体験」から作家たちは生れた (The "Camus" of Japan: writers born of the "repatriate experience"). *Shokun* 諸君 7 (1979): 198–225.

Igarashi, Yoshikuni. "Belated Homecomings: Japanese Prisoners of War in Siberia and their Return to Postwar Japan." In *Prisoners of War, Prisoners of Peace: Captivity, Homecoming and Memory in World War II*, ed. Bob Moore and Barbara Hately-Broad, 105–121. New York: Berg, 2005.

———. *Bodies of Memory: Narratives of War in Postwar Japanese Culture, 1945–1970*. Princeton, NJ: Princeton University Press, 2000.

Iiyama Tatsuo 飯山達雄. *Haisen, hikiage no dōkoku* 敗戦・引揚げの慟哭 (A lament for defeat and repatriation). Vol. 3 of *Harukanaru Chūgoku tairiku shashinshū* 遥かなる中国大陸写真集 (Photographs from the distant Chinese continent). Tokyo: Kokusho kankōkai, 1979.

———. "Kimin 41-nen no kokka sekinin, zoku: Chūgoku zanryū koji ni Kantōgun kazoku wa inai" 棄民 41 年の国家責任、続：中国残留孤児に関東軍家族はいない (State responsibility for abandoned peoples 41 years ago, continued: among the orphans left behind in China, there are no family members of the Kwantun Army). *Asahi jānaru* 朝日ジャーナル 28, no. 25 (1986): 88–92.

Imai Shūji 今井脩二. "Rira saku gogatsu to nareba" リラ咲く五月とねれば (When May arrives and the lilacs bloom). *Minato* みなと (June 1947): 20–30.

Inaba Jurō 稲葉寿郎. "Hikiagesha no sengo: Tsuchiura hikiageryō o chūshin ni" 引揚者の戦後：土浦引揚寮を中心に (Postwar for the repatriates: the Tsuchiura repatriate dormitory). In *Kokumin kokka no kōzu* 国民国家の構図 (The structure of the nation state), ed. Ōhama Tetsuya 大浜徹也, 283–306. Tokyo: Yūzankaku, 1999.

Iriye, Akira. *The Cold War in Asia: A Historical Introduction.* Englewood Cliffs, NJ: Prentice Hall, 1974.

Ishikawa Hiroyoshi 石川弘義 et al., eds. *Taishū bunka jiten* 大衆文化事典 (Dictionary of popular culture). Tokyo: Kōbundo, 1991.

Itsuki Hiroyuki 五木寛之. *Unmei no ashioto* 運命の足音 (Fate's footsteps). Tokyo: Gentōsha, 2003.

Iwanami shoten henshūbu 岩波書店編集部, ed. *Kindai Nihon sōgō nenpyō* 近代日本総合年表 (Timeline of modern Japanese history). Third edition. Tokyo: Iwanami shoten, 1991.

Iwasaki Jirō 岩崎爾郎. *Bukka no sesō 100-nen* 物価の世相 100 年 (A hundred-year social history of the cost of living). Tokyo: Yomiuri shinbunsha, 1982.

James, D. Clayton. *The Years of MacArthur.* Vol. 3. Boston, MA: Houghton Mifflin, 1985.

Jiji shinpō 時事新報, 1949.

Johnston, William. *The Modern Epidemic: A History of Tuberculosis in Japan.* Cambridge, MA: Council on East Asian Studies, Harvard University, 1995.

Judt, Tony. *Postwar: A History of Europe Since 1945.* New York: Penguin, 2005.

Kaigai hikiage shinbun 海外引揚新聞, 1946–.

Kajiyama Toshiyuki. *The Clan Records: Five Stories of Korea.* Trans. Yoshiko Kurata Dykstra. Honolulu, HI: University of Hawai'i Press, 1961 [1995].

Kami Shōichirō 上笙一郎. *Man-Mō kaitaku seishōnen giyūgun* 満蒙開拓青少年義勇軍 (The Manchurian and Mongolian youth corps brigades). Tokyo: Chūkō shinsho, 1973.

Kaminogō Toshiaki 上之郷利昭. "Tokushū 2: mō hitotsu no shūsen shori Sasebo hikiage engokyoku 140-nin no monogatari: '1000-nen mirai toshi' ni

nemuru senzen, senchū, sengo" 特集 2 もう一つの終戦処理 佐世保
引揚援護局・一四〇人の物語：「一〇〇〇年の未来都市」に眠る
戦前・戦中・戦後 (Special issue 2: another postwar cleanup the Sasebo
regional repatriation center stories of 140 people: the prewar, wartime, and
postwar that sleeps in the "future city of 1,000 years"). *Rekishi kaidō* 歴史
街道 (September 1998): 78–87.

Kamitsubo Takashi 上坪隆. *Mizuko no uta: dokyumento hikiage koji to onnatachi*
水子の譜: ドキュメント引揚孤児と女たち (The song of the fetus: a
documentary look at repatriate orphans and women). Tokyo: Shakai shisōsha,
1993.

———. *Mizuko no uta: hikiage koji to okasareta onnatachi no kiroku Shōwa shi no ki-
roku* 水子の譜: 引揚孤児と犯された女たちの記録　昭和史の記録
(The song of the fetus: a record of repatriate orphans and violated women).
Tokyo: Gendai shi shuppankai, 1979.

Kang Chae-ŏn 姜在彦 and Kim Tong-hun 金東勲. *Zainichi Kankoku/Chōsenjin:
rekishi to tenbō* 在日韓国・朝鮮人—歴史と展望 (South and North Korean
residents in Japan: history and prospects). Tokyo: Rōdō keizaisha, 1989.

Katō Kiyofumi 加藤聖文, ed. *Kaigai hikiage kankei shiryō shūsei* 海外引揚関係
史料集成 (Collection of historical documents on repatriation from overseas). Tokyo: Yumani shobō, 2002.

Katō Yōko 加藤陽子. "Haisha no kikan: Chūgoku kara no fukuin, hikiage
mondai no tenkai" 敗者の帰還: 中国からの復員・引揚問題の展開
(Demobilization and repatriation of Japanese armed forces in China). *Kokusai
seiji* 国際政治 (May 1995): 110–25.

Kawachi Sensuke. "Sazanka." In *Ukiyo: Stories of Postwar Japan*, ed. Jay Gluck,
195–202. New York: Grosset's Universal Library, 1964.

Kawahara Isao 河原功. *Taiwan hikiage ryūyō kiroku* 台湾引揚留用記録 (The
record of repatriation and staying behind in Taiwan). 10 vols. Tokyo: Yumani
shobō, 1997–98.

Kawamoto Saburō 川本三郎. "Sarai shinema rebyū nozoku: Maizurukō wa
samazama na 'sengo' no dorama o unda" サライシネマレビュー覗く：
舞鶴港は様々な「戦後」のドラマを生んだ (Sarai movie review:
a look at the "postwar" dramas created by the Maizuru harbor). *Sarai* サライ
(September 17, 1992): 116–17.

Kawamura Minato 川村湊. *Ikyō no Shōwa bungaku: "Manshū" to kindai Nihon*
異郷の昭和文学:「満州」と近代日本 (Shōwa literature from another
land: "Manshū" and modern Japan). Tokyo: Iwanami shinsho, 1990.

———. *Sakubun no naka no dai Nippon teikoku* 作文のなかの大日本帝国 (The
Japanese empire in Japanese writing). Tokyo: Iwanami shoten, 2000.

————. *Sengo bungaku o tou: sono taiken to rinen* 戦後文学を問う：その体験と理念 (An inquiry into postwar literature: experience and ideas). Tokyo: Iwanami shinsho, 1995.

"Kikokusen o meguru shinbun gassen" 帰国船をめぐる新聞合戦 (The newspaper war over returning ships). *Chūō kōron* 中央公論 (May 1953): 152–61.

Kim, Key-Hiuk. *The Last Phase of the East Asian World Order: Korea, Japan, and the Chinese Empire, 1860–1882*. Berkeley and Los Angeles, CA: University of California Press, 1980.

Kimoto Itaru 木本至. *Zasshi de yomu sengo shi* 雑誌で読む戦後史 (Postwar history through reading magazines). Tokyo: Shinchō sencho, 1985.

Kimura Hideaki 木村秀明. *Aru sengo shi no joshō: MRU hikiage iryō no kiroku* ある戦後史の序章：MRU 引揚医療の記録 (A prologue to postwar history: a record of the Mobile Relief Unit for treating repatriates). Fukuoka: Nishi Nihon toshokan konsarutanto kyōkai, 1980.

Kimura Takuji 木村卓滋. "Demobilization and the Dismantling of the Japanese Imperial Military." Paper presented at the AAS annual convention, Washington, DC, April 6, 2002.

————. "Sensōbyōsha senbotsusha izoku tō engohō no seitei to gunjin onkyū no fukkatsu: kyū gunjin kanren dantai e no eikyō o chūshin ni" 戦傷病者戦没者遺族等援護法の制定と軍人恩給の復活 ： 旧軍人関連団体への影響を中心に (The establishment of the law for aiding injured and sick veterans and bereaved family members and the revival of pensions for military men: influence on veterans' organizations). *Jinmin no rekishigaku* 人民の歴史学 (1997): 1–10.

Kinema junpōsha キネマ旬報社, ed. *Nihon eiga terebi kantoku zenshū* 日本映画テレビ監督全集 (Film and television directors in Japan). Tokyo: Kinema junpōsha, 1988.

Kobayashi Masaki 小林正樹, dir. *Ningen no jōken* 人間の条件 (The human condition). 3 parts. Tokyo: Shōchiku, 1958, 1960, 1961.

Kokusaijin 国際人, 1947–48.

Komiya Kiyoshi 小宮清. *Manshū memorī mappu* 満州メモリー・マップ (A "memory map" of Manchuria). Tokyo: Chikuma shobō, 1990.

Konpeki 紺碧, 1954–.

Kōseishō engokyoku 厚生省援護局. *Chūgoku zanryū koji: kore made no sokuseki to kore kara no michinori* 中国残留孤児：これまでの足跡とこれからの道のり. Tokyo: Gyōsei, 1987.

Kōseishō engokyoku 厚生省援護局. *Hikiage to engo 30-nen no ayumi* 引揚げと援護三十年の歩み (A thirty-year history of repatriation and aid). Tokyo: Kōseishō, 1977.

Kōseishō 50-nen shi henshū iinkai 厚生省五十年史編集委員会, ed. *Kōseishō 50-nen shi, shiryō hen* 厚生省五十年史 資料篇 (A fifty-year history of the Ministry of Health and Welfare, documents). Tokyo: Kōseishō 50-nen shi henshū iinkai, 1988.

Kōseishō hikiage engokyoku 厚生省引揚援護局. *Zoku hikiage engo no kiroku* 続：引揚援護の記録 (A record of repatriation and aid, vol. 2). Tokyo: Kōseishō, 1955.

──────. *Zoku zoku: hikiage engo no kiroku* 続々：引揚援護の記録 (A record of repatriation and aid, vol. 3). Tokyo: Kōseishō, 1963.

Kōseishō Senzaki hikiage engokyoku 厚生省仙崎引揚援護局. *Senzaki hikiage engokyoku shi* 仙崎引揚援護局史 (The history of the Senzaki regional repatriation center). Senzaki: Kōseishō Senzaki hikiage engokyoku, 1946.

Kōseishō shakai engokyoku 厚生省社会援護局. *Engo 50-nen shi* 援護 50 年史 (A fifty-year history of aid). Tokyo: Gyōsei, 1997.

Koshiro, Yukiko. *Trans-Pacific Racisms and the U.S. Occupation of Japan.* New York: Columbia University Press, 1999.

Krieger, Paul Henry. "The Fantastic Stories of Abe Kōbō: A Study of Three Early Short Stories, with Translations." Ph.D. diss., University of Minnesota, 1991.

Kunihiro Yasuo 国弘威雄. *Korotō daikenhen: Nihonjin nanmin 105-man hikiage no kiroku* 葫蘆島大遣返：日本人難民１０５万引揚げの記録 (The great deportation from Huludao: the record of the repatriation of 1,050,000 Japanese refugees). Documentary, 1998.

──────. "Korotō daikenhen: Nihonjin nanmin 105-man hikiage no kiroku" 葫蘆島大遣返：日本人難民 105 万引揚げの記録. *Shinario* シナリオ, no. 4 (1998): 72–103.

Kuramoto, Kazuko. *Manchurian Legacy: Memoirs of a Japanese Colonist.* East Lansing, MI: Michigan State University Press, 1999.

Kushner, Barak. *The Thought War: Japanese Imperial Propaganda.* Honolulu, HI: University of Hawai'i Press, 2006.

Kuznetsov, S. I. "The Ideological Indoctrination of Japanese Prisoners of War in the Stalinist Camps of the Soviet Union." Trans. Mary E. Glantz. *Journal of Slavic Military Studies* 10, no. 4 (December 1997): 86–103.

──────. "The Situation of Japanese Prisoners of War in Soviet Camps (1945–1956)." Trans. Col. David M. Glantz. *Journal of Slavic Military Studies* 8, no. 3 (September 1995): 612–29.

Lamley, Harry J. "Taiwan Under Japanese Rule, 1895–1945: The Vicissitudes of Colonialism." In *Taiwan: A New History*, ed. Murray A. Rubinstein, 201–60. Armonk, NY: M. E. Sharpe, 1999.

Lee, Changsoo and George De Vos. *Koreans in Japan: Ethnic Conflict and Accommodation.* Berkeley and Los Angeles, CA: University of California Press, 1981.

Lie, John. *Multiethnic Japan.* Cambridge, MA: Harvard University Press, 2001.

Lone, Stewart. *Japan's First Modern War.* London: St. Martin's Press, 1994.

Lynn, Hyung Gu. "Malthusian Dreams, Colonial Imagery: The Oriental Development Company and Japanese Emigration to Korea." In *Settler Colonialism in the Twentieth Century: Projects, Practices, Legacies,* ed. Caroline Elkins and Susan Pedersen, 25–40. New York and London: Routledge, 2005.

Machi Jurō 町樹郎. "Kin-ken shūchūei" 錦県集中営 (The Kin-ken refugee camp). *Minato* みなと 19 (February 1948): 28–33.

Magnier, Mark. "Tokyo Governor Assails Critics, Says Remarks Were Misunderstood." *Los Angeles Times,* April 13, 2000.

Maizuru chihō hikiage engokyoku 舞鶴地方引揚援護局. *Maizuru chihō hikiage engokyoku shi* 舞鶴地方引揚援護局史 (The history of the Maizuru regional repatriation center). Tokyo: Kōseishō hikiage engokyoku, 1961.

Maizuru-shi 舞鶴市, ed. *Hikiagekō Maizuru no kiroku* 引揚港舞鶴の記録 (A record of Maizuru as a repatriation harbor). Maizuru: Maizuru-shi, 1990.

Maizuru hikiage kinenkan 舞鶴引揚記念館. *Haha naru minato Maizuru* 母なる港舞鶴 (Our mother harbor Maizuru). Maizuru: Maizuru hikiage kinenkan, 1995.

Man-Mō dōhō engokai 満蒙同胞援護会, ed. *Man-Mō shūsen shi* 満蒙終戦史 (The end of the war in Manchuria and Mongolia). Tokyo: Kawade shobō, 1962.

Marrus, Michael R. *The Unwanted: European Refugees in the Twentieth Century.* New York: Oxford University Press, 1985.

Matsusaka, Yoshihisa Tak. *The Making of Japanese Manchuria, 1904–1932.* Cambridge, MA: Harvard University Asia Center, 2001.

Mayo, Marlene. "The War of Words Continues: American Radio Guidance in Occupied Japan." In *The Occupation of Japan: Arts and Culture,* ed. Thomas W. Burkman, 45–83. Norfolk, VA: General Douglas MacArthur Foundation, 1988.

McWilliams, Wayne C. *Homeward Bound: Repatriation of Japanese from Korea.* Hong Kong: Asian Research Service, 1988.

Minakawa Takahira 皆川考平. "Hikiagesha mondai ni yosete" 引揚者問題に寄せて (Addressing the repatriation problem). Addendum to *Hadaka no 600-mannin: Manshū hikiagesha no shuki* 裸の六百万人：満洲引揚者の手記 (The naked six million: the notes of a Manchurian repatriate), by Tamana Katsuo 玉名勝夫, 125–35. Tokyo: Shunkōsha, 1948.

Minato みなと, 1946–.

Mitchell, Richard. *The Korean Minority in Japan*. Berkeley and Los Angeles, CA: University of California Press, 1967.

Moeller, Robert G. *War Stories: The Search for a Usable Past in the Federal Republic of Germany*. Berkeley and Los Angeles, CA: University of California Press, 2001.

Molasky, Michael S. *The American Occupation of Japan and Okinawa: Literature and Memory*. New York: Routledge, 1999.

Morita Yoshio 森田芳夫. *Chōsen Shūsen no Kiroku: Bei-So ryōgun no shinchū to Nihonjin no hikiage* 朝鮮終戦の記録：米ソ両軍の進駐と日本人の引揚げ (A record of the end of the war in Korea: the American and Soviet Occupation and the repatriation of Japanese). Tokyo: Gannandō shoten, 1967.

Morris-Suzuki, Tessa. "A Descent into the Past: The Frontier in the Construction of Japanese Identity." In *Multicultural Japan: Paleolithic to Postmodern*, ed. Donald Denoon and Gavan McCormack, 81–94. Cambridge, UK: Cambridge University Press, 1997.

———. *Exodus to North Korea: Shadows from Japan's Cold War*, Lanham, MD: Rowman and Littlefield, 2007.

———. "Northern Lights: The Making and Unmaking of Karafuto Identity." *Journal of Asian Studies* 60, no. 3 (August 2001): 645–71.

Murakami Haruki. *The Wind-Up Bird Chronicle*. Trans. Jay Rubin. New York: Knopf, 1997. Originally published in three volumes as *Nejimakidori kuronikuru*. Tokyo: Shinchōsha, 1994–95.

Myers, Ramon H. and Mark R. Peattie, eds. *The Japanese Colonial Empire, 1895–1945*. Princeton, NJ: Princeton University Press, 1984.

Nagano-ken kaitaku jikōkai Manshū kaitaku shi kankōkai 長野県開拓自興会満州開拓史刊行会, ed. *Nagano-ken Manshū kaitaku shi* 長野県満州開拓史 (The history of Nagano Prefecture agricultural settlements in Manchuria). 3 vols. Nagano: Nagano-ken kaitaku jikōkai Manshū kaitaku shi kankōkai, 1984.

Naikaku sōri daijin kanbō kanrishitsu 内閣総理大臣官房管理室. *Zaigai zaisan mondai no shori kiroku: hikiagesha tokubetsu kōfukin no shikyū* 在外財産問題の処理記録：引揚者特別交付金の支給 (The record of addressing the problem of overseas assets: the repatriate special subsidy allowance law). Tokyo: Naikaku sōri daijin kanbō kanrishitsu, 1973.

Naimark, Norman. *Fires of Hatred: Ethnic Cleansing in the Twentieth Century*. Cambridge, MA: Harvard University Press, 2001.

Natsume Sōseki. "Travels in Manchuria and Korea." In *Rediscovering Natsume Sōseki,* trans. Inger Sigrun Brodey and Sammy Tsunematsu. Kent, UK: Global Books, 2000.

"Nenpu" 年譜. In *Shin'ei bungaku sōsho* 新鋭文学叢書. Vol. 2. *Abe Kōbō shū* 安部公房集. Tokyo: Chikuma shobō, 1960.

NHK. *Saikai: 35-nenme no tairiku no ko* 再会: 35年目の大陸の子 (To meet again: children of the continent after 35 years). Documentary. Originally aired on NHK on September 9, 1980.

Nihon keizai shinbun 日本経済新聞, 1949–50.

Nimmo, William F. *Behind a Curtain of Silence: Japanese in Soviet Custody, 1945–1956*. Westport, CT: Greenwood Press, 1988.

Norgren, Tiana. *Abortion Before Birth Control*. Princeton, NJ: Princeton University Press, 2001.

Odaka Kōnosuke 尾高煌之助. "Hikiagesha to sensō chokugo no rōdōryoku" 引揚者と戦争直後の労働力 (Repatriates and the labor force immediately after the war). *Tōkyō Daigaku shakaigaku kenkyūjo kiyō* 東京大学社会学研究所紀要 (April 1996): 135–44.

Oguma Eiji 小熊英二. *A Genealogy of "Japanese" Self-Images*. Trans. David Askew. Melbourne: Trans Pacific Press, 2002.

———. *Tan'itsu minzoku shinwa no kigen* 単一民族神話の起源 (The myth of the homogeneous nation). Tokyo: Shin'yōsha, 1995.

Okamoto, Koichi. "Imaginary Settings: Sino-Japanese-U.S. Relations during the Occupation Years." Ph.D. diss., Columbia University, 2001.

Ōkubo Maki 大久保真紀. *Chūgoku zanryū Nihonjin: "kimin" no keika to kikokugo no kunan* 中国残留日本人: 「棄民」の経過と、帰国後の苦難 (Japanese left behind in China: the process of becoming "abandoned people" and troubles after returning to Japan). Tokyo: Tōbunken, 2006.

Okuizumi Eizaburō, ed. *User's Guide to the Gordon W. Prange Collection: Microfilm Edition of Censored Periodicals, 1945–1949*. Tokyo: Yūshōdō shoten, 1982.

Ōkurashō kanrikyoku 大蔵省管理局. *Nihonjin no kaigai katsudō ni kansuru rekishiteki chōsa* 日本人の海外活動に関する歴史的調査 (A historical survey of the overseas activities of Japanese nationals). 12 Volumes. Seoul: Kōrai shorin, 1983 [1947].

Onshi zaidan engo kaihō 恩賜財団同胞援護会報, 1949–.

Ōnuma Yasuaki 大沼保昭. *Saharin kimin: sengo sekinin no tenkei* サハリン棄民: 戦後責任の点景 (The abandoned on Sakhalin: a look at postwar responsibility). Tokyo: Chūkō shinsho, 1992.

Orr, James J. *The Victim as Hero: Ideologies of Peace and National Identity in Postwar Japan*. Honolulu, HI: University of Hawai'i Press, 2001.

Ōshima Nagisa 大島渚, dir. *Gishiki* 儀式 (Ceremony). Tokyo: ATG, 1971.

———. "Kieta Nagano-ken no Yomikaki-mura" 消えた長野県の読書村 (The village of Yomikaki from Nagano Prefecture that disappeared). *Ushio* 潮 (August 1971): 196–207.

Ōta Masahide. "The U.S. Occupation of Okinawa and Postwar Reforms in Japan Proper." In *Democratizing Japan: The Allied Occupation*, ed. Robert E. Ward and Sakamoto Yoshikazu, 284–305. Honolulu, HI: University of Hawai'i Press, 1987.

Ōtani Susumu 大谷進. *Ikiteiru: Ueno chikadō no jittai* 生きてゐる：上野地下道 の実態 (Surviving: the reality of the Ueno underpass). Tokyo: Sengo Nihon shakai setai shi, 1948.

Ozaki Kazuo 尾崎一雄, Kanbayashi Akatsuki 上林暁, and Tonomura Shigeru 外村繁. "Sōsaku gappyō" 創作合評 (A joint review of works). *Gunzō* 群像 12, no. 5 (1957): 240–52.

Ozawa Seiji 小澤征爾. *Chichi o kataru* 父を語る (Speaking of my father). To-kyo: Chūō kōron jigyō shuppan, 1972.

"Ozawa's Vienna Debut Will Be a Waltz Worth the Wait." *Boston Globe*, January 1, 2002.

Parrott, Lindesay. "Japan to Punish Red Repatriates." Special to the *New York Times*, August 10, 1949.

————. "Japanese Repatriated by Soviet Sworn to Communize Homeland." Special to the *New York Times*, June 28, 1949.

Pepper, Suzanne. *Civil War in China: The Political Struggle, 1945–1949.* Berkeley and Los Angeles, CA: University of California Press, 1978.

Phillips, Steven E. *Between Assimilation and Independence: The Taiwanese Encounter Nationalist China, 1945–1950.* Stanford, CA: Stanford University Press, 2003.

Radtke, K. W. "Negotiations between the PRC and Japan on the Return of Japanese Civilians and the Repatriation of Japanese Prisoners of War." In *Leyden Studies in Sinology: Papers Presented at the Conference held in Celebration of the Fiftieth Anniversary of the Sinological Institute of Leyden University, December 8–12, 1980,* ed. W. L. Idema, 190–213. Leyden: Brill, 1981.

Ravina, Mark. *The Last Samurai: The Life and Battles of Saigō Takamori.* Hoboken, NJ: John Wiley & Sons, 2003.

Reischauer, Edwin O. "Forward." In *The Korean Minority in Japan, 1904–1950,* by Edward D. Wagner. New York: Institute of Pacific Relations, 1951.

Reishi shinbun 励志新聞, 1947.

Rogaski, Ruth. *Hygienic Modernity: Meanings of Health and Disease in Treaty-Port China.* Berkeley and Los Angeles, CA: University of California Press, 2004.

Roseman, Mark. "Refugees and Ruhr Miners: A Case Study of the Impact of the Refugees on Post-War German Society." In *Refugees in the Age of Total War*, ed. Anna C. Bramwell, 185–98. London: Unwin Hyman, 1988.

Ross, Kristin. *Fast Cars, Clean Bodies: Decolonization and the Reordering of French Culture.* Cambridge, MA: The MIT Press, 1996.

"Rupo: hikiagete wa kita keredo ルポ：引揚げてはきたけれど (I was repatriated, but . . .)." *Chūō kōron* 中央公論 (February 1949): 29–35.

"Ruporutāju: hikiagete wa mita keredo" ルポルタージュ：引揚げてはみた
けれど (I was repatriated, but . . .). *Nihon shūhō* 日本週報 (May 1949): 8–13.

Saraki Yoshihisa 皿木喜久. "ZOOM UP: jūnen no danshō o tōshite miete kuru
sengo 50-nen, soshite kono kuni no 'rinkaku.'" ZOOM UP: 10 年の断章を
通して見えてくる戦後 50 年、そしてこの国の「輪郭」 (ZOOM
UP: what we can see of the 50 postwar years by looking in ten year fragments,
and the "contours" of this country). *Shūkan SPA!* 週刊 SPA! (February 1,
1995), 26–28.

Sasebo hikiage engokyoku jōhōka 佐世保引揚援護局情報課. *Sasebo hikiage
engokyoku shi* 佐世保引揚援護局史 (The history of the Sasebo regional repatriation center). Vols. 1 and 2. Sasebo hikiage engokyoku, 1949.

"Sasebo-shi Uragashira hikiage kinen heiwa kōen" 佐世保市浦頭引揚記念平
和公園 (The Sasebo Uragashira repatriation memorial park). Undated pamphlet. Sasebo: Uragashira hikiage kinen heiwa kōen, shiryōkan.

Saunders, E. Dale. "Abe Kōbō." In *Kodansha Encyclopedia of Japan*, vol. 1, 2–3. Tokyo: Kodansha, 1983.

Sawachi Hisae 沢地久枝. *Mō hitotsu no Manshū* もうひとつの満洲 (Another
Manshū). Tokyo: Bungei shunjū, 1986.

Schaller, Michael. *The American Occupation of Japan: The Origins of the Cold War in
Asia.* New York: Oxford University Press, 1985.

Schlesinger, Jacob M. *Shadow Shoguns: The Rise and Fall of Japan's Postwar Political
Machine.* New York: Simon & Schuster, 1997.

Sengo kaitaku shi hensan iinkai 戦後開拓史編纂委員会. *Sengo kaitaku shi* 戦
後開拓史 (A history of postwar agricultural pioneering). 3 vols. Tokyo: Zenkoku kaitaku nōgyō kyōdō kumiai rengōkai, 1967.

Sensaisha jihō 戦災者時報, 1946.

Sensō giseisha 戦争犠牲者, 1946.

Seraphim, Franziska. *War Memory and Social Politics in Japan, 1945–2005.* Cambridge, MA: Harvard University Asia Center, 2006.

Shibusawa, Naoko. *America's Geisha Ally: Reimagining the Japanese Enemy.* Cambridge, MA: Harvard University Press, 2006.

Shimane-ken gaichi hikiage minpō 島根県外地引揚民報, 1946–47.

Shinkensetsu 新建設, 1946.

Shinonoi heiwa katsudō iinkai 篠ノ井平和活動委員会. "Kodomotachi ni ikasareta 85-nen" 子どもたちに生かされた 85 年 (85 years of being kept
alive by children). *Pīsu messēji* ピースメッセージ, 37–41. Locally published
pamphlet. Nagano: Kōpu Nagano, 1996.

Shūkan Asahi 週刊朝日, ed. *Nedanshi nenpyō: Meiji, Taishō, Shōwa* 値段史年表：
明治・大正・昭和 (A timeline of the history of prices in Meiji, Taishō, and
Shōwa). Tokyo: Asahi shinbunsha, 1988.

Smith, Andrea L., ed. *Europe's Invisible Migrants*. Amsterdam: Amsterdam University Press, 2003.

Sorlin, Pierre. "Children as War Victims in Postwar European Cinema." In *War and Remembrance in the Twentieth Century*, ed. Jay Winter and Emmanuel Sivan, 104–24. Cambridge, UK: Cambridge University Press, 1999.

"Stardust: 'Hikiage' kara hanseki: Hakatakō ni tōjō shita Toyofuku Tomonori no kinenhi" 「引き揚げ」から半世紀: 博多港に登場した豊福知徳の記念碑 (The appearance of Toyofuka Tomonori's memorial in Hakata harbor, a half a century after "repatriation"). *Geijutsu shinchō* 芸術新潮 5 (1996): 123–24.

Stora, Benjamin. *Algeria, 1830–2000: A Short History*. Trans. Jane Marie Todd. Ithaca, NY: Cornell University Press, 2001.

———. "The 'Southern' World of the *Pieds Noirs*: References to and Representations of Europeans in Colonial Algeria." In *Settler Colonialism in the Twentieth Century: Projects, Practices, Legacies*, ed. Caroline Elkins and Susan Pedersen, 225–41. New York and London: Routledge, 2005.

Sun Jae-won 宣在源. "Nihon no koyō seido: fukkōki (1945–49) no koyō chōsei" 日本の雇用制度—復興期 (1945–49 年)の雇用調整 (The employment system in Japan—an employment adjustment during the reconstruction period [1945–49]). *Keizaigaku ronshū* 経済学論集 (April 1998): 17–48.

———. "The Reverse Impact of Colonialism: Repatriation and Resettlement of Japanese Entrepeneurs after the Second World War." In *Japanese Settler Colonialism in Japan: Advancing, Settling Down, and Returning to Japan, 1905–1950*, ed. Andrew Gordon, 23–31. Reischauer Institute of Japanese Studies, Occasional Papers in Japanese Studies, no. 2002–03. Cambridge, MA: Reischauer Institute of Japanese Studies, Harvard University, 2002.

Supreme Commander for the Allied Powers. *Reports of General MacArthur: MacArthur in Japan: The Occupation, Military Phase*. Vol. 1, Supplement. Washington, DC: U.S. Government Printing Office, 1966 [1950].

Suzuki Takashi 鈴木隆史. *Nihon teikokushugi to Manshū: 1900–1945* 日本帝国主義と満州: 1900–1945 (Japanese imperialism and Manchuria). Vol. 2. Tokyo: Hanawa shobō, 1992.

Tabata Yoshio 田端義夫 and Seshi Bonta 世志凡太. "Sore ga tōi rekishi ni naru mae ni: 'Kaeribune' ni takushita senchū sengo" それが、遠い歴史になる前に「かえり船」に託した戦中・戦後 (Before that became ancient history: the wartime and postwar behind the song "Kaeribune"). *Rekishi kaidō* 歴史街道 (April 2000): 123–29.

Taira, Koji. "Troubled National Identity: The Ryukyuans/Okinawans." In *Japan's Minorities: The Illusion of Homogeneity*, ed. Michael Weiner, 140–77. New York: Routledge, 1997.

Takahashi Saburō 高橋三郎. *"Senki mono" o yomu: sensō taiken to sengo Nihon shakai* 「戦記もの」を読む: 戦争体験と戦後日本社会 (Reading "war stories": war experiences and postwar Japan). Kyoto: Academia shuppankai, 1988.

Takeda Shigetarō 武田繁太郎. *Chinmoku no 40-nen: hikiage josei kyōsei chūzetsu no kiroku* 沈黙の四十年: 引き揚げ女性強制中絶の記録 (Forty years of silence: a record of the forced abortions on repatriated women). Tokyo: Chūō kōronsha, 1985.

Takemae Eiji 竹前栄治, ed. *GHQ shirei sōshūsei* GHQ 指令総集成 (Complete compilation of SCAPINs). 15 vols. Tokyo: Emutei shuppan, 1993.

———. *Inside GHQ: The Allied Occupation of Japan and Its Legacy.* Trans. and adapted by Robert Rickets and Sebastian Swann. New York: Continuum, 2002.

Tamana Katsuo 玉名勝夫. *Hadaka no 600-mannin: Manshū hikiagesha no shuki* 裸の六百万人: 満洲引揚者の手記 (The naked six million: the notes of a Manchurian repatriate). Tokyo: Shunkōsha, 1948.

Tamanoi, Mariko. "Knowledge, Power, and Racial Classification: The 'Japanese' in 'Manchuria.'" *Journal of Asian Studies* 59, no. 2 (May 2000): 248–76.

———. "A Road to a Redeemed Mankind: The Politics of Memory among the Former Peasant Settlers in Manchuria." *South Atlantic Quarterly* 99, no. 1 (2001): 143–71.

Tanaka Hiroshi 田中宏. *Zainichi gaikokujin: hō no kabe, kokoro no mizo* 在日外国人: 法の壁、心の溝 (Resident foreigners in Japan: legal and psychological obstacles to equality). Tokyo: Iwanami shinsho, 1995.

Tanizaki Jun'ichirō. *The Makioka Sisters.* Trans. Edward G. Seidensticker. New York: Vintage, 1995.

———. *Sasameyuki* 細雪. Tōkyō: Ōbunsha, 1969.

Tōhoku dōhō 東北導報. Shenyang and Changchun editions, 1946–48.

Tokuda Tsuneo 徳田恒夫. "Kaigai hikiagesha wa uttaeru" 海外引揚者は訴へる (Protests of overseas repatriates). *Minshū no hata* 民衆の旗 (November 1946): 38–41.

Tōkyō shinbun 東京新聞, 1949–80.

Tōkyō-to 東京都. *Okaerinasai kikan no minasama* おかえりなさい帰還の皆様 (Welcome home, returnees). Tokyo: Tominshitsu kōhōbu minseikyoku hogobu. 1953.

Toyama-ken kōseibu shakai fukushika 富山県厚生部社会福祉課, ed. *Toyama-ken shūsen shori shi* 富山県終戦処理史 (The history of managing the end of the war in Toyama Prefecture). Toyama: Toyama-ken, 1975.

Tōyō keizai shinpōsha 東洋経済新報社, ed. *Kanketsu Shōwa kokusei sōran.* 完結 昭和国勢総覧 (Complete overview of national population in the Shōwa period). Vol. 3. Tokyo: Tōyō keizai shinpōsha, 1991.

Tsukada Asae 塚田浅江. "Haisen zengo no Senzan Sarashinagō kaitakudan hinan jōkyō kiroku" 敗戦前後の尖山更級郷開拓団避難状況記録 (A record of the flight of the Senzan Sarashina agricultural settlement before and after the war). Diary written in the Ueyamada Hospital, Nagano Prefecture, November 1946.

―――. "Kaitaku gakkō no omoide" 開拓学校の思い出 (Recollections of the school in the Manchurian agricultural settlement). In *Man-Mō kaitaku no shuki: Nagano kenjin no kiroku* 満蒙開拓の手記 長野県人の記録 (Notes from the Manchurian and Mongolian agricultural settlements: records from the people of Nagano Prefecture), ed. Nozoe Kenji 野添憲治, 332–39. Tokyo: Nihon hōsō shuppan kyōkai, 1979.

Uchida, Jun. "Brokers of Empire: Japanese and Korean Business Elites in Colonial Korea." In *Settler Colonialism in the Twentieth Century: Projects, Practices, Legacies,* ed. Caroline Elkins and Susan Pedersen, 153–71. New York and London: Routledge, 2005.

Ueno, Chizuko. "The Politics of Memory: Nation, Individual and Self." *History & Memory* 11, no. 2 (Winter/Fall 1999): 129–52.

United States Air Force. *Japanese Repatriates, Ōtake* (film footage). RG 342, Frames 11026–28, April 1946.

United States Army Military Government in Korea (USAMGIK), Headquarters. "Repatriation from 25 September 1945 to 31 December 1945. Report. Prepared by William J. Gane. Seoul: United States Army, 1946.

United States, Office of Strategic Services, Research and Analysis Branch. "Japanese Civilians Overseas." (Report no. 2691). Washington, 1945.

Wagner, Edward D. *The Korean Minority in Japan, 1904–1950.* New York: Institute of Pacific Relations, 1951.

Wakatsuki Yasuo 若槻泰雄. *Sengo hikiage no kiroku* 戦後引揚げの記録 (A record of postwar repatriation). Tokyo: Jiji tsūshinsha, 1991.

Wolff, Stefan. *The German Question since 1919: An Analysis with Key Documents.* Westport, CT: Praeger, 2003.

Yamakawa Akira 山川暁. *Manshū ni kieta bunson: Chichibu Nakagawamura kaitakudan tenmatsuki* 満洲に消えた分村：秩父・中川村開拓団顛末記 (A village that disappeared in Manchuria: a record of the demise of the Chichibu Nakagawamura agricultural settlement). Tokyo: Sōshisha, 1995.

Yamamoto Jishō 山本慈昭 and Hara Yasuji 原安治. *Saikai: Chūgoku zanryū koji no saigetsu* 再会：中国残留孤児の歳月 (To meet again: the lives of the orphans left behind in China over the years). Tokyo: Nihon hōsō shuppan kyō-kai, 1981.

Yamasaki Toyoko 山崎豊子. *The Barren Zone*. Trans. James T. Araki. Honolulu, HI: University of Hawai'i Press, 1985. Originally published as *Fumō chitai* 不毛地帯. Tokyo: Kōdansha, 1976.

———. *Daichi no ko* 大地の子 (Child of the continent). 4 vols. Tokyo: Bungei shunjū, 1994. Originally published serially in the magazine *Bungei shunjū*, April 1988–April 1989.

———. *"Daichi no ko" to watashi* 「大地の子」と私 (*Child of the continent and me*). Tokyo: Bungei shunjū, 1999.

Yang, Daqing. "Resurrecting the Empire? Japanese Technicians in Postwar China, 1945–1949." In *The Japanese Empire in East Asia and Its Postwar Legacy*, ed. Harald Fuess, 185–205. Munich: Deutches Institut für Japanstudien, 1998.

Yomiuri shinbunsha Ōsaka shakaibu, ed. 読売新聞大阪社会部. *Chūgoku koji* 中国孤児 (Orphans left behind in China). Tokyo: Kadokawa shoten, 1985.

Yosano Akiko. *Travels in Manchuria and Mongolia*. Trans. Joshua Fogel. New York: Columbia University Press, 2001.

Yoshida, Takashi. *The Making of the "Rape of Nanking": History and Memory in Japan, China, and the United States*. Oxford, UK: Oxford University Press, 2006.

Young, Louise. *Japan's Total Empire: Manchuria and the Culture of Wartime Imperialism*. Berkeley and Los Angeles, CA: University of California Press, 1998.

Yūkan Fukunichi 夕刊フクニチ, 1946.

Oral History Interviews

October 27, 1999; Sagami

December 21, 1999; Yokohama

February 14, 2000; Tokyo

February 18, 2000; Hakodate

February 22, 2000; Nagano

February 24, 2000; Nagano

May 29, 2000; Kokura

May 30, 2000; Imari, Saga

May 31, 2000; Sasebo

July 14, 2000; Tokyo

August 14, 2000; Kyoto

November 19, 2000; Utsunomiya

November 20, 2000; Tokyo

Index

Harvard East Asian Monographs
(*out-of-print)

22039405